Foreword by

JACK CANFIELD

D1594953

PROJECT

HEAVEN

ON

EARTH

The 3 simple questions
that will help you change the world ... easily

MARTIN RUTTE

Co-author of *The New York Times* bestseller *Chicken Soup for the Soul®at Work*

"Deep in our souls, don't we all want Heaven on Earth? Now is the time for us to be deliberate creators of the kind of world we long for. We don't have to take huge leaps to create this; we just have to take baby steps every day and keep on taking them. Martin Rutte is the Heaven on Earth visionary and coach helping us in this worthy mission."

– Marci Shimoff
New York Times #1 Best Selling Author, *Happy for No Reason*

"Your work on Heaven on Earth is powerful and timely. You are a Wayshower. I love you for that. Very glad you're having this important impact."

– Barnet Bain
Director, *Milton's Secret*
Producer, *What Dreams May Come*
Author, *The Book of Doing and Being: Rediscovering Creativity in Life, Love and Work*

"Martin is a crucial change agent; his work is nothing less than the vision of a new human society. I can't imagine how you could bring more meaning and joy to your life than to join Martin and become an active participant in the Great Turning. You can either be at the effect of a changing world or one of its co-creators!"

– Tim Kelley
Global Change Agent
Author, *True Purpose*

"When I first heard Martin speak about Heaven on Earth years ago, it honestly seemed too mystical to me, but now I love it — I love this whole field you are establishing for us all. Thanks, Martin, for being such a key part of the new story."

– Barbara Marx Hubbard
Visionary, Social Innovator, and Evolutionary Thinker
www.Evolve.org

"Heaven on Earth is the new human story. And you can participate in it by simply giving and honoring your word that you are. Martin Rutte is a clear leader in this emerging story."

– don Miguel Ruiz
Author, *The Four Agreements*

"Martin Rutte is a brilliant guide and explorer in the new territory of how we co-create Heaven on Earth. My wife, Kathlyn, and I have been studying the art of co-creation for 35 years now, and it's our experience that it is absolutely crucial to fulfillment as individuals and planetary citizens. Martin's leadership, based on his rich life experience and professional expertise, will guarantee you an exhilarating journey to a new perspective."

> **– Gay Hendricks**
> **Author, *The Big Leap***
> **www.hendricks.com**

"There is perhaps no more ancient desire in human history than that of creating Heaven on Earth. Yet, for perhaps the first time in those thousands of years, we can truly imagine a world where the problems of yesterday and today (war, scarcity, starvation, exploitation, mass suffering) are no more, and humans are free to thrive as never before on this planet. And if we can imagine it, we can make it so.

"For several decades, Martin Rutte has been passionately pursuing the all-important question of what Heaven on Earth might truly look like. I know of no one more capable of leading us on a transformational journey into this vast and wonderful subject. Prepare to feel hopeful and inspired!"

> **– Carter Phipps**
> **Author, *Evolutionaries***

"Martin Rutte tells the new story with passionate clarity. He brings inspiration and hope in the way people look at their lives and their place in the world. It is life changing for those who hear and embrace the compelling story of Heaven on Earth that he tells."

> **– Peggy Holman**
> **Author, *Engaging Emergence: Turning Upheaval into Opportunity***
> **Co-author, *The Change Handbook***

"It is a tremendous accomplishment and I think it will be one of the documents that can matter — like the Source Document for the Hunger Project and the UN Millennial Charter.

"I was reminded of the phrase 'a world that works for everyone with no one left out' and while I have said that many times in blogs and talks, it's a phrase that had become a bit stale and lost some of it's power to inspire me and call me forth. In reading your book, it all came back that Heaven on Earth is possible and if we live it one day at a time, we'll help cultivate it and have faith that it is manifesting around us every moment.

"Heaven on Earth is a powerful movement and an opening for anyone to connect to a deeper level of awareness and responsibility for our world and the opportunity each of us has to make a difference — to make the world what we would want it to be if it were perfect. Martin Rutte has reduced ancient teachings and traditions to a few simple questions, which when answered from the heart, show us who we are and that our lives and our world is a choice that each of us make every moment of every day. Bravo."

– Jim Selman
Coach, Facilitator, and Consultant
Founder, Paracomm.com

"Heaven on Earth gave me a language that is both universal and common. It brought out into the open the whole notion that we as human beings are continually creating results we don't want and that we can instead focus our attention on creating the world we do want.

"It made it very simple by calling it Heaven on Earth — people seem to know what that is without a big explanation — people just know…and can actually talk about it fairly readily.

"It spurred me to an idea I wouldn't have had. I have for a long time been very disturbed by the violence against women happening in the world — both locally and globally. In one of the teleseminar sessions Martin and another participant stimulated a simple yet powerful idea, involving a penny a day, to create the world we want. This idea, Making Change, became an initiative in the county where I live. We have distributed jars in the community in a campaign to keep this issue in peoples' consciousness by contributing even just a penny every day to end violence against women. ('I pledge to make change by giving change to end violence against women and girls in Lunenburg/Queens counties.')

"What a brave soul Martin is to take this message of Heaven on Earth across the world — his commitment is relentless and unwavering."

– Sue Bookchin
www.BeThePeace.ca

"Martin and I share an absolute devotion to the glorious and never-ending process of humbly participating in creating 'heaven on earth.' He is a brilliant teacher and a bright light shining inspiration and illumination on the path of his students' discovery of what 'heaven on earth' is for them."

– Patricia Albere
Evolutionary Collective

"I brought Martin's Heaven on Earth questions to a troubled, fractured team of medical leaders. Within an hour, they became aligned around values; they had looked deeply into their own personal motivations for being in the medical world; and they coalesced into a trusting, connected, and generous group. It was an amazing and touching experience — for the group and for me. And, the benefits of the work will be felt by 5,000 of their employees and countless patients. Heaven on Earth is powerful work."

> **– Rick Foster**
> **Consultant and Co-author, *How We Choose to Be Happy* and *Happiness & Health***

"Co-creating heaven on earth isn't just a nice catchphrase, it's a way of life for Martin Rutte. Martin has been consciously inspiring and living heaven on earth since I've known him. Martin's simple questions show you how to make small, easy tweaks, daily, to create more heaven on earth. He did it with me and in others I've witnessed. Martin inspired me to craft my own version of heaven on earth, "Heaven on Earth for Law Enforcement," and he can do the same for you. Are you ready to start experiencing heaven on earth?"

> **– Justin Criner**
> **Police Officer**

"What is Heaven on Earth FOR YOU? In that question, Martin takes a heady, philosophical discussion and brings it right down to earth, right into the heart. I remember vividly when he asked me his three Heaven on Earth questions. It was life transforming. I realized that Heaven on Earth was something that could be done right now, today! Give Martin a few moments and he will show your heaven, hiding right here, in plain sight. Then you won't have to look for it anymore. You will just share it with the rest of us."

> **– GP Walsh**
> **Spiritual Teacher, Founder of the MasterHEART Institute**
> **Creator of Inner Reconciliation**

"Martin's ability to clear that which limits individuals and groups is truly remarkable. He is both acutely direct and one of the deepest listeners I have ever met. Though, ultimately, what makes him so able to assist others see in themselves what is possible, is that he is unrelentingly committed to his own and all other's living heaven on earth now."

> **– Kele Redmond**
> **Healer – Artist – Social Animator**

"I can't imagine a more important human activity than envisioning Heaven on Earth — so that we may then collaboratively create the better world we imagine. Nor can I imagine a better spokesman to promote this movement than passionate, articulate, and fully, authentically human, Martin Rutte."

> **– Mark Belfry**
> **Author, *The Suncaster***

"Martin is a friend, a colleague, and a valued advisor with honest simplicity and keen insight. The power of spirit illuminates his work."

> **– Jack Canfield**
> **Co-author of The Success Principles™ and**
> **Co-creator of the *Chicken Soup for the Soul*® series**

"Because we create what we expect, when you look for Heaven on Earth, you find it. Regular ordinary moments become expanded, joyful, and euphoric moments. A moment of being cuddled by my two sons, or a beautiful hug from my husband are no longer just moments, they are moments when I experience Heaven on Earth. Thank you Martin for creating this perspective and teaching each of us how to create a new experience of life. This is a must read for any spiritual seeker."

> **– Christy Whitman**
> ***The New York Times* Best Selling author, *The Art of Having It All***
> **www.christywhitman.com**

"We all dream of a better life — for ourselves, loved ones, and the world. Turning our images of 'heaven on earth' into a reality, fulfilling our mission in life, requires mastery. Martin Rutte's *Project Heaven on Earth* is a clear roadmap for both uncovering and realizing our dreams for a better life."

> **– Dr. Ken Druck**
> **Author, *Courageous Aging: Your Best Years Ever Reimagined* and**
> **the original Executive Coach**

"Anything less than Heaven on Earth is beneath us."

> **– Rinaldo S. Brutoco**
> **Founder & President, World Business Academy**
> **www.worldbusiness.org**

Project Heaven on Earth:
The 3 simple questions that will help you change the world … easily

3 Questions Publishing

www.ProjectHeavenOnEarth.com

Martin@ProjectHeavenOnEarth.com

Special discounts apply when 50 or more books are purchased.
For ordering information, please visit
www.ProjectHeavenOnEarth.com/book

Printed in U.S.A.
First Edition

Cover design by: Paul Bartlett, www.PJBart.com

Headshot photo of Martin Rutte by: Michael Gomez, www.GomezPhotography.com

Interior book design: David Christel

ISBN- 978-0-692-07362-9

Library of Congress Control Number on File.

Permission was granted for use of all the stories included in the *Project Heaven on Earth* book.

Earthrise (p. 3) by NASA: www.nasa.gov/image-feature/apollo-8-earthrise
Photo of Earth (pp. 6 and 185) by NASA/ GSFC/ NOAA/ USGS [Public domain], via Wikimedia Commons: http://commons.wikimedia.org/wiki/File:Nasa_blue_marble.jpg

Ch. 11, pp. 113 - 117:
    Photos of Natalie Alexia and Jack Canfield taken by Adam Carroll. All other photos taken by Natalie Alexia.

Dedicated to

My Father of Blessed Memory	My Mother of Blessed Memory
Tzvi ben Moshe	Fiygeh Rivka Liah
Harry (Hershel) Rutte	Lily Rutte

Contents

Project Heaven on Earth

Foreword

Jack Canfield

Co-author of *The Success Principles*™ and
Co-creator of the *Chicken Soup for the Soul*® series

Several years ago, my family and I were visiting Cameroon, a country in Africa just south of Nigeria. We were staying in a beautiful home by the sea.

One morning I went for a walk on the beach by myself. As I wandered down the beach I started collecting shells. At one point, I looked up and saw a man coming out of a tiny little shack, very poor, very third world.

He walked up to me and reached out holding a handful of shells and said, "I see you're collecting shells. May I offer these to you as a gift?"

"Yes." I answered. "Thank you very much."

He told me he was a fisherman who had been living in Equatorial Guinea, the country south of Cameroon. The fish there had all been fished out or polluted out so he had moved his family up the coast to Cameroon where there were more fish and which offered him a chance of making a better living and better supporting his family.

We talked about what it was like being a fisherman in Cameroon. "It's not very good. I catch whatever fish I can, and then I lay them out on a piece of canvas on the side of the road to sell them." People drive by and sometimes stop to buy.

"What's the hardest part of your life?" I asked.

He said, "Having children who are sick and not being able to afford to take them to the doctor or buy medicine for them."

I thought to myself, Oh my God, that's the same thing any parent in the world wants — to love your children and have them be healthy. In that moment, I felt an instant, deep, and powerful connection with him. I was profoundly moved by our shared humanity.

Today's media — through documentary movies, television, and the Internet — give us the ability to have a similar level of connectedness with people all around the world. It has allowed us to realize that we truly are all one human family. And with that realization, we can begin to dream about the kind of life and the kind of world we want to live in for our own family and for our larger global family. And if we're going to dream, why not dream the ultimate? Why not unleash our full potential to create the kind of world we all deeply long for — Heaven on Earth?

I first met Martin Rutte about 30 years ago. A mutual friend had told me about him and suggested that Martin would be a great person to speak at an upcoming workshop I was giving. We spoke on the phone and discovered that we were both going to be in the San Francisco area at the same time, so I invited him to attend a speech I was giving at Mills College in Oakland.

After the speech, he came up to introduce himself, and I asked him what he thought of my presentation. He asked me if I wanted the truth. I said, "Yes."

He told me he really didn't like my talk because it was too focused on my marketing my books and tapes.

No one had ever spoken to me like that before. I appreciated his honesty and thanked him for his courage in telling me the truth. He lit up and thanked me for being so gracious.

I instantly fell in love with Martin because he was such a combination of love, compassion, and honesty. Over time we've become very good, close friends.

Twelve years ago, when I started the Transformational Leadership Council (an association of trainers, coaches, writers and film makers doing transformational work in the areas of human potential, leadership, and social change), I asked Martin to be a founding member. Over the years, Martin has spoken numerous times at our international conferences, and always, everyone in the audience is completely captivated by his compassion, his humor, the depth and breadth of his knowledge, and his passionate commitment to creating Heaven on Earth.

What's exciting about Martin's vision is that when you ask anybody if they would like to have Heaven on Earth, they always say, "Yes!" And if you then ask them what Heaven on Earth is, they always have an answer. And their answers always transcend political divides and divergent philosophies. People instantly, deeply, and clearly know what Heaven on Earth is; they clearly know the essence of what it means. Bringing that knowing publicly out into the world now is so very important and so very needed.

Wanting Heaven on Earth is natural for us. Deep inside, we all believe in it because when you say the phrase Heaven on Earth, people respond, "Yeah, we want that."

To me, Heaven on Earth taps into something universal, fundamental, and beyond what is learned. It reveals something that's essential to our basic human nature — the Divine spark that exists deep within all of us looking for expression in the outer world. It's what we all desire and what we would all like to create, but obviously, we've not yet done it.

Why haven't we? I believe it's because we've all, in our own unique ways, been wounded in childhood. And we've been conditioned by the different belief systems of our cultures. As a result, we are often unconsciously run by our fear rather than by our true nature, which is naturally cooperative and loving. But deep down, underneath all the wounding and all the conditioning, we all want to live in peace, we want to love and be loved, and we want the freedom to express our true selves. It doesn't matter where you go in the world, we all tear up or get goose bumps when people do things that are compassionate, kind, and loving because that is a fundamental part of our human nature.

What Martin has done for all of us in this book is take our Soul's deep longing for the kind of world we all want — Heaven on Earth — and made it simple, easy, and concrete for us to begin creating and experiencing it. And the timing is perfect.

I believe learning how to create Heaven on Earth is more important now than it has ever been in history, because we live in a time where there is a rapidly accelerating convergence of many, many cultures, traditions and belief systems that, on the surface at least, often conflict with each other. Now more than ever we desperately need a solution that creates a public awareness of our common humanity. When you add to this that we are now armed to the teeth with nuclear weapons, and we live with the possibility that more and more people have access to these weapons, it's vitally imperative that we figure out as soon as possible how to make our world work so that these weapons are never used.

Add to this the threat of environmental catastrophe because of climate change, the mass migrations of people from numerous war zones, the large-scale breakdown of economic and governmental systems, the rapid population growth, the disruptions and unemployment caused by technology, and all the other things that are challenging us at this time. And the result of all of this is a tremendous amount of fear that everyone senses.

It's time we transcend that fear by committing, believing and trusting that we can in fact work together to create our new story, what Martin calls, "The new story of what it means to be a human and what it means to be humanity."

Story is vital. It's the container that gives meaning to the circumstances of our lives. If our story is one of limitation, pessimism and hopelessness, our lives and the world reflect that. If our story is one of hopefulness, expansiveness and energy, what we experience and express in our lives and in the world is vitality, purpose, and service.

About five or ten years ago, a lot of people started saying, "The current story is not working. We need a new story." And then we stopped hearing that. I think the reason we stopped hearing it is because nobody could identify or name the new story. If you keep saying we need a new story, but can't identify or name it, it becomes a source of frustration.

Fortunately, what Martin has done in this book is name the new story: Project Heaven on Earth.

Victor Hugo once said, "Nothing is as powerful as an idea whose time has come," and Project Heaven on Earth is an idea whose time has clearly come.

What I love about this book is that it is not just a treatise on the subject. It is a practical guidebook on how to actually create Heaven on Earth...now. Martin will show you a collection of different "Gateways" for taking action, which he's discovered by talking to thousands of people. A Gateway is a doorway, an entrance, a portal into a new story, a new life, a new world.

You are going to learn about and work with Internal Gateways, Relationship Gateways, and Outer World Gateways.

You'll also learn how you can directly experience Heaven on Earth starting right here, right now. And you'll read about inspiring examples of people from all over the world who are making Heaven on Earth real right now.

As you read this book, I encourage you to make a commitment — in the smallest, simplest, easiest way — to take action on making Heaven on Earth real. By doing that, you are directly contributing to Heaven on Earth. And know that a growing number of others all around the world are doing the same thing. Acting together, in hundreds of simple, small and unique ways, we can each do our part to finally create the world we all secretly yearn for.

I promise you that you are about to embark on perhaps the most important journey of your life, perhaps the most important journey of all our lives, because if we fail…well, you know what the opposite of Heaven is.

We don't need to wait any longer; in fact, we can't wait. The time is now. We need to take this heartfelt dream that we've long thought impossible and make it our new human story.

Project Heaven on Earth brilliantly shows what we, all of humanity, can do if we set our minds to it — co-create the world of our deepest yearnings…a true Heaven on Earth.

Enjoy the journey.

Preface

Why are we here? What is Humanity's job?

Haven't we had enough of the hells on Earth?

Isn't it time to make our world Heaven on Earth?

Imagine being given a magic wand and with it you can create Heaven on Earth. Wouldn't you want to not only lessen the amount of wars in the world but really end all wars? And wouldn't you want to do the same with hunger, poverty, homelessness, crime, addiction, abuse, and so on and so on? I know the vast majority of Humanity would.

In 1998 I was graced with an epiphany and realized what my next assignment in life was: "I'm going to take on changing the story of what it means to be a human and what it means to be Humanity so that we collectively experience co-creating Heaven on Earth."

Let me tell you a little bit about my journey and what brought me to this realization.

I was born and raised in a lower middle-class family of Jewish immigrants in Hamilton, Canada. My mother was from Poland, my father from the Ukraine. My native tongue was Yiddish. I learned English on the streets. I learned French and Latin in high school, Hebrew in Hebrew school, and a smattering of other languages (Polish, Ukrainian, Russian) that my parents spoke when they didn't want my sister and me to understand what they were saying.

I tell you this because I've always had an ability to understand and translate between people and world-views. This ability helps me see how people perceive the world and thus what's unique to them as individuals and what's common to us all as humanity.

I started my career working for the Canadian government. My job was to fund innovative programs to reduce substance abuse. That taught me about influence and leverage, how a little effort, in the right place, could produce a dramatic impact.

I then started my own business, focusing on personal growth workshops, consulting, and speaking. The emphasis was on helping people distinguish between their mind/ego and the Soul. When you set goals from your mind/ego, you set your sights on what you believe is possible. When you do the same thing from your Soul, from your deep inner being, what you want in life is usually beyond what your mind/ego believes is possible.

My work was to have people and organizations set their vision/goals from "beyond what they believed possible," yet still deeply desired. The results people achieved were amazing. They were inspiring to themselves and others. Over and over again they proved you can actually do something in life that you don't believe is possible.

In the late 1980s I had a deeply spiritual experience and realized I wanted to bring spirituality into business. I don't mean spirituality in a proselytizing way, as in "I know what spirituality is and you don't." I mean it as an ongoing inquiry. Just as a business person asks every day, "How can I make my business more successful?" we can also engage, if we choose, in the inquiry, "How can I experience more of the spiritual in my work?"

I spent almost thirty years taking this conversation into the world of business. I helped set up and speak at conferences, I did a ton of media, and I was the co-founder and Chair of the Centre for Spirituality and the Workplace in the Sobey School of Business at Saint Mary's University in Halifax, Canada. The purpose of the Centre was: "Positively and strategically influencing the conversation and accomplishments about spirituality and the workplace globally." The essence of the Centre's work was to foster a new worldwide conversation, and we did.

I also became an author, co-authoring *Chicken Soup for the Soul at Work*. The idea for this book started in the mid-90s when I observed the massive structural changes occurring in business. There was a very palpable malaise in the workplace. I thought something had to be done, so I proposed the book title to my friend Jack Canfield of *Chicken Soup* fame. He loved the idea and said, "Do it!"

The book was published and became a *New York Times* business bestseller. After that happened, I had a conversation with my co-authors, my wife Maida Rogerson and my friend Tim Clauss, telling them that I didn't think merely having the book published was enough to begin turning around the malaise I was seeing in the workplace. That's when Tim came up with the brilliant idea of doing *Chicken Soup in the Workplace* story sessions for companies. I called several clients. They loved the idea and brought us in to do workshops.

In every session we did, people were eager to share their own stories. What they were really doing, I discovered, was sharing values they felt were important in their workplaces.

Essentially, stories are a storehouse for values. We pass values on through our stories.

Toward the end of each session, we would move from telling and hearing people's stories to looking at the overall story of their workplace. Every workplace has a story. Parts of that story work and parts don't. By asking people to metaphorically step up into a forest ranger station and look down onto their workplace, they gained a higher level perspective and could very easily see, describe, and understand the story.

Now that they knew the story of their workplace, they began discovering they could nurture and expand the parts of the story that worked, and change the parts that didn't. We then spoke about using the same process to discover the story of their own lives, their families, and their nation.

I believe the time has now come to do the same thing with the story of our world.

We've heard it said many times that the old story isn't working — disease, wars, poverty, and other sufferings continue and continue. What we need is a new story — but notice that no one ever says what that new story is. It's never named.

Let's name the world's new story and make it a grand and noble new story. Let's make it an ambitious and splendid story about what it means for us to be a human and what it means for us to be Humanity. Let's make it a story that engages people, that enrolls them from deep within their hearts and Souls, that makes them want to pitch in and contribute to make this new story work because it has touched something in the very essence of who we are.

This new global story will usher in a new era of promise, creativity, responsibility, dedication, and devotion — our Souls' deepest desire. We can do it. That's what this book is about.

Introduction

Humanity is at a crossroads. I'm deeply concerned about the state of our world and pained about the direction we've been taking. The sufferings of the world seem overwhelming, they continue and continue — war, hunger, poverty, the threat of global financial collapse. Resignation is being stockpiled. Hope is in short supply. Optimism hides in a cave.

Where are our priorities? Recall the massacre of 800,000 people in Rwanda, the 180,000 people killed and 3 million driven from their homes in the Darfur region of Sudan. And what about the Israeli–Palestinian situation, the civil war in Syria — and on it goes.

We have enough nuclear arms to blow ourselves up many times over while the environment continues to deteriorate. But these two problems are different than any others we've had in the past...these problems can end all life on Earth.

What will it take for us to get it?

The option we have is to continue the same story or we can start a new story with new possibilities and a new trajectory. The choice really is up to us.

But what can one human being do to change the course of history...not much! Yet, when we stop to think about it, what has changed the course of history, with the exception of natural calamities, is human beings. The power to change the course of history, the power to change our story, resides in us — individually and collectively.

We have deeply held dreams for the kind of world we want — dreams for peace, prosperity, safety, health, a clean and sustainable environment, freedom, and more. Each of us clearly knows the basic components of what it would take to make the world work.

Isn't it time for us to make these dreams real?

This book says, "YES, it's time!" and offers an opening to a new pathway to accomplish our dreams.

What if there were capacities within us that we could access to activate the "make-our-dreams-a-reality" potential in ourselves and others? These capacities are real. They're just waiting to be called upon.

I believe what's needed to move us forward at this point in our evolution is the birthing of a new possibility for our world — a new story of what it means to be human (an individual) and what it means to be Humanity (the human community). (I capitalize "Humanity" because I want us to start thinking and experiencing us as one family with extraordinary potential.)

This new story needs to engage our deepest core. It needs to ignite a move from resignation to engagement, from stagnation to creativity, from inaction and observation to action. This book is about discovering that potential within you and inviting you to turn it "ON."

My intentions for you are that:

- you experience the clarity of why you are here on Earth, and why we are all here;

- you experience a renewed optimism, a greatly expanded sense of what is possible, and a feeling of sustainable hope for the world;

- your heart's desire for the world, your vision for Humanity, becomes possible and you begin making that real; and

- your dream for the world and making that real becomes an acceptable topic of public conversation and action.

My intentions for us all, for Humanity, are that:

- we experience why we are here and what we are here to do;

- we understand what our work together is — creating a world that works — and we begin being of service in accomplishing that; and

- we choose to move to our next evolutionary level.

We can choose to continue believing that we can't make a difference, that we have to resign ourselves to live in a world without hope for the future, that we are insignificant, that life is overwhelming. Or, we can choose to use our energies to have the kind of world we deeply long for.

The first choice is fearful, shut down, polarized, vengeful, and mired in negativity. The second choice overflows with possibility, energy, hope, accomplishment, and heart.

Imagine harnessing our collective human capacities and taking this planet to its next evolutionary level. By doing that, we would unleash an era of momentum, hope, inventiveness, and creativity.

As humans, we can focus our life energies. As Humanity, we can do the same and alter the planet and people's lives for the better.

This book is about choosing and helping to shape the future we want — about opening a new possibility for what life can be.

This book is also a tool you can use as your contribution to change the current story and the world. I call it Project Heaven on Earth. That's right. If we're going to dream, let's dream big, let's go for the "whole enchilada." Let's discover what we really deeply want for our world and let's start taking the simple, easy, concrete steps that will get us on this path.

As the chapters of this book unfold, my desire is that your deepest inner dream for our world is re-ignited, that your passion for the world you long for erupts, and that your engagement comes charging out of the starting gate.

"The future we create is the only future we share."
Suresh Pandit

"I had a dream once of a long dining table, yards long,
at which guests carried on animated,
fascinating conversations with one another.
I sat in on many of them, wide-eyed like a child,
taking in all the exciting ideas flying around the table.
People were talking about how the world could be
and what it would take to create Heaven on Earth."
Marianne Williamson

PROJECT

HEAVEN

ON

EARTH

The 3 simple questions
that will help you change the world ... easily

MARTIN RUTTE

Prelude

This book honors a young girl I met in Fortaleza, Brazil. She was in a children's hunger rehabilitation program called IPREDE.

IPREDE takes in starving children, nourishes them, and brings them back to the normal weight for their age. It also works with their mothers, teaching them how to properly feed their children, grow food and medicinal herbs, and realize that they can positively impact the health and well-being of their children.

I was taken, along with my wife Maida, to IPREDE to see the children by my dear friend, Roberto Braga. We met the director, Ana Maria Teles de Norões, a wonderful, deeply spiritual, committed woman, who took us on a tour. I'd seen pictures of starving children on TV, but had never been with any in real life. The two are *not* the same. These children and their condition moved me to my very core.

And then I met her. A child about 10 − 12 years old sitting on the floor by herself, malnourished, catatonic, cigarette burns on her body. I sat down to be with her. I picked up a little stuffed toy animal and passed it to her in an attempt to make contact. She immediately pulled away. It was impossible to get physically close and comfort her. I didn't know what to do. I decided the only thing I could do was send her my thoughts. In my mind I said to her that what had been done to her was completely unacceptable. It was wrong. It was an aberration of what it means to be human. And then I sent her my love.

I had never been in the presence of such indescribable cruelty and suffering. I promised I would do something about this situation in the world so that she and others would never have to suffer so profoundly.

I got up to leave and walked outside the room, feeling my knees begin to buckle. Roberto saw me and I could see the look of anguished concern on his face. I was so furious, I felt I could have killed the person who had done this to her.

But being with her had broken open something new in me. She immeasurably strengthened my resolve to end the senseless, cruel, immoral, and unnecessary suffering in our world. There is just too much hell on Earth.

I choose to create Heaven on Earth.

Chapter 1

Birthing Our New Story

For years I have been speaking to thousands of people about the kind of world they want and one blazing desire stands out: There is a desire, a longing in each of us, for a world that works.

There is a desire, a longing in each of us, for the unnecessary, immoral, and reoccurring problems of the planet — war, hunger, poverty, disease, hatred, addictions, abuse, crime, pollution, etc. — not just to get better, but to once and for all end.

We've suppressed these yearnings that arise from our soul, yearnings for a world that inspires hope, creativity, and engagement. What keeps this self-censoring in place is a culture that believes having the kind of world we yearn for simply is not possible.

Yet, from our most profound core, we continue to know the kind of world we want. This comes from thousands of people I've spoken with who, when given an opportunity to speak about the world of their dreams, share the same longings. We want a world moving in a direction that satisfies and feeds our deepest being. We want a world that is life affirming, ennobling, energizing, engaging, and hopeful. This is the world we long to see and feel and live in.

This kind of world *is* possible. It *is* realizable.

There is a process now emerging in our global culture to support this desire. Fundamentally, it calls for a re-envisioning of who we are as humans and as Humanity. As this process continues unfolding, it acts as an opening allowing us — for the first time — to consciously choose and create our new, collective "story."

We know we have it within ourselves to tackle the overwhelming problems of the world. The human spirit has already:

- Sent and returned a man from the moon

- Knocked down the Berlin Wall

- Stopped smallpox and leprosy epidemics

- Brought about a peaceful transition to democracy in South Africa

- Invented the Internet with its endless possibilities (PayPal, Skype, Facebook, etc.)

- Detected gravitational waves for the first time

- Launched an interplanetary probe that sent back the first close-up pictures of Pluto

- Developed nanotechnology

- Delved into the far reaches of the micro-universe (confirmation of the Higgs boson) and the macro-universe (observed light from just after the Big Bang)

Accomplishments such as these, and many others, are a testament to the ingenuity of the human spirit. They are the positive, caring, and creative part of Humanity's story at this turning point in our evolution. They illustrate our phenomenal drive, imagination, and accomplishments.

And, our current human story also contains elements that do not work: fear, prejudice, tremendous heartache, divisiveness, evil, and horror. Pick any major suffering — war, terrorism, homelessness, disease, poverty — and you can see these elements vividly present. Because these sufferings have been with us for centuries, we conclude that that's just the way life is — we can never really end them. The underlying belief is that we're unable to make a true, deep, and lasting difference in having the world work. Clearly, this is not the part of our story we want to continue engaging with, tolerating, and empowering.

At our core, what we hunger for is a new context, a new vision for the third millennium — one that inspires and enlivens us. In short, a new story for all Humanity.

A story shapes our perception of reality. We create our own individual life story in order to give meaning and purpose to our lives. We then tell our story to others so we can share, connect, and continue defining who we are. "Telling" is an aspect of story.

"Doing" is another aspect of story. Doing emerges from story. Story gives rise to events and actions. Martin Luther King, Jr.'s "I Have a Dream" speech was an action that arose out of the emancipation movement story; Mother Teresa saw the story of extreme poverty in Calcutta, chose to change it and founded a new order, the Missionaries of Charity. The order now extends throughout the world helping the poorest of the poor.

There is no doing without an underlying and informing story: story shapes the content and manner of "what" we do and also provides the context, the "why" we do what we do.

If we add together our more than seven billion human stories — the telling and the doing — we begin to get a sense of the collective story of Humanity. We are also able to appreciate and reflect upon the evolution of Humanity's story over time.

And what is now emerging is the next era in our evolutionary progression. We know we want to do something from deep in our hearts, deep in our souls, that will truly support and take our planet to its next evolutionary level — the next chapter in our collective story.

There are many examples of Humanity expanding into a new story: the Magna Carta, the Renaissance, and the Industrial Revolution. A more recent example is the famous photo of the Earth rising over the moon's horizon. This was the first time we saw our entire home planet as one. We were both the observer and the observed. We were able to look skyward and see the marbled face of the moon, while simultaneously a picture was beamed back to us of our world — a swirling blue and white jewel in the blackness of space.

What was suddenly birthed with that iconic photo was a new realization of who we, Humanity, are. Frank White, in his book *The Overview Effect*, interviewed astronauts from many nations and asked about their experience of being in space. They reported that the first thing they did was look for the lights of their home town at night. Then they looked for the next larger context. For U.S. astronauts, it was their home state…but there are no lines on Earth defining states when you're looking down from several hundred miles up. The astronauts would then look for the border of their country and, again (with the exception of island countries such as Australia and Ireland), there are no countries. They would then look to geographical boundaries like North America and Africa. And then they would *all* jump to the next level, to the level of the whole of our home planet Earth…to the overview effect.

When you can't see separating lines, what you see is the totality. The environment is one. The economy is global. The Internet is planetary. We've made up the lines! This is one Earth, we are one family.

"Once a photograph of the Earth, taken from the outside, is available… a new idea as powerful as any in history will be let loose."

Sir Fred Hoyle, 1948

Now that we can see and experience the whole of our Earth and ourselves, we can also ask questions in relation to the whole: What is our purpose — why are we here, *and* what is our vision — what do we aspire to, what are we to become?

Our current story speaks volumes about our inventiveness, our tenacity, our expansiveness, and our brilliance. It also connects us to our roots, all the way back to the beginning. But, our current story needs to evolve. It is no longer sufficient for our needs, our awareness, and our dreamed-of potential.

Our new story is to now make our "one" work.

We have it within our power to consciously change and evolve our own personal story. And now, because of global technology and the higher level of global consciousness, we can do the same for Humanity as a whole. We can create a new story that will positively impact our collective future.

For the first time, Humanity can, with awareness, actually choose a global story, a unified narrative that inspires, engages, and uplifts. Now is the time for a new civilization-fueling vision to elevate Humanity to its next evolutionary stage.

The world is ready, the world is waiting. What is required is a shift in perception about our potential and our possibilities. What is needed are contributions and actions that begin producing the world we want. What is wanted is the feeling that we're moving in the right direction, infusing Humanity with a renewed sense of hope, optimism, and meaningful accomplishment.

I believe that given the tools the vast majority of us would want to participate in the formation of a new human story that inspires hope for the future, gives us the feeling of positive momentum, and ushers in a sense of expansiveness. United, we can co-create a grand, planetary adventure, each person adding their inspiration, spirit, voice, and gifts.

We can't wait any longer — we don't need to. Now is the time to begin the next chapter in the collective story of Humanity's evolution, a positive chapter we've been waiting and longing for. The time is now, the place is here, the person is you.

Chapter 2

The Work of Humanity

Oscar Motomura, president of Amana-Key, a management training company in Sao Paulo, Brazil, once spoke about the effects of technology on the world. "With global air travel, the Internet and instantaneous global communications, the concept of Humanity is now tangible."

In years past we would sympathize with someone's dire situation in a country half-way around the world, but because of the existing technology, this was delayed days or even weeks from when the event actually occurred. Today's technology brings us immediate coverage of the world's sufferings. Parents crying in despair over the loss of their child in an earthquake or a grandmother whose entire crop has been wiped out by a tsunami can be viewed thousands of miles away instantaneously. The heart, compassion, and humane aspect of Humanity is now profoundly tangible.

A couple of years after Oscar's talk and unaware of what he'd said, Rob Lehman, former president of the charitable Fetzer Institute, wrote a paper in which he asked, "What is the common work of Humanity?"

For me, there was a quantum evolutionary leap from Oscar's statement to Rob's. Oscar had introduced the notion of Humanity as existing and tangible. Rob then asked what are we, Humanity, here to do?

It was a life-changing question: Why are we all here? What's our mission, our vision? What is Humanity's purpose?

And I began wondering: What if others, lots and lots of others, began answering Rob's question? We could use what would be revealed to help the world discover the next chapter in Humanity's evolution.

A Civilization-Fueling Vision

Swedish author Karl-Erik Edris writes about "a civilization-fueling vision" and its reality-defining function:

> "...when a civilization-fueling vision is vibrant and functions well, it includes the individual in a great cosmic context, which in principle lends meaning to his life and aids him in finding reconciliation with the grim realities of life.

> "The civilization-fueling vision brings a strong sense of meaningfulness in human endeavors. No matter how many difficulties a person may experience in life, these difficulties do not usually overpower the superior, meaningful order he imagines himself being part of."

At this critical juncture in our collective evolution, I believe our task is the birthing of a new global vision, the conscious creation of a new story for Humanity. Now is the time to birth this new model of existence, this new collective purpose — this new civilization-fueling vision.

For me, the answer to Rob's question, "What is the common work of Humanity?" has to do with creating a world that works. "But what does that mean?" I asked myself. Then it came to me: What if we established Heaven on Earth?

What if we established Heaven on Earth?

Heaven on Earth?

I remember the first time the thought of Heaven on Earth occurred to me. My initial concern was that people would think I was crazy. But as I thought more deeply about it, I realized we can and do talk about hell on Earth, but why can't our primary conversations be about Heaven on Earth? What if we were to really consider establishing Heaven on Earth? Imagine the kinds of conversations we would have. Imagine the possibilities that would open up.

I became more intrigued. What if we had a world that lived up to our dreams and ideals? What if we had faith in the direction Humanity was moving? What if we could engage people in a new vision of what is possible for Humanity? What would it feel and look like to have Humanity truly acting in concert expressing a shared purpose — the co-creation of Heaven on Earth?

The more I thought about it, the more I liked it, and the more I felt the time *is* now.

By choosing to have our collective story be the creation of Heaven on Earth, a new global force is unleashed. We can experience it carrying us, enlivening us, and giving us the support and courage to express and put into action our deepest longings for the kind of world we want.

This is a story big enough for Humanity to full-heartedly engage in.

My friend Richard Porter, a consultant and observer of the human condition, says, "Heaven on Earth is our destiny."

Project Heaven on Earth

Heaven on Earth is an idea that can unleash and engage our deepest longings. Pragmatists, visionaries, scientists, idealists, engineers, hairdressers, philosophers, truck drivers, homemakers, farmers, youth — anyone — can identify with, feel in their gut, and intellectually grasp this fundamental desire to have the world of their dreams.

But how could I take an intangible idea and make it concrete? What was the vehicle for turning this vision into reality?

I went back to Richard with this problem and we came up with "Project Heaven on Earth."

Everything fell into place. Here was a vehicle that was both pragmatic and pure, visionary and tangible, theoretical and doable. Why? Because the word "Project" is both a noun and a verb? What if we then considered the phrase "Project Heaven on Earth" to be both a noun and a verb?

"Project Heaven on Earth" as a Noun: This Project is a thing you do, something you put your energy into. It's a vehicle for the alignment of Humanity.

"Project Heaven on Earth" as a Verb: You project yourself, your Being, your intention, into the world to build the world of your dreams and yearnings.

Project Heaven on Earth creates the union, of noun and verb, through which we make our vision for our world real and make our new story come alive.

The intention of Project Heaven on Earth is to collectively change Humanity's current story from one that doesn't work for a great number of people (hunger, war, poverty, etc.) to one that works for you, me, everyone.

Imagine that you've just bought a new piece of computer software. You install it, launch it, and are presented with a new set of possibilities and opportunities. You can suddenly do things you've never been able to do before. All you have to do is add your own unique content.

Think of Project Heaven on Earth as a piece of metaphorical software. It, too, opens up all kinds of new possibilities into which we can put our own distinct selves — our ideas, our acts of service and contribution, our talents, our brilliance, our gifts. Into this Project, citizens of our world can put their actions that individually and collectively contribute to helping co-create Heaven on Earth — the work of Humanity.

The dawn of the next chapter in our collective story is here — Project Heaven on Earth. The work of Humanity now is to consciously and collectively envision and then live this new story.

Let's begin.

"Heaven on Earth is...

being plugged into Creation."

Mark Kerr
Editor
USA

"...the place where soul and community intersect: our stories."

Gertrude Mueller Nelson

"Heaven on Earth is...

seeking us out."

Ross Foti
Healer
USA

"...today we are witnessing the birth of a new ethic
that originates from a central place of synthesis,
where all dreams, aspirations and values of humankind converge. This is new.
It constitutes one of the greatest and most exciting attempts
at total human fulfillment in the entire evolution of the human race."

Robert Muller
former UN Assistant Secretary-General

Chapter 3

Discovering Heaven on Earth

As I began my journey of inquiry into Heaven on Earth, I realized I knew what "Earth" was, but what about "Heaven"?

I certainly had my own ideas about Heaven — where it is, what it is. Rather than holding on tightly to my ideas like they were inside my closed fist, I thought it might be better if I opened my hand and held those notions lightly in my palm so I could examine them more easily and with greater clarity.

For me, and a great many other people, Heaven is usually thought of as the place where God and the angels live, and the place we go to after death. *The Oxford English Dictionary* defines "Heaven" as a noun:

> "The celestial abode of immortal beings;
> the habitation of God and his angels, and of beatified spirits,
> usually placed in the realms beyond the sky;
> the state of the blessed hereafter."

From ancient times Heaven was imagined as a canopy which, like a large sphere, encapsulated the Earth. It was immediately visible above us. The stars, the sun, the moon, and the visible planets orbited within this sphere. Heaven was thought to exist from a couple of inches above the Earth up to the canopy. In other words, Heaven was here, now.

Many philosophers and astrologers, including Aristotle and Ptolemy, taught that the Earth and the surrounding canopy were the Universe. Then, in 1543, Nikolaus Copernicus released his study announcing that the Earth circled the sun. This challenged the very idea that Heaven surrounded the Earth. About fifty years later, Galileo, using the newly invented telescope, confirmed that the Earth did indeed travel around the sun.

Both men's work pushed Heaven, which had been in the sky above, further out...beyond what we could see, beyond the telescope's range. Much more importantly, Heaven had become not here, not now. It was no longer immediately available.

In my research on Heaven, though, I discovered there is an additional way to describe it. *The Oxford English Dictionary* also defines "Heaven" as a verb:

> "To make heavenly in character,
> to transport or transform into heaven;
> also, to bless with heaven, beatify, render supremely happy."

To be more precise, Heaven is a transitive verb (a transitive verb requires a direct object — a noun, pronoun, or noun phrase — to complete a sentence's meaning). We have to *Heaven* someone or something. We can go around *heavening* all day. We can transform our relationship with people into a *heavenly* one. We can transform our relationship with problems into a *heavenly* one. We can transform our relationship with life itself into a *heavenly* one.

As a verb, *Heavening* brings Heaven back into the here and now. Whitney Roberson, a friend and Episcopal priest, says, "We can go about Heavening Earth."

Now that I had a new, more immediate appreciation of Heaven, I turned my attention to Heaven on Earth. I first wondered if I had actually ever experienced Heaven on Earth. The answer was a definite yes when I'm:

- Feeling the love and enjoying the beauty of my wife Maida.

- Seeing my favorite flower: a heliconia. I remember the first time I saw one. It was a moment of pure magic. Maida and I were on vacation in the British Virgin Islands. The shape of the flower was unlike anything I'd ever seen. The colors were deep and rich. There were bright reds and yellows, and soft pinks and light greens. Heliconias continue to take my breath away to this day.

- Listening to tenor Jussi Björling and baritone Robert Merrill sing the duet, "Au Fond du Temple Saint," from the opera *The Pearl Fishers*. When they begin, you hear each man singing separately. Then, as they join voices, you continue hearing each voice distinctly yet, at the same time, you hear a new, third "voice" produced by their singing in perfect harmony — two men producing three sounds. It's transcendent. I've heard this piece of music hundreds of times and I still get tears in my eyes at the sound of the opening notes.

- Putting my *tallis*, my prayer shawl, over my head in synagogue and reciting the silent prayer, the Amidah. I feel I'm entering into the Divine.

- Producing a fine piece of art. I do a form of print making called monotype, which produces a one-of-a-kind print. Every time a new print emerges from the press, I feel I'm present at a birth. A stillness falls over the room as I lift the paper from the inked plate and behold the new work.

- Seeing my great-niece and great-nephew, hearing the first bird sing at sunrise, listening to Robin Williams do one of his comedy routines.

These are just a few of the times I have and do experience Heaven on Earth.

Let's Discover if You've Ever Had a Heaven on Earth Experience

Have you ever had moments when everything seemed perfect, when everything was just right? It may have been when you were smelling a rose, when something you worked on for a long time came to fruition, or when you were in love.

Some people experience Heaven on Earth when they see a newborn baby, enjoy a fine meal, walk in nature, have someone smile at them, experience the perfection of it all.

Question 1: Recall a time when you experienced Heaven on Earth. What was happening?

Describe in the space below what happened, how it felt, how you perceived the world. What was your experience of yourself, of others, of life?

_____

_____

_____

_____

_____

_____

_____

_____

_____

_____

_____

_____

_____

_____

Please share what you've written and any insights you've gained with someone else.
The act of sharing strengthens your experience and engages you at a deeper level.

Whenever I ask someone Question 1, whether they're in a workshop I'm leading or sitting beside me on an airplane, they almost always simply answer the question. They don't ask, "What do you mean by Heaven on Earth?"

In order for you to have answered this question, there must be what I call an "Already Knowing" about Heaven on Earth within you. There must be a place in you, deep within you, that already knows.

Just as love is always and eternally love, so are peace, joy, beauty, and so on — eternal and innate. Each cannot be anything else. They exist as the presence of a particular quality, and only that quality. Heaven on Earth is in the same realm. That's how we know and recognize it.

What happens when you're asked Question 1 is that you go inside yourself and scan your life for those times when you've experienced Heaven on Earth. And effortlessly, a time or times pop into your awareness. It's that simple — you have had a time or times when you've experienced Heaven on Earth.

Ask your family, friends, and co-workers this simple question, listen to their answers, and observe that they, too, have had a Heaven on Earth experience.

Let's expand your experience of the presence of Heaven on Earth.

Have you ever watched a magician using a magic wand? Suppose you have a magic wand and can create anything you want with it. A magic wand relieves you of the necessity of knowing how something will be achieved because that's the wand's job. This gives you tremendous freedom. You don't have to be constrained by knowing how something will get done. You can let your imagination take flight. You can discover deeper levels of your heart's desire.

Question 2: Imagine you have a magic wand and with it you can create Heaven on Earth. What is Heaven on Earth for you?

Take as much time as you need with this. Open your heart. Let your mind go. Marinate in what Heaven on Earth is for you. What would be present, what would disappear and no longer exist, and what would newly appear? In the space below, describe what Heaven on Earth is for you in words, pictures, or symbols.

_____

_____

_____

_____

_____

_____

_____

_____

_____

_____

_____

_____

_____

_____

_____

Please share this with at least one other person.

I am always deeply touched when people share what Heaven on Earth is for them. I always experience truth, purity, directness, and authenticity. People are very present — they're right here, right now.

I used to say it's a deeper part of themselves speaking. Then I felt it's something even deeper than that, it's their souls speaking. As I listened to more and more people answering this question, I realized it is the essence of their souls speaking. Now I believe it's the Divine Presence in them speaking.

Ask people Question 2. Listen to the content of their answers, to the feeling and tone. I personally feel it's a privilege to be let into something so very personal and intimate. Please be respectful and honoring of their answers. Don't agree or disagree with them. Be supportive. For them, this is what Heaven on Earth is.

Making Heaven on Earth Real…One Step at a Time

Imagine you're home alone one Sunday afternoon and you hear a knock at the door. You open it and see three masked people, each pointing a banana at you. You recognize the people as your friends and begin laughing as they say, "Hands up." You decide to go along with the joke and put your hands up.

They tell you to get in their car and they drive out to a field where there's a helicopter with its engine going and its blades spinning. They tell you to get in. They blindfold you. The helicopter takes off. You have no idea where you're going. Finally, they take the blindfold off and you see that you're flying over a field of lush green grass that stretches for miles in every direction. In the distance, you notice a white square. The helicopter flies to it and then hovers high above it. You see the square has four equal walls enormous in length and stretching into the distance. Only one of the walls has a door in it.

Your friends blindfold you again and the helicopter spins round and round. Then it lands. One of your friends takes the blindfold off and tells you that you're in the middle of the white square you saw from the air. You look around, but can't see any of the four walls you saw from the air. You ask your friends about this and they all promise you that you are in the middle of that huge square. You believe them.

Your friends ask you to step out of the helicopter. They then give you one simple instruction, "Leave the square." You look at them and one of them says, "Don't worry, we'll pick you up after you leave the square." "OK," you say, and step out of the helicopter. You walk away from it and it takes off with your three friends inside.

You decide to leave the square as your friends have asked, but there's one problem. Because the square is so big, you can't see any of the four walls and you don't know which one has the door in it. What do you do, where do you start, where do you begin?

You begin by taking the first step. That's also how you begin creating Heaven on Earth.

Project Heaven on Earth

Question 3 takes your deep knowing about what Heaven on Earth is for you and starts making that real in the world. How? *You begin.* You begin by asking:

Question 3: What simple, easy, concrete step(s) will you take in the next 24 hours to make Heaven on Earth real?

By making the step simple, by making it one you know you can do and by doing it within 24 hours, you've actually begun creating Heaven on Earth. Take a baby step. It's as simple as that.

In the space below, please answer question 3.

_____

_____

_____

_____

_____

_____

_____

_____

_____

_____

_____

_____

_____

And then the day after tomorrow, you take another simple, easy, concrete step — and so on and so on. Little steps taken one after another over time are what make big differences!

Congratulations —
You've Begun Creating Heaven on Earth!

It really is that simple and easy. You can now play your part, making your unique contribution. You can start acting on it, speaking about it, engaging with it, and continually expanding it — you can be Heavening Earth.

Ask your friends, family, and colleagues the three Heaven on Earth questions:

1. Recall a time when you experienced Heaven on Earth. What was happening?

2. Imagine you have a magic wand and with it you can create Heaven on Earth. What is Heaven on Earth for you?

3. What simple, easy, concrete step(s) will you take in the next 24 hours to make Heaven on Earth real?

I've asked thousands of people to tell me a time when they've experienced Heaven on Earth, and I've observed several very interesting patterns in their answers. First of all, people do not ask me to explain what I mean by Heaven on Earth. Instead, they immediately tell me the time or times when they've experienced it. They instinctively know what it is.

The repeated ease of answering the first question tells me there already exists within us a template, a reference point, a built-in standard by which we *know* what Heaven on Earth is. We then search for those experiences in our lives matching that. It's the "Already Knowing" about what Heaven on Earth is deep within us. We know. We simply know.

When I then tell people they have a magic wand and can create Heaven on Earth with it, what they say Heaven on Earth is for them and how they say it is profound. People are still and peaceful when they answer. There is an experience I feel from them of truth, clarity, immediacy, and genuineness. I feel they're sharing from their divine essence.

There are patterns to their answers, and we'll be talking more about that later on, but the energy and tone of their answers is always the same.

The more you engage with Heaven on Earth, the more people you talk to about it, the more comfortable with it you become, the more you'll begin looking for signs of progress (both tiny and large), the more the momentum will grow. Begin with simple steps that are easy and comfortable for you. And over time, Heaven on Earth will spread, it will flower, it will become *our* reality.

Heaven on Earth for Barry Spilchuk

Dear Martin,

I took a few days to think about your question, "What, at its very essence, is Heaven on Earth?" I kept thinking about it…

AND THEN…

I experienced it…

while sitting with a dear friend having lunch on Monday of this week…we were having an amazing conversation…it lasted three hours. Our waitress was awesome. She knew exactly when to "play" with us and when to leave us alone.

At the three-hour mark, my friend, Ann, called her friend Caroline and asked her to come and meet with us in the restaurant. She arrived in six or seven minutes. As soon as she arrived, we said hello and I felt something. At that precise moment, our waitress, Debbie, came back to the table. Here I was, surrounded by three amazing children of God…Ann, Caroline, and Debbie.

Ann and I had previously been discussing your question, so I asked Caroline and Debbie if they had ever heard of Heaven on Earth. They acknowledged that they had. I then blurted out, "Would you mind if I share a Heaven on Earth experience that I'm having at this moment?"

"Please do," they said.

"It's the ability to express to someone that you love them even if you've just met!" I said. "Caroline, you and I have known each other for three minutes. Debbie, we've known each other for three hours. Ann, it's been 12 years. I love you all very much!"

I felt that the feeling was mutual from all three ladies. In that moment, I felt so complete, so at peace, so full.

So, Martin, I guess my answer would be…

Heaven on Earth is…to be able to express love and feel love at any given moment.

Thanks for asking!

Barry

"Heaven on Earth is...

for me, this week was:
Brilliant colours emblazoning the evening sky
and sharing the delights of this with another.
The freshness, vitality, and hope
pregnant in the early morning walk.
Creative ideas bursting forth in the backdrop of my mind
forming new linkages and possibilities.
Experiencing a sense of expanded consciousness.
The warm touch of a friend's hand as we walk silently in the dark
amongst the tall trees."

Jasbindar Singh
Management Psychologist
New Zealand

"We are all faced with a series of great opportunities
brilliantly disguised as impossible situations."

Chuck Swindoll

Chapter 4

Overcoming Roadblocks
and Mis-beliefs

When we consider creating Heaven on Earth, roadblocks sometimes emerge — so, let's examine them. What are roadblocks, how do they work, what is their purpose, and, most importantly, how can we use them to help create Heaven on Earth?

Here are some possible roadblocks that may have popped into your head as you think more about Heaven on Earth:

You might also experience one of these roadblocks:

- People will think I'm crazy, that I've gone off the deep end. I'll be laughed at.

- I can only change what I can change and I know I can't change the world.

- I'd be embarrassed to talk about it.

- You can only have Heaven after you die. What makes you think we can create it now?

- I don't know how to do it.

- I have enough problems in my life to handle before I start taking on the world.

- I don't have any real power or authority.

How Roadblocks Work

Whenever we consider accomplishing a major objective, roadblocks come out of hiding. We may have no idea they're even there until we choose to take action on an objective. Imagine for a moment really setting the objective of creating Heaven on Earth. Notice what roadblocks immediately come to mind.

My roadblocks: _____

_____

_____

When a roadblock appears, many people think they should wait for it to either diminish or disappear before they begin working on their objective. But this isn't effective. Here's why: **Objectives and roadblocks are connected and are often directly proportional — the larger the objective, the larger the roadblock.** Another way of saying this is:

Larger roadblocks are a sign of larger objectives.

The larger your objectives, the more engaged you become with a greater sense of accomplishment and the more you discover what you have to offer. You experience a more expansive range of your gifts and capacities to contribute. You also experience a reciprocating relationship between your accomplishments and wanting to contribute even more. This is how Heaven on Earth, or any large objective, continues developing momentum.

When I first started speaking about creating Heaven on Earth, I had my own fears about what others would think and say. These were my internal roadblocks. There were also many times I experienced external roadblocks, such as people saying, "That's unrealistic," "That's too big an idea," or "It's impossible." They were simply commenting on my idea, but I took their comments personally...thereby creating yet another roadblock.

You have two options when it comes to a roadblock. You can either use it as a wall that stops you or you can reposition the very same roadblock and use it as a stepping-stone to achieve the result you want. The same roadblock can either slow/stop you, or it can empower you. We've all seen people who've become victims to their roadblocks and we've also seen people who've become victors over their roadblocks. The key to your relationship with a roadblock is your commitment. Which of the two options will you commit to: the roadblock or the result?

As you proceed along the path of creating Heaven on Earth, there will be roadblocks, but as long as your commitment to Heaven on Earth is stronger than your commitment to the roadblock, you'll keep moving forward.

And how do you create a commitment to your objective? Simple. Give your word — to yourself, someone else, or a group — and then honor your word. Honoring your word, your commitment, instead of falling victim to the roadblock will unleash a flood of positive new energies.

To review: Be clear about your objective; know that if the objective is large, the roadblock may be proportionately as large; and know that your commitment to the result needs to be stronger than your commitment to the roadblock. With these three factors in place, you're well on your way. (Also see Appendix 1, Section c, p. 254: The Five Most Common Roadblocks and What You Can Do about Them.)

"How wonderful it is that nobody need wait a single moment before starting to improve the world."

Anne Frank

Here are three additional perspectives that can support you in achieving your Heaven on Earth result: (1) Moving from Belief to Commitment, (2) Being Responsible, and (3) Achieving a Result Beyond What You Believe Is Possible.

Moving from Belief to Commitment

Why do people believe they can't bring about Heaven on Earth — believe that it's impossible for Humanity to get it together and choose to have the entire world work?

"Well," they say, "look at the evidence: war, poverty, crime, violence, hunger, inefficiencies, injustice, cruelty, pollution, and so on. Many of these issues have been with us since the beginning of recorded history, and it's obvious they're still here. So, we have proof that we didn't have Heaven on Earth in the past and we certainly don't have it now. We can then logically conclude and believe we won't have it in the future."

Believing that we can't have Heaven on Earth is just like any other limiting belief. It's the same as: I believe I can't create enough money, I believe I don't have enough time, I believe I'm not good enough, and other similar beliefs.

Why would someone purposely set out to prove that life isn't and can never be Heaven on Earth? Why would a person want to continually prove that life doesn't work, that it can't work, that that's the very nature of existence?

Somewhere along the line, we have chosen — unknowingly, without awareness — to believe and live out of the belief that "Life is not and cannot be Heaven on Earth."

But consider for a moment a more empowering alternative. What if we simply made a commitment, gave our word, that from this moment on, this life, this world, *is* Heaven on Earth? What if we then looked for and created examples and evidence of this new commitment? Wouldn't that be to our individual and collective advantage?

What if our positive commitment drove us instead of our negative belief? What would happen? What would change in our lives this minute, tomorrow, next year? How would the world begin to change for the better?

What if we commit to increasing the visible amount of what works in the world? What if we use Heaven on Earth as our Civilization-Fueling Vision?

As more and more people deliberately choose "We are creating Heaven on Earth," the commitment expands globally. Since we want to have results consistent with our commitment, we will naturally look for and create results that show Heaven on Earth is here and is expanding.

Your choice of the story within which life occurs can either be "This is not Heaven on Earth and it can never be" or "We are creating Heaven on Earth." The choice is yours. I invite you to simply be willing to commit to living your life as though Heaven on Earth is showing up all around you, and then set out to prove it.

Being Responsible

*"We can choose to be audacious enough
to take responsibility for the entire human family."*
Werner Erhard

To produce a result, you need to be responsible for it being produced. Setting an objective for yourself and being responsible for accomplishing it energizes you and others. When you accomplish what you've set out to accomplish, you move forward, you feel a sense of momentum, you expand your capacity.

In creating Heaven on Earth, we are going to confront the need to be responsible for problems, issues, roadblocks, and opportunities that are not in our normal realm of responsibility. If I asked you right now to be responsible for ensuring there were no more wars on the planet...ever, what would you think? What would you feel? Or if I asked you to be responsible for ensuring an end to all disease or an end to all environmental pollution?

If each of the more than seven billion people in our world today think we are individually not responsible for ending war, then we have a global mind-set that will at best only produce interim solutions to selected wars. We won't have a global mind-set that is committed to and responsible for ending war *once and for all*. Imagine all of us actually being responsible for ending war. How long do you think the existence of war would last? That's exactly the kind of thinking and perspective needed to help create Heaven on Earth.

If expanding our sense of responsibility can give us new benefits — the end of war, the end of poverty, the end of disease, the end of hunger — why are we so reluctant to expand what we are responsible for? Why are we willing to be responsible only for certain things and not others?

It's because our beliefs tell us there are certain things we are not and cannot be responsible for: "I'm not responsible for ending an armed conflict between two groups." "I'm not responsible for ending world hunger." "I'm not responsible for ending homelessness, environmental pollution, slavery, or torture." Why do we draw a line where our responsibility ends, *especially* if we would really like to see these issues ended?

Take a moment to look at your life and see what you are not willing to be responsible for. Where do you draw the line separating what you are and are not willing to be responsible for?

Why do people continue being not responsible? Because when they think about being responsible for additional issues, there is an association of responsibility with blame, shame, guilt, or burden. Phrases shouted in anger like, "Who's responsible for this?" or embarrassingly mumbled like, "I am responsible for that," have led us to be apprehensive of, frightened by, or overwhelmed by the idea of being responsible for some aspects of life. We may feel that being more responsible means taking on more burdens or more blame or guilt, and who wants that?

Let me be clear here. I am not talking about *taking* responsibility, I'm talking about *being* responsible. Taking responsibility implies added burden. Being responsible implies a willingness to be responsible for producing a chosen result. It doesn't mean *you* have to do it all. It does, however, mean it has to get done.

And, it's easier than you think. As my dear friend Bob Branscom, a management trainer and author, used to say, "You don't have to be 100% responsible 100% of the time for 100% of it all. All it takes is a willingness to operate *as though* you are responsible." You don't even have to believe you are responsible in order to be responsible. All you have to do is live life as though you are responsible for bringing about a chosen result and observe what happens.

> Let's try a little experiment. Name an issue in your life, work or in the world, that you'd like to see resolved, or cleared up. It can be an issue that's been bothering you or one that hasn't been working. Make it an issue that you don't feel responsible for.
>
> Look and see what or who is responsible for it.
>
> Notice that as long as someone or something else is responsible, the situation stays pretty much the same — stuck.
>
> Since this is an experiment, would you be willing to live as though you are responsible for solving this issue? The "as though" allows the situation to become unstuck, it allows for some initial movement.

If the answer is "no," then just lightly notice your unwillingness.

If the answer is "yes," then what's the first, simple, easy, concrete step you can take to create some progress? Do that and watch what happens.

Living from "I am *not* responsible," you are at the effect of life. Life does it to you. Living from "I *am* responsible," you are at cause in life. You are in your center of power and creativity. You are making the kind of difference in the world that gives you the pleasure of accomplishment.

I'm asking you to be willing to operate as though you are responsible for creating Heaven on Earth.

Along with a growing number of others around the world, you can become what Raquel Santilli Villares, a social entrepreneur in Brazil, calls "co-responsible."

My friend, author, philosopher, teacher, Gordon Allan says:

> "As we evolve individually and collectively, so, too, does our notion of 'responsibility.' Responsibility has evolved from the non-responsible, 'Do as you're told,' to the hyper-responsible, 'It's all up to you.' The first asks people to be less responsible than they are and the latter asks people to be more responsible than they can be. Ultimately, both leave people alone and disempowered.
>
> "However, when we begin to view responsibility as a lived way of being, a new paradigm of responsibility arises, which transcends the prior two and results in people having an expanded willingness to engage the unknown together.
>
> "This new view of responsibility arises directly out of the notion of Humanity as a living entity with individuals being analogous to the cells of the collective human organism. Each person, each part of Humanity, has a specific task, but can't live or function independently of others, nor can Humanity as a whole function independent of each of us.
>
> "Responsibility at this level is a paradox that by its nature cannot be rationally understood but can be intuited. The following statement illustrates this: 'Humanity is engaged in an extraordinary transformation. Whether or not it succeeds is [y]our responsibility.' Viewed from this relational context, we are responsible, both individually and collectively, for the co-creation of Heaven on Earth."

"…we all share responsibility for the current state of the world.
We also all share responsibility for the shape of the future."
David Woolfson

Achieving a Result Beyond What You Believe Is Possible!

Many people believe that, in order to do something, they need to believe that they can do it. They say, "In order for me to do X, I need to *believe* that I can do X." Belief then is a prerequisite for accomplishment. But this is not necessarily true. Let me explain.

If we think we need to believe we can do something in order to do it, then we will only do those things we believe we can do. But what if we wanted to do something and believed we couldn't do it? What if we wanted to end world hunger but didn't believe we could do it? Aren't we constantly seeing scenes of starving children on TV? Or what if we wanted to end war but didn't believe we could? There have always been wars and there are wars now. Therefore, there will always be wars.

According to this operating assumption, we have to wait until we believe we can do something in order to do it. The result is that our time is spent either waiting for or trying to create the belief.

One way we try to avoid this assumption is to make our objective smaller. This makes it easier to believe we can accomplish it. We do achieve a result, but the result is smaller than what we originally wanted. Another way we try to avoid our assumption is to move the date for the completion of the objective farther into the future. This also makes it easier to believe we can accomplish it. Again, we achieve a result, but it's farther away than we originally wanted.

In both of these attempts, we achieve a result, but we haven't gone for what we really want, we've settled for less. "Waiting for the belief to be there" still exerts its control over us.

Waiting for the belief to be present doesn't give us what we want. While we're waiting to have the belief that we can end hunger or war, hunger and war persist — people are suffering, children continue to die, and families, cities, and countries are destroyed. The fact that we don't believe it's possible to end hunger or abolish war, and the fact that we think we need to believe it's possible before we begin, becomes more important and powerful than our actually ending them! The necessity for the belief to first be present prevents us from getting into action.

There is another, much more useful way to engage with this. What if we say we don't believe we can end hunger or end war and we do it anyway? What if we say having the belief that we can do something is not a necessary prerequisite to producing a result? What if we make taking action on ending hunger or war far more important than waiting to have the belief that we can end it?

Let's relate this to your own life. Have you ever seen someone do something amazing and then they say, "I don't believe I did that"? Have you ever done something so amazing yourself and then said, "I don't believe I did that"? How can this be? How can you continue having experiences in your life where you, or others, actually accomplish something and then say, "I don't believe I did it"?

How do people achieve something *without* believing they can? Doesn't this fly directly in the face of the basic assumption that we have to believe we can do something in order to do it? Why is this so?

The reason is:

**It is not necessary
to believe you can accomplish something
in order to accomplish it.**

It's nice if it's there, but it's not necessary. You don't have to believe that you can do something in order to do it. What you need in order to do something is to *do it!*

In the mid-1980s, I decided to run a full 26.2-mile marathon. I'd never run one before. The most I'd ever run was 5 miles, which is what I believed I'd probably do in the marathon. I phoned two friends, Bryan and Jim, and asked them to join me.

The day of the marathon was beautiful and sunny. There were about 2,000 runners at the starting line and we all took off at the sound of the starter's gun. I was running at a faster pace than I ever had. Bryan, Jim, and I talked and laughed and sang and joked as we ran. Whenever I felt tired, the two of them would urge me on and vice versa.

We passed the 5-mile mark, the 6, then the 7-mile mark. Things were going fine. Then came miles 8, 9, and 10. Then miles 11, 12, 13, and 14. Even at 15 miles, we were all going strong. At 16 miles, a funny thing happened. I was still running, but when I looked around me, everything was standing still. How could that be? I didn't understand. Then I looked down at my legs and immediately understood. They weren't moving! I was running from the waist up, not from the waist down — I'd hit "the wall." And so the marathon ended for me (Jim and Bryan kept going).

Here I was with a belief that I could only run 5 miles because that's the most I'd ever done. Yet on that day I ran 16. And to this very day, I still don't believe I did it. It was so far beyond my belief of what I thought I could do. But so what? I did it. The limiting belief hadn't won, the accomplishment had won — I'd won!

Do you see the freedom this gives you? You can say, "I am going to end hunger in the world and I don't believe I can do it," and then you set out to end it. You can say, "I am going to end war in the world" (or end disease, or end hatred), not believe you can, and then set out to end it.

Looking at belief in this way allows you to begin, allows you to take action to solve the problem, allows you to produce your deeply desired result. Would it be all right with you if hunger ended in the world and you didn't believe it was possible? Would it be all right with you if war and poverty and disease ended in the world and you didn't believe it was possible? Of course it would.

Imagine our world as more and more people live from this perspective: more and more people taking on their heart's desires in spite of not believing they can achieve them, rather than sitting around waiting to believe they can. How different would our world be? Wouldn't we be well on our way to *co-creating* Heaven on Earth?

My invitation is that you be more committed to producing the seemingly impossible results in your life and in the world — those results that you don't believe are possible to achieve, yet you still want them — than setting out to prove how you have to believe you can do something before you actually do it.

Remember: It's not necessary to believe you can accomplish something in order to accomplish it.

If You Show Up, They Will Build It!

In the spring of 1998 Claire Warhaftig and her husband, Irving, traveled to Mexico to the artists' city of San Miguel d'Allende. The sponsoring organization was Patronato Pro Niños. The Americans living there open their homes to guests to house and feed them. They also provide tours and escorted shopping sprees. All the fees go to charity.

One day all the guests were invited to visit two poor rural areas. Of the 25 people in the group, only Claire, Irving, and one other person went.

They visited what Claire described as not a village, but a cluster of thatched cottages called Rosa Blanca. Attached to one of the cottages was a shoddy bamboo structure out of which peered children dressed in ragged clothing. It was the schoolhouse.

Claire was very upset with the condition of the school, which had no electricity, water, or light. She asked the teacher, Minerva, what the students needed: pens, pencils, etc.? "No," said Minerva, "the Mexican government gives us all the supplies we need. What we really need is a new schoolhouse."

"I can't do that," thought Claire. But the idea stuck in her mind and began gnawing at her. She spoke to the Patronato Pro Niños people and asked, "If I decide to help, what should I do?" They said she should build a two-room schoolhouse, one for regular students and one for preschoolers. She asked how much it would cost and was told $1,000. She responded from her heart. "Ok, I'll do it."

Claire returned to the U.S. and sent out a letter to all her friends asking for donations. She then contacted Patronato Pro Niños again, asking how they thought she should proceed. One man said hesitatingly, "The materials will be stolen." Another replied, "There are no men in Rosa Blanca who can build it."

Claire had never done anything like this before, but she had this immense faith that the building would be built. She made the commitment, took the initiative, followed through, and did a fund-raising mailing. She didn't raise $1,000 — she raised $4,500!

So, the building began. The building materials were not stolen. There were men who could and did build the schoolhouse. What problems there were involved communication between Mexico and the U.S. To put it mildly, they were very difficult. It took weeks for letters to be received and translated. Throughout all of this, building proceeded.

Sixteen months later, the schoolhouse was completed. The cost: $2,500. Claire used the rest of the money to buy books, audiotapes, even a Spanish encyclopedia. One day, Claire was in Denver and discovered a store that sold Spanish globes. She also found a miniature plastic skeleton with all the body parts labeled in Spanish. She bought them both and sent them to Santa Rosa.

On their next trip, Claire and Irving visited the completed school. One old grandmother joyfully said to her, "It's a milagro (miracle), it's a milagro. I have a school for my grandchildren."

The people felt that somebody cared about them, somebody saw them. They felt they mattered, that they now counted.

Claire took individual pictures of all the children, had each one framed, and placed them on a wall of the school.

She then asked, "Now what?" She was told they needed two toilets, one for the boys and one for the girls. They now have the two toilets. The children and everyone else in Rosa Blanca — all 39 people — also needed shoes. Claire and Irv got the exact shoe measurements of each person, went to the local flea market, and bought shoes for every single person.

On their third visit, in March of 2000, something new happened. This time the women in Rosa Blanca told Claire, "We'd like to give you something. Tomorrow, we are going to bring lunch."

The next day, they brought chicken and cactus and rice and, of course, a little home brew. It was more than a meal, it was a celebration of their combined spirit.

Again Claire asked, "Now what?" They began to talk about having running water. Again, Claire said, "Ok, I'll do it." This was becoming a habit.

The women of the village were deeply touched. They asked when Claire would come back and she replied, "When there's water, I'll come back and shower with you."

Claire returned home and began her own "drilling" for water. She found David Douglas of Waterlines, an organization that arranges to bring water to villages. David speaks Spanish, knows people in the area, and he promised Claire money for the water (Waterlines is funded by different Presbyterian churches, each providing funding to bring water to a specific village).

David paid to have a hydrologist, a water expert, visit Rosa Blanca and test to see how deep the well would have to be to have a permanent supply. The hydrologist reported back that, unfortunately, the well would have to be dug so deep that the money could be better used building an entire hospital.

Claire was disappointed…but we're talking about Claire and Rosa Blanca. Several weeks later David phoned back and said that the county of San Miguel would pay to bring a water line out from the city if Rosa Blanca hooked up with another community. No problem!

Claire again asked Minerva, "What now?" Minerva responded, "A library."

"Okay," said Claire.

This time Claire was forced to start sending grant proposals to foundations, another thing she'd never done before. She began writing foundations and talking to a man who might fund not only this library, but a new library system for all of Mexico.

Claire's new idea is to get others around the world to adopt similar communities. She has asked people to visit a country or an area that is less well off. "Find your own Rosa Blanca," she says. "Make it yours. Make it your family. Make it work."

At one of her meetings with Minerva, Claire was asked, "How do you want the new school to be named?" Not wanting to be forward, Minerva was actually asking if Claire would like the school named after her. Without pause, Claire answered, "I want it called Escuela Milagrosa Numero Uno (Miracle School #1)."

Claire sees this school as the first of many such Miracle Schools around the world.

"To keep resisting Heaven on Earth takes more energy and yields more pain than simply creating it."

Rinaldo Brutoco

Going Viral with Heaven on Earth

When you're living from the context of co-creating Heaven on Earth, all contributions play a part. When I asked my friend Gordon Allan for his definition of Heaven on Earth, he jokingly said, "Ask someone else." After I laughed, I began to think that wasn't such a bad idea. I then expanded on it and thought, *"What if we asked just two people the three Heaven on Earth questions?"*

1. Recall a time when you experienced Heaven on Earth. What was happening?

2. Imagine you have a magic wand and with it you can create Heaven on Earth. What is Heaven on Earth for you?

3. What simple, easy, concrete step(s) will you take in the next 24 hours to make Heaven on Earth real?

Engaging people with these three questions will get them thinking, talking, and doing — it will start a global conversation and movement.

Suppose you ask two people today, and ask them each to do the same with two people tomorrow. On the third day the four people ask two new people each, and so on and so on. And let's suppose everyone participates. How long do you think it would take to contact all of the more than seven billion people on the planet — 100 days...300 days...two years...seven years...?

It would take just 32 days to reach the entire world!

Day	Number of people spoken to that day	Total spoken to
Day 1	**2**	**2**
Day 2	4	6
Day 3	8	14
Day 4	16	30
Day 5	32	62
Day 6	64	126
Day 7	128	254
Day 8	256	510
Day 9	512	1,022
Day 10	1,024	2,046
Day 11	2,048	4,094
Day 12	4,096	8,190
Day 13	8,192	16,382
Day 14	16,384	32,766
Day 15	32,768	65,534
Day 16	65,536	131,070
Day 17	131,072	262,142
Day 18	262,144	524,286
Day 19	**524,288**	**1,048,574**
Day 20	1,048,576	2,097,150
Day 21	2,097,152	4,194,302
Day 22	4,194,304	8,388,606
Day 23	8,388,608	16,777,214
Day 24	16,777,216	33,554,430
Day 25	33,554,432	67,108,862
Day 26	67,108,864	134,217,726
Day 27	134,217,728	268,435,454
Day 28	268,435,456	536,870,910
Day 29	**536,870,912**	**1,073,741,822**
Day 30	1,073,741,824	2,147,483,646
Day 31	2,147,483,648	4,294,967,294
Day 32	4,294,967,296	8,589,934,590

It takes 19 days to reach the first million people, but only 10 more days to reach the first billion.

Here's how it works:

• On Day 1, you talk to 2 people.

• On Day 2, the 2 people from Day 1 each talk to 2 people for a total of 4 people spoken to. The **total** number of people spoken to in 2 days equals 6 (2 from Day 1 + 4 from Day 2).

• On Day 3, the 4 people spoken to on day 2 each talk to 2 new people for a total of 8 people. The total number of people spoken to in 3 days then equals 14 (2 from Day 1 + 4 from Day 2 + 8 from Day 3 = 14).

The process of each person speaking to just 2 people mushrooms exponentially.

Let's look at a graph of this chart….

TOTAL NUMBER OF PEOPLE SPOKEN TO

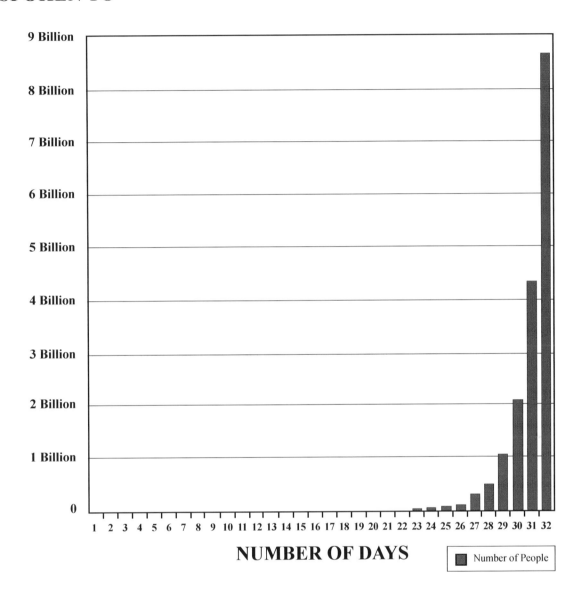

Nothing appears to be happening on this chart until day 23, when it bursts out and takes off like a rocket. Thomas Petinger, Jr. once wrote "You can heat water from 33 degrees to 211 degrees without seeing much change, but raise the temperature just one more degree and a totally new thing appears."

Are you willing to ask two people the three Heaven on Earth questions today? Who are your two people?

"Heaven on Earth is...

when we realize our responsibility to help each other
to maximize our human potential—
what a quantum leap that would be
for the collective quality of humanity."

Philip J. Krawitz
Chief Executive Officer
Cape Union Mart Group of Companies
South Africa

"...our conversations organize the processes and structures,
which shape our collective futures."

Peter Senge

Chapter 5

The Voice of Humanity

There are people, in history and today, who speak for the whole of Humanity — Nelson Mandela, the Dalai Lama, Mother Teresa, Archbishop Tutu, Václav Havel, Helen Keller, Buckminster Fuller, the Pope and the Secretary-General of the United Nations, among many others.

What allows these people to speak for Humanity is:

- They have achieved status by virtue of their position.

- They have credibility because of their commitment and results.

- They have stepped forward to lead in times of great collective adversity.

- They are in a line of authority that has traditionally spoken for Humanity.

We give them our committed listening — when they speak, we listen.

Speaking for Humanity is not limited to just these people. Each of us also possesses the ability to speak for and to Humanity. It's just that we haven't been made aware that we have this ability or been trained to express it. We haven't exercised this voice because we haven't recognized it as an innate capacity within ourselves.

Because we are members of the human family and share the experience of our common Humanity, we can speak on its behalf. Our hearts are touched when we see a starving infant, an avalanche burying people, or a fire destroying someone's home. Even if these events occur in another country, another culture, we instinctively know and share the feeling of the mother who has lost her child, the soldier wounded in battle, the grandmother forced to flee her lifelong home. We do feel another's suffering. We do experience the commonality of being human. We can speak for the whole, to the whole.

It's now time to discover our collective voice that gives expression to our commonality. It's time to nurture the expression of this ability already innate within each of us. It's time to put into practice our capacity to speak and listen to "The Voice of Humanity." What's needed in our evolution is to bring this out so that it is globally heard, experienced, and known.

When we stop and reflect on where we as Humanity have been, where we are and where we're going, then using our voice becomes vital as one of the foundations for our positive collective future. It's time to give our voice a more public expression. How can we make this happen?

Celebration is one expression of the Voice of Humanity. On December 31, 1999, we watched the dawning of the third millennium in the Julian calendar. I was struck by how we observed universal expressions, no matter the language, no matter the country: dance, music, ceremony, fireworks, joy, and celebration. These were common to all people and places on Earth. When we celebrate, the human commonality underlying our various forms of celebration is evident.

Speaking as One

The Voice of Humanity can be expressed in many ways. Let's bring it forth into our collective public expression using words, images, symbols and experiences that are felt, understood, and have meaning globally. We want to express that which uplifts the human condition and inspires us.

We could:

- Launch a YouTube channel where people can speak to and on behalf of Humanity.

- Start "The Voice of Humanity" programs in public schools, colleges, and universities. (See Appendix 2: A Four-Year Undergraduate University Degree in Co-Creating Heaven on Earth.)

- Create a "This Is How I Inspire Humanity" contest. The winning entries would be posted on a website and featured in newspaper and magazine articles.

- Hold a contest to depict, in any art form, what people want to say to Humanity. The winning entries would be posted online and the originals would travel the world in a Voice of Humanity exhibit.

- Showcase people and groups speaking on behalf of Humanity on TV and in newspapers and magazines.

- Establish a program for both children and adults at the United Nations where they speak from the dais to the entire UN.

- Convene a conference of the world's Faith Traditions on "The Purpose of Humanity" and then expand the global conversation about it.

The possibilities are endless. What could you do to support the cultural blooming of the Voice of Humanity in your own unique way? Speaking as one, we evolve the discourse of Heaven on Earth to merge the individual with the global, the public with the personal.

In the same way that the introduction and development of language helped move evolution forward, the introduction of "The Voice of Humanity" will help move us to our next evolutionary level.

The Voice of Humanity

You can speak to all of Humanity.
What will you say?

You can speak on behalf of all Humanity.
What will you say?

"Heaven on Earth is...

humankind consciously connected to
its spiritual source."

Tim Clauss
Management Consultant
& Spiritual Counselor
USA

"…if we pass a strainer through the world's religions
to lift out their conclusions about reality and how life should be lived,
those conclusions begin to look like the winnowed wisdom of the human race."

Huston Smith

Chapter 6

Heaven on Earth:
What the Faith Traditions Say

Over the years I've asked thousands of people the three Heaven on Earth questions. Their answers gave me the opportunity to delve deeper and deeper into this inquiry and see patterns and commonality.

In addition to individuals, I wanted to know if any institution had thought about and reflected on Heaven on Earth. It seemed to me that collectively the Faith Traditions would be the institution that would have done the most exploration into this topic and would have the most distilled wisdom to offer.

Originally I'd thought of exploring the three Abrahamic Traditions (Judaism, Christianity, and Islam), along with some of the other more populous ones. But then it dawned on me that it would be more impactful to include a broader range of Traditions and put them in alphabetical order. This would allow us to see the broad scope and grandeur that the Traditions have as a collective institution when they speak about Heaven on Earth.

Where possible in this chapter, I begin with a quote from a sacred text followed by quotes from people writing in that Tradition.

I haven't done an all-inclusive search of every Tradition, nor a definitive search within each one. There is, however, enough material in this chapter to observe that the Traditions do speak about both the idea and the reality of Heaven on Earth, whether the phrase is used specifically, as an allegory, or as a myth.

As you read through the quotes from each Tradition, experience what moves you, explore what reveals new clarity, and reflect on new revelations or insights.

I invite you to find Heaven on Earth references in your own Tradition. I'd love to see what you find. Please send them to me at: www.ProjectHeavenOnEarth.com

In their collective voice, the Traditions provide, for me, a power and a moral authority. In their collective clarity, there is an elemental, transcendent, and connecting call. And in their combined expression, there is the ancient, the modern, and the visionary. Taken together, the Faith Traditions are another dimension of the Voice of Humanity speaking about the experience and for the co-creation of Heaven on Earth.

BAHA'I

"Today, this Servant has assuredly come to vivify the world and to bring into unity all who are on the face of the Earth. That which God willeth shall come to pass and thou shalt see the Earth as the Abhá (Most Glorious) Paradise."

Baha'u'llah
Tablet to Ra'is

"...in this marvelous cycle, the Earth will be transformed, and the world of humanity arrayed in tranquility and beauty. Disputes, quarrels, and murders will be replaced by peace, truth, and concord; among the nations, people, races, and countries, love and amity will appear. Co-operation and union will be established, and finally war will be entirely suppressed.... Universal peace will raise its tent in the center of the Earth...."

`Abdu'l-Bahá

"In these days, the East is in need of material progress and the West is in need of a spiritual ideal. It would be well for the West to turn to the East for illumination, and to give in exchange its scientific knowledge. There must be this interchange of gifts. The East and the West must unite to give each other what is lacking.... This union will bring about true civilization where the spiritual is expressed and carried out in the material. Receiving thus, the one from the other, the greatest harmony will prevail, all people will be united, a state of great perfection will be attained, there will be a firm cementing, and this world will become a shining mirror for the reflection of the attributes of God."

`Abdu'l-Bahá

BUDDHISM

"...all living beings are the Buddha-Land sought by all Bodhisattvas."
The Vimalakirti Nirdesa Sutra

"While everyone has a responsibility to help the world, we can create additional chaos if we try to impose our ideas or our help upon others. Many people have theories about what the world needs. Some people think that the world needs communism; some people think that the world needs democracy; some people think that technology will save the world; some people think that technology will destroy the world. The Shambhala teachings are not based on converting the world to another theory. The premise of Shambhala vision is that, in order to establish an enlightened society for others, we need to discover what inherently we have to offer the world. So, to begin with, we should make an effort to examine our own experience, in order to see what it contains that is of value in helping ourselves and others to uplift their existence."

Chögyam Trungpa Rinpoche

"The ordinary conception of the soul's being transported to Paradise and born there was merely a figure of speech...the fact being that neither Amida [Buddha], nor the sainted beings [Bodhisattvas]... are to be conceived as existing 'over there' at all, because the Pure Land is the ultimate and absolute reality, and that is everywhere, so that we may be identified with it right here where we are."

Ryoyo Shogei

CHRISTIANITY

"May your Kingdom come. May your will be done on earth, as it is in heaven."

Luke 11:2 (World English Bible)

"The Kingdom of God is still a collective conception, involving the whole social life of man. It is not a matter of saving human atoms, but of saving the social organism. It is not a matter of getting individuals to heaven, but of transforming the life on earth into the harmony of heaven."

Walter Rauschenbusch
Christianity and the Social Crisis

"If we could see the holy in every reality, we should be in the Kingdom of God."

Paul Tillich

"Heaven and earth are threads from the same loom."

A Shaker saying

"The Kingdom of God is not to be found in some other world beyond, but in the midst of this world…. God wants us to honor Him in our fellow man — and nowhere else."

Dietrich Bonhoeffer

"Working toward Heaven on Earth is entering into communion with God and so enabling Him to work His divine will through us."

Anglican Bishop Henry Hill

"Heaven is wherever God is. The word 'heaven' does not designate a place but, rather, indicates God's presence, which is not bound by space and time.

"We should not look for heaven above the clouds. Wherever we turn to God in his glory and to our neighbor in his need; wherever we experience the joys of love; whenever we convert and allow ourselves to be reconciled with God, heaven opens there. 'Not that God is where heaven is, but rather heaven is where God is' (Gerhard Ebeling)."

YOUCAT question 518

CONFUCIANISM

"Heaven means to be one with God."

Confucius

"The great man regards Heaven and Earth and the myriad things as one body. He regards the world as one family and the country as one person…. That the great man can regard Heaven, Earth, and the myriad things as one body is not because he deliberately wants to do so, but because it is natural to the humane nature of his mind that he do so…. Such a mind is rooted in his Heaven-endowed nature…."

The Great Learning

"The Confucian path to human flourishing, neither a spiritual journey to the other shore nor a salvation in the next life, is rooted in the improvability of this world and this life."

Wei-ming Tu

"To bring to completion without acting, to obtain without seeking — this is the work of Heaven."

Hsün Tzu

"When the work of Heaven has been established and its accomplishments brought to completion, when the form of man is whole and his spirit born, then love and hate, delight and anger, sorrow and joy find lodging in him."

Hsün Tzu

HINDUISM

"Truly, as far as the space of this [universe] extends, that far extends the space within the heart. Within it are held both Heaven and Earth...."

The Chandogya Upanishad

"Only spiritual consciousness — realization of God's presence in oneself and in every other living being — can save the world. I see no chance for peace without it. Begin with yourself. There is no time to waste. It is your duty to do your part to bring God's kingdom on Earth."

Paramahansa Yogananda

"...the world famous Sri Meenakshi Sundareswarar Temple standing out as a glorious monument creating a feeling of heaven on earth."

Shastry V. Mallady

(This quote begins with a shloka/verse, a morning prayer: "I do not ask for temporal power, nor do I ask to go to heaven, nor even to attain *nirvana*. What I ask for is that I may be able to relieve the pain of those who are in pain.")
To which Gandhi adds: "The prayer, you will note, is not exclusive. It is not restricted to one's own caste or community. It is all-inclusive. It comprehends the whole of humanity. Its realization would thus mean the establishment of the Kingdom of Heaven on Earth."

Mahatma Gandhi
Harijan

INDIGENOUS

"Once you feel what it means to live in a state of bliss, you will love it. You will know that Heaven on Earth is truth — that Heaven truly exists. This way of life is possible and it's in your hands. Moses called it the Promised Land, Buddha called it Nirvana, Jesus called it Heaven, and the Toltecs call it a New Dream."

don Miguel Ruiz
The Four Agreements

"All of us alive on Lady Gaia at this time have the opportunity to be an active part of the Rainbow of Light that creates the bridge into a new and Golden Time for All Our Relations and us. At this point in human history, we have the opportunity to literally bring Heaven to Earth. Our ability to visualize and believe it is possible for us to lift ourselves up, to pick up the profound work of our earthly ancestors and move responsibly into our own piece of the action, and to fully embody Spirit is what will make this ascension possible. The exciting part is that we have the opportunity to complete something Mother Earth and humanity have been working on for eons."

Brooke Medicine Eagle
The Last Ghost Dance: A Guide for Earth Mages

"To me Turangawaewae describes heaven on earth. Turangawaewae is where the tipuna have woven a standing place for my sacred print (tu — stand, ranga — weave, waewae — feet). Tipuna are all the ancestral beings who have contributed to my presence on earth. They are the source of my growth (tipu — grow, puna — source). They include Wai (Water), Hau (Wind), Maunga (Mountain), Whenua (Land), Rakau (Tree). They are the elders. Humans are the youngest in the evolutionary chain. The weavings of the elder's sacred print has created this beautiful planet as a turangawaewae for all mokopuna (moko — blueprint, puna — source). When younger remembers elder with respect and gratitude, younger experiences turangawaewae as heaven on earth."

Makuini Ruth Tai, Maori
Aotearoa/New Zealand

ISLAM

"Verily God does not change that state of a people till they change themselves."

The Qur-an: Surah 13.11

"A man's true wealth is the good he does in the world."

Prophet Mohammed (PBUH)

"We Muslims believe we need to live our earthly life in a heavenly way. To create Heaven on Earth is obligatory in Islam, it is ordered. What we do in this life will shape our life in Heaven. We should contribute to creating all the features of Heaven here on Earth. We will be rewarded after death for this. Thus everyone is being tested to see if they are making Earth a better world. Remember, what you do in this world shapes your lot in the world to come. This is the test of man to make it a better world."

Dr. Hassan Hathout
The Islamic Center of
Southern California

"The goals of Islam (maqasid al-Shari'ah)… are…based on its own concepts of human well-being (falah) and good life (hayat tayyibah) which give utmost importance to brotherhood and socio-economic justice and require a balanced satisfaction of both the material and the spiritual needs of all human beings. This is because of the belief that all human beings are equal in being God's viceregents on earth and His dependents, and cannot feel inner happiness and tranquility until the real well-being of all has been attained through the satisfaction of both spiritual and material needs."

Dr. Muhammad Umer Chapra

"Let the beauty we love be what we do!"

Rumi

JAINISM

"Jain Dharma teaches you Heaven is in your hands as is Hell. If you don't experience Heaven, life has no meaning. Where we are living now is Heaven. It's all Heaven. People have to know Heaven is not a concept. It's all these things that create harmony in life, and the things that are conducive to living peacefully are Heavenly things.

"It's YOUR CHOICE to have Heaven or Hell in every moment in your life. There are four fundamental things that create Heavenly feelings: things that create Heavenly feelings in you, place, time, and what you experience.

"We have to untie the knots preventing our experience of Heaven: anger, ego, selfishness/deceitfulness, and greed. When you have no knots inside or outside, that's how you feel Heavenly. The Kingdom of Heaven is within us. So, wherever we go, we have Heaven. You have freedom of choice and your choices will create Heaven or Hell. You can go from Heaven here on Earth to Heaven there in Heaven."

Pujyashri Chitrabhanu

"In Jainism, it is the pious duty of a householder to fix a limit to his possessions, as well as for his consumption and to use his extra money for the service of mankind. It is through the observation of these vows that we can restore peace and harmony in human society and eradicate economic inequality and class conflicts."

Professor Sagarmal Jain
*The Solutions of World Problems
from a Jain Perspective*

JUDAISM

"The Golden Age of Humanity is not in the past, but in the future (Isaiah II and XI); and all the children of men are destined to help in the establishment of that Kingdom of God on earth."

Edited by Dr. J. H. Hertz, C.H.
Late Chief Rabbi of the British Empire
The Pentateuch and Haftorahs,
Hebrew Text English Translation and Commentary
2nd Edition

"…man's return to God and the restoration of Paradise on earth require…a revival of devotion to duty, an effort within the capacity of every human being…."

Samson Raphael Hirsch
T'RUMATH TZVI

"When we reflect on the suffering in the world… we know this is not the way the world should be. It is not what God intended for us. Judaism teaches us not to accept the status quo and never to give up our dreams for a better world."

Melinda Ribner
New Age Judaism: Ancient Wisdom for the Modern World

Rabbi Tarfon taught: "It is not your responsibility to finish the work of perfecting the world, but you are not free to desist from trying."

The Pirke Avot, 2:21
as interpreted by Larry Kahaner in
Values, Prosperity and the Talmud:
Business Lessons from the Ancient Rabbis

"We are not waiting for some great revelation from above to save us from our incompetence as guardians of this world and put everything in order. Rather, we are waiting to see the sun rise over everything we have done, to see the fruits of our labors blossom in an eternal spring."

Compiled and interpreted
by Tzvi Freeman
Bringing Heaven Down to Earth:
365 Meditations from the Wisdom of
the Rebbe Menachem M. Schneerson

MORMONISM

"God help us to build homes in which the spirit of Heaven on Earth may be experienced. You and I know that this is possible; it is not a dream; it is not a theory."

Gospel Ideals: Selections from
the Discourses of David O. McKay

"We know that the kingdom of God, which is established among us, will continue to spread…until it covers the Earth."

John Taylor

"When the opportunity to serve is recognized as a blessing, where thoughtfulness, courtesy, tolerance, kindness, consideration are habitual, where duties become privileges, where virtues are recognized and gratefully mentioned, where faults are minimized or overlooked, where the home is enveloped by love and hallowed by prayer, there is Heaven on Earth."

Hugh B. Brown
Continuing the Quest

"Generally speaking, the Mormon Church considers the home to be the place that Heaven on Earth can be experienced. Because the foundation belief is that we are here on Earth to gain a physical body, and have our spirit become completely one with our human mind and body, we individually and collectively can also become Heaven on Earth."

Richard James
in a letter to Martin Rutte

NEW SPIRITUAL THOUGHT

"Remember, you create your own reality by the choices you make in the moment. Today, go for more moments of creating 'Heaven on Earth.' It's your choice. Efficient decisions from the heart will take you there."

Doc Childre and Sara Paddison
HeartMath Discovery Program

"We create exclusively in accordance with our Heart — we become the co-creators of the universe and are in the flow of Life. We know our power transforms the world. Our positive feelings, thoughts, and actions clear negativity and pollution. We envision peace on Earth. We align with others with the same vision. We give birth to the future and create Heaven on Earth."

Silvana Maria Pagani
Founder, Ministry of Angels

"These…chapters endeavor to bring to light the true meaning and significance of non-duality. They attempt to reveal the deeply mysterious relationship and simultaneous non-difference between Heaven and Earth, between enlightenment and the human experience."

Andrew Cohen
Embracing Heaven and Earth

"Heaven on Earth is the birthright of every individual. It is not necessary to wait until after life to enjoy the life of Heaven. Wishful thinking about living life in Heaven at a time in the future is a waste of the present and a waste of the glorious gift of human life."

Maharishi Mahesh Yogi

"The Kingdom of Heaven is now manifesting on Earth."

Declaration of
"Our Awakened World 2001" Conference

"When the earth is filled with those who have altruistic love to others and put altruistic ways of living into practice in their daily life, the world will become Paradise."

Sekai Mahikari Bunmei Kyodan-USA

SHINTOISM

"According to the Kojiki, the mythological chronology of Japan, the gods of the Shinto religion are believed to have created Japan as their image of paradise on earth…."

N. Alice Yamada

The Omoto Maxim
"Kami is the spirit which pervades the entire universe, and man is the focus of the workings of heaven and earth. When Kami and man become one, infinite power will become manifest."

Onisaburo Deguchi

"Regard heaven as your father, earth as your mother, and all things as your brothers and sisters."

Oracle of the Kami of Atsuta

"To be helpful to others and in the world at large through deeds of service without thought of rewards, and to seek the advancement of the world as one whose life mediates the will of Kami."

Jinja Honcho
Association of Shinto Shrines

"In the Shinto view, the natural state of the cosmos is one of harmony in which divine, natural, and human elements are all intimately related."

Paul Watt

SIKHISM

"Wherever God's Name is chanted, that is heaven. One is filled with bliss when one sees God within oneself."

"I sing the Glorious Praises of the One God forever."

"The City of heaven is where people of Truth dwell."

Siri Guru Granth Sahib
English translation by
Guruka Singh Khalsa

"Amid the nights and seasons, dates and days, amid air, water, fire and netherworlds, the earth is placed as the place for righteous action."

Guru Nanak

TAOISM

"Were marquises and kings able to maintain [the Tao], then ten thousand things would submit to them on their own, and Heaven and Earth would unite to send fourth sweet dew."

Tao Te Ching

"With your body complete and your vitality made whole again, you may become one with Heaven…. When the body and vitality are without flaw, this is called being able to shift. Vitality added to vitality, you return to become the Helper of Heaven."

Chuang-Tzu

"Do not try to develop what is natural to man; develop what is natural to Heaven. He who develops Heaven benefits life; he who develops man injures life. Do not reject what is of Heaven, do not neglect what is of man, and the people will be close to the attainment of Truth."

Chuang-Tzu

ZOROASTRIANISM

"Taking the first step with a good thought, the second step with a good word, and the third with a good deed, I entered Paradise."

Zoroaster

"Thus may we be those who will make existence brilliant, O Wise One and You [other] Ahuras, with the bringer of changes and with truth, when [our] thoughts will have become concentrated (on the place) where insight may be present."

Yasna Gatha 30.9

"Through Your power make real the existence which is brilliant in my imagination, O Ahura."

Yasna Gatha 34.15

"Holiness is the best of all good; it is also happiness. Happy the man who is holy with perfect holiness."
"Which is really meant to say that such a man is in Heaven or, to put it another way, has Heaven in him."

Zend Avesta
with commentary
by Miles M. Dawson

After reading the Faith Traditions quotes, what is clearer for you, what insights did you gain, what three major points impressed you?

_____

_____

_____

_____

_____

Here's what Michael Owens, a PhD student in religion, had to say after he researched the Faith Traditions for me.

> "…'heaven on earth' is clearly not a new idea. …[it] is not something we have recently discovered and no culture can lay claim to its invention. Man has been talking about, theorizing about, desiring, and working towards 'heaven on earth' for as far back as we have written records. One might say that it was not the goal of Jesus or the Buddha to establish Heaven on Earth, but just to get the ball rolling in that direction, to hand over the torch…to others who would carry on the fight. So perhaps the point is not that we live in a Heaven here on Earth, but that we are moving towards it….
>
> "…I think it's important to ask yourself why others have failed, what can I learn from them, and how can I succeed."

When I read what the Faith Traditions have to say, I realized that there is an underlying thread, a constant, common, and collective storyline both ancient and current.

Here are my thoughts after reading all the quotes:

- They illuminate why and how we can achieve Heaven on Earth.

- They describe what will be present and what will be absent.

- The creation of Heaven on Earth has begun.

- Heaven on Earth is possible as an actual, real result. It's more than a dream or theory.

- Heaven on Earth has been worked on for a long time by individuals and small groups. We now have the opportunity to have it be the work of all Humanity.

- It's now time to powerfully go public with this and join with others who share this human destiny and make it happen.

- It's what we're here to do.

- It's our belief that "We can't have Heaven on Earth" that stops us from engaging in creating and having it.

- Heaven on Earth is in our hearts.

- Earth is in Heaven, Earth is not separate from Heaven — Heaven is in Earth, Heaven is not separate from Earth.

- Creating Heaven on Earth is expressing the beauty we love.

- It's already present, right here, right now.

- Don't be concerned only with the next world, make this world work.

- The Work of Heaven is here on Earth.

- It's God's will for us.

- God is ready to bring Heaven on Earth. All we have to do is welcome it, embrace it, and live it.

- Be of service to others and life.

- Discover and give your unique talents/contribution in order to make it happen.

- Don't think Heaven can't happen here. It's here and you are invited to be part of it.

- Heaven on Earth needs to come in through the body.

- We all want to enjoy the fruits of our individual and collective labors — actually seeing Heaven on Earth dawn on Earth.

Transforming Our World Into The Garden of Eden

One day I wondered if there had ever been a time when all of Humanity had experienced Heaven on Earth? "Yes," I thought, "when Adam and Eve, who were all of Humanity, lived in the Garden of Eden. There was enough food and water. There were trees, those that were beautiful to look at and those that provided fruit to eat. There was a river that watered the Garden. There were birds and various kinds of animals. There was no shame, no strife, no disease. It was beautiful to behold. It was Paradise on Earth."

Amidst all this, there was only one prohibition. God told Adam and Eve they could not eat from the Tree of the Knowledge of Good and Evil. All they had to do was simply obey this one decree. But they didn't, they disobeyed. They ate from the Tree, refused to be responsible (they tried to hide, Adam blamed Eve, Eve blamed the serpent), and they were kicked out.

Whether you believe the Garden of Eden is literal/historical or metaphorical, I ask that you please follow along with my exploration here since it is our first earthly experience and memory of Heaven on Earth and since it plays such a defining role in the three Abrahamic religions: Judaism, Christianity, and Islam.

I continued my exploration by asking, "Who was cast out? Was it Adam and Eve or was it them along with the entirety of Humanity that followed?" To answer this, I asked a local Orthodox rabbi who explained that in the original Hebrew text, the word "Adam" is not used by itself. Rather, what is written is "ha Adam," which translates as "the Adam." "The use of the definite article," he said, "implies *all* Adam, all of Humanity. So, when Adam and Eve were expelled from the Garden, all of Humanity was expelled."

"All right," I said to him, "if we're out, we're out." Then a fascinating notion popped into my head. "After we were kicked out," I asked, "does it say anywhere in the Torah (the Bible) that we can't go back in? Does it say we cannot re-enter?" The rabbi said he'd never been asked this before and he'd have to get back to me. The next day he called and said, "No, it doesn't say we can't go back in."

I was flabbergasted. I literally thought I was going to fall off my chair.

What instantly became clear to me was that a mis-belief, an erroneous myth, had been created — we believed that because we had been expelled, we would never be able to return. Yet the Torah *does not* say this. Nowhere does it state that God said we could not come back — *we concluded it*. This insight was myth shattering.

Genesis 3:24 says that God drove Adam and Eve out of the Garden. I wanted to know what the Hebrew for "drive out" is and what it precisely means. I thought that if I went back to the original Hebrew, it might give me more clarity. The Hebrew word used is *vahyihgaresh*, "and He drove out." The root of the verb is *garash*, which translates as: to chase out, drive out, expel, cast out, divorce, drive away.

I called the rabbi again and asked if *garash* implies being "driven out" in only one direction — is the verb one-way or is there a chance of return? He said it does not imply a one-way direction.

It was now clear to me that *garash* does *not* mean driven out *without* any possibility of returning.

I called another rabbi and asked about Genesis 3:23, which says, again referring to Adam, that God *sent him forth* from the Garden to till the ground from whence he was taken. The word, in Hebrew, is *vahyishalchayhoo*, "and He sent him forth." The root of the verb is *shalach*, meaning to send, stretch out, extend, direct, let loose, let go, set free, to send forth. The rabbi said it can be interpreted that man's job is to go out with a mission to accomplish, namely to raise up this world to a higher spiritual level. My interpretation is that we have been sent out of the Garden with the specific mission of making the world outside of the Garden *into* the Garden, of making this world be the Heaven on Earth that Eden was. (To review, the verb in Genesis 3:23 is to "send out with a mission" and the verb in 3:24 is to "send out" but with the possibility of returning.) These interpretations give us an empowering possibility along with a much larger opportunity for the Work of Humanity.

Having explored Judaism, I then turned my attention to Christianity.

I asked my learned Christian friends about this. They replied that the New Testament does not state anywhere that we cannot re-enter the Garden. In fact, just the opposite is true. The way back, they said, is through Christ: "I am the gate; whoever enters through me will be saved." (John 10:9). My interpretation is that "being saved" is experiencing Heaven here on Earth.

TheBibleProject.com, in their YouTube video, "Animated Explanation of Heaven & Earth," says:

> "The union of Heaven and Earth is what the story of the Bible is all about. How they were once fully united and then driven apart and about how God is bringing them back together once again. …The focus of the Bible story is on how Heaven and Earth are being re-united through Jesus and will be completely brought together one day when he returns."

N.T. "Tom" Wright, Anglican Bishop of Durham, England, says:

> "At no point do the resurrection narratives in the four Gospels say, 'Jesus has been raised, therefore we are all going to heaven.' It says that Christ is coming here, to join together the heavens and the Earth in an act of new creation."

Glenn Paauw, Executive Director of the Biblica Institute for Bible Reading makes three additional comments from the Christian perspective:

> "…if we turn our eyes upon the real Jesus of the Bible — the incarnate, embodied, fully human Jesus — the things of earth might just grow strangely clear, and we'd see how to help heaven come to earth in the here and now."

> "Heaven (God's realm) and earth (our realm) are somewhat separated for now, in this era of in-between. But the promised future is always heaven and earth reunited. Time will bring the estranged places back together."

> "We are in a new creation story, not a post-creation story or end-of-creation story."

Having now discovered what both Judaism and Christianity offer, I then moved on to the third Abrahamic religion, Islam.

In Islam, THE HOLY QUR-ĀN (Koran)[1] in Surat (chapter) 2, Ayat (verse) 36, states:

> "Then did Satan make them slip
> From the (Garden), and get them out
> Of the state (of felicity) in which
> They had been. And We said:
> 'Get ye down, all (ye people),
> With enmity between yourselves.
> On earth will be your dwelling place
> And your means of livelihood —
> For a time.'"

In line 5, "all (ye people)," indicates (and the commentary by the English translator of this volume supports this) that all of Humanity was kicked out of the Garden.

---

1. *THE HOLY QUR-ĀN*. English translation of the meanings and Commentary, King Fahd Holy Qur-ān Printing Complex, AL-Madinah AL-Munawarah, The Kingdom of Saudi Arabia, 1410H.

The key question was what the phrase, "For a time" (again repeated in Surat 7, Ayat 24), meant. I asked an Islamic scholar who said that "For a time" is generally interpreted as "for your time here on earth, that is, for your life." What he was saying was that it was not possible to return to the Garden, to have Heaven here on Earth. It was only possible after death.

I then spoke with a Sufi teacher (Sufism is the mystical tradition of Islam) who gave me another interpretation of "For a time" and death. He explained that there are two types of death: death of the physical body and death of the ego. By giving up the ego, i.e., our sense of self, we experience a death and then we immediately experience Heaven on Earth. "You can have the death of the sense of self and [the] sense of separation from God and the world. You can be with God in the Now. …In the Sufi Hadith, the Prophet Mohammed, Peace Be Upon Him, is quoted as saying, 'Die before you die.'"

In this interpretation of death, we experience being in the Garden while we are alive. We experience Heaven on Earth.

I now had all three Abrahamic religions saying it was possible to return to the Garden. I had evidence that dissolved one of the foundational mis-beliefs of Judaic, Christian, and Islamic thinking. The conclusion that we could not re-enter had evolved over time into a myth, which had informed all three Faiths, and thus most of the Western world — but this is not accurate.

I then wondered, "Was there evidence that we *could* re-enter?" The Bible says, in Genesis 3:24, that God placed cherubim (a type of angel) on the east side of the Garden of Eden and a flaming sword that turned in every direction, to guard the way back to the Tree of Life.

Why are there cherubim guarding the way to the Tree of Life? "To guard" is to prevent entry. Adam, Eve and we, Humanity, are not allowed to re-enter because the cherubim are preventing entry.

I did some further research and found another eye-opening interpretation. The renowned Jewish authority on the Bible, Rabbi Samson Raphael Hirsch, wrote:

> "To guard the way to the Tree of Life can mean either to guard the way to the Tree of Life so that man will not be able to find the tree, or to guard the way so that the way should not be lost to man, so that some day man may be able to return to it. … God severed His direct contacts with man, but He appointed the cherubim and the sword to preserve for man the path to the Tree of Life."[2]

The cherubim's job is to guard the way so that the way remains in place and is not lost to us. When we choose to return, which we can choose right now, the way is still there.

And what about the flaming sword that turned every way? The second rabbi I spoke to asked me, "Suppose you were going to try to re-enter the Garden of Eden and you saw an ever-turning flaming sword? What would you do?" He explained that from the perspective of your ego, you wouldn't dare re-enter because you'd be afraid of being chopped up, burned, and killed. The flaming sword is to prevent those who are only living for themselves from

---

2. *The Pentateuch: Trumath Tzvi. Translation of the text and excerpts from the commentary of Samson Raphael Hirsch with all Haftoroth and the Five Megilloth,* Judaica Press, 1986.

entering. However, people who are living from their higher purpose, their Soul, know they haven't anything to fear or lose. From the perspective of the Soul, they trust God/The Divine to protect them as they re-enter.

Both the cherubim and the turning, flaming sword keep the entry open to the Garden, the Tree of Life, and Paradise here on Earth for all of us.

When we, Humanity, were in the Garden, we were in Heaven on Earth — we were in original innocence.

We left the Garden with the task of transforming everything outside the Garden into the Garden. On our journey, we've experienced problems, sufferings, accomplishments, and joys. With our original innocence now combined with a collective, tempered maturity, we're realizing that we *can* and we *are* fulfilling our noble mission.

Heaven on Earth has been in us and with us in our cellular and collective memory since the Garden. Now, by choosing and committing to do so, we can be back in the Garden in this moment and forever — co-experiencing and Co-creating Heaven here on Earth now and for all time.

What Is Our Role? What Is God's Role?

What part do we play and what part does God, Divine Grace, or Spirit play in the creation of Heaven on Earth? (If *God* is a comfortable word for you, please use it. If *God* is not, please use the word or phrase that is. Matthew Fox says, "…whatever name we give the Source of sources, the Artist of artists, the Creator of creation, all are accurate and none are sufficient.")

I believe we play our part in the ongoing co-creation and unfolding of Heaven on Earth in several ways:

- We become aware and responsive to what God asks of us. We do this through discovering and living our life's calling, through prayer, sacred texts, meditation, intuitive insights, the gift of grace, and the wise advice of others. We then respond through our choices and actions.

- We give our gifts, talents and wisdom unconditionally, with integrity, excellence, graciousness, joy, play, and conscious intention. We connect with others around the world doing the same.

- We harness our individual and collective free will for the common good.

And the rest is up to God.

As attorney Donna Boris says, "By doing our duty, we invite Grace in."

Angels Can Be Anywhere

Sylvia Hill has a degree in counseling and runs a shoe shine stand at the Delta commuter terminal in Boston's Logan Airport. Along with the usual tools of her trade — brushes, rags, and polish — Sylvia also carries a Bible and a notebook. The Bible is for her own inspiration, and the notebook is for prayer requests from her customers. The notebook lists people's first names and the problems they're facing — health issues, marital problems, job turmoil, and so on.

While Sylvia is polishing shoes, she is also fulfilling her calling as a counselor, encourager, minister, and listener. "I didn't want to just come to the airport and shine shoes," Hill says. "I wanted to provide service to people, and I wanted to make a difference, and God has answered my prayers."

She never offends customers by pushing her religious views on them. "I don't proselytize or do anything like that. But I might say something like 'God is good,' or 'Aren't we blessed,' or 'Praise God,' and that might open up the conversation. They see me as a shoe shine person so they don't really feel threatened." Her warm personality and cheery energy encourage a feeling of intimacy. People share their problems, and with her degree in counseling and her Christian faith, Sylvia is ready to offer any help she can. She believes God intended for her to be right where she is.

A gentleman arrived one morning obviously upset. As Sylvia tells it: "I don't even remember how it was that he started to tell me his story, but he said he was worried about his son who earned over $200,000 a year and yet was addicted to cocaine. We talked a little and I prayed with him for his son, Jeffrey. I told him I'd continue praying for Jeffrey and that I felt that God was big enough to handle this problem. I also shared a couple of scriptures to encourage the father. About six weeks later, the son acknowledged his drug problem to his family.

"Jeffrey went into a residential treatment program and later continued with outpatient treatment and going to groups. He also joined a local church. He lost weight. He became the son that restored his parents' pride.

"Well, it's been about a year now and Jeffrey's been doing well despite one setback. I gave a book of stories to his father to read and to share with Jeffrey as I felt it would boost both their souls."

The next time you're at the Delta Shuttle at Logan Airport, think of Sylvia Hill, a genuine Heaven Maker.

"Heaven on Earth is...

discovering your spirit and expressing your unique gifts."

Tracy L. Warren
Student
USA

"...that breathtaking attempt to build, out of simple acts and ordinary lives,
a fragment of heaven on earth."

Rabbi Professor Jonathan Sacks

Chapter 7

Heavening & Heaven Makers

Have you ever met someone and had the most remarkably good feeling about who they are and what they're doing in their lives? These are people who have found their niche in life, the one made just for them. They've jumped in fullheartedly and are loving what they're doing. When you're with them, you experience Heaven on Earth. I call them Heaven Makers.

A Heaven Maker is someone who is helping co-create Heaven on Earth. They help create pathways to and experiences of Heaven on Earth for others. Heaven on Earth is their heart's desire. It's an essential part of their Soul's intention and service to life. It enlivens a vibrant dynamic within them. It's what they're here to do. It's their contribution to the creation of Humanity's new story — they're heavening Earth.

- In Mexico, Sylvia Padelford talked to two people every day for 33 days about Project Heaven on Earth, creating a multiplier effect through her sharing.

- In Ireland, Frances Tolton, a consultant who works throughout Europe, carries a form she hands out to people asking them to write their description of Heaven on Earth.

- In Brazil, Sônia Café wrote a book, *64 Poderes: e as muitas maneiras de criar o CÉU NA TERRA*, which translates as *64 Powers: and the many ways to create Heaven on Earth.*

Around the globe, there are an increasing number of Heaven Makers co-creating Heaven on Earth. They're adding ideas and coming up with their own unique contributions. Here are a few of them:

The Heaven on Earth Video Contest

Laurie and Jacob Teitelbaum want to help spread Heaven on Earth around the world and they're using technology to do it. They've created the Heaven on Earth Video Contest, with a Grand Prize of $5,000 and more than $10,000 in total prizes.

"Our judges are looking for a 2-5 minute, nonreligious video that can open up people's minds to 'Heaven on Earth' occurring in our real world. Your video will offer a vision — your vision — of what the ultimate experience would be. Your video will help open the doors of imagination to this new world, and will ideally enable others to think 'I want that!' Vision and desire is what makes the ultimate world possible!"

Messages you can convey with your video:

1. Heaven on Earth would be an incredible experience.

2. Heaven on Earth is a reality that is possible *now*.

3. Heaven on Earth can happen easily and gracefully (no catastrophes needed).

4. Heaven on Earth is for absolutely everyone!

You can view the previous winning entries and learn how you can enter the contest here: tinyurl.com/HonEVideoContest

Heaven on Earth for Policing

I asked Justin Criner, a police officer in Texas, what Heaven on Earth is for policing. He looked at me and instantly said, "The end of crime, and everyone helping each other in acts of kindness."

Justin then created a 16-page manual, *Discovering Heaven on Earth for Law Enforcement*, that helps anyone begin the process of ending crime in their own community, whether they are in law enforcement or not.

It's available for free here: tinyurl.com/HonEPolice

The Web of Life

Alima Susan Friar is a microgreen farmer in Paonia, Colorado. Microgreens are tiny plants that go from seed to table in 7–10 days. In answer to Question 2, "What is Heaven on Earth for you?" she wrote: "Heaven on Earth is creating food sustainability by nurturing and tilling the soil of our earthly Garden every day with love and seeing us all as part of the same village co-creating together."

She came up with the idea of embedding her answer onto the end of every e-mail she sends. It took about a minute to set up and now every time she sends out an e-mail, she's doing her part in co-creating Heaven on Earth.

In Chile, Diane Alméras has also added her Heaven on Earth description to the end of her e-mails. In addition, she includes the second Heaven on Earth question so her recipients can see the question and answer it for themselves.

Because of Diane, Alima was inspired to add the second question.

What Good Would a Penny Do?

I was doing a global Heaven on Earth teleseminar and we were looking at the various sufferings in the world and what could be done to end them. Sue Bookchin, one of the participants, spoke about how violence against women on a global scale was deeply disturbing to her and was the issue that "makes my blood boil. It makes me shake with outrage." She found it barely tolerable to even think about the ways in which women were the object of violence. She also spoke about sexual slavery, the use of rape as a weapon of war, and the lifelong trauma women experience as a result.

On the local level, she was on the board of Second Story Women's Centre in Lunenburg, Nova Scotia, Canada. It was clear to her that violence against women was also an issue locally.

While commemorations for fourteen women killed in 1989 by a male student at École Polytechnique in Montreal were held every year in Lunenburg County, the prevalence and attitudes about violence against women had not really changed much in decades. Then, Sue added, "And the day after we hold the commemoration, everyone goes back to life as usual and nobody does anything different."

In a tone of great frustration, she said, "What would you do, Martin?"

I replied, "Sue, I don't know your financial situation. You could donate $5,000 or you could donate a penny."

With even greater frustration, she blurted out, "What good would a penny do?"

One of the other participants on the call, Deahni, chimed in and said, "What if everyone in your county gave a penny a day to help end violence against women?" Sue responded, "Oh my goodness, what a great idea. A penny a day will keep this issue in people's consciousness every day, and a penny is affordable to everyone, even school children."

In October of 2010, Sue and Second Story Women's Centre launched, "Making Change." The idea is simple: They handed out Mason jars with the Making Change logo on it and asked people to donate a minimum of a penny a day to help end violence against women locally. Some people in the neighboring county of Queens also took jars.

On September 3, 2013, Sue updated me:

"As we were in the midst of formulating next steps for 'Making Change' (it raised about $2,500), there was a call for proposals from the federal government's Status of Women Canada for exactly what we wanted to do. Second Story applied for and was awarded $300,000 over three years, starting in April 2012, for a coordinated community response to violence against women and girls in Lunenburg County. We are in the second year, and as co-coordinator of the Be the Peace project, as it is now called, it has pretty much taken over my life!!! Have a look at the website: www.bethepeace.ca. There is also a cool YouTube video of our first public forum in July 2012: tinyurl.com/HonEBeThePeace

"From that meeting came ten different community working groups.

"When we began 'Making Change,' we discovered that people really did want to talk about violence against women and not have it hide in the shadows any more. And once they had a forum where they could talk about it, they wanted to take action to end it.

"Today, almost everyone we talk to knows about the Be the Peace project, and asks, 'How can we help?'"

I'm Committed to Making My Nation a Heaven on Earth Nation

A growing group of people around the world have chosen to make their country a Heaven on Earth Nation.

In Denmark, Susanne Frandsen has started a Facebook page, in both Danish and English, called Project Heaven on Earth — i Denmark, Europa & Verden (in Denmark, Europe, and the World).

She: was featured in a six-page article for a Danish online magazine, created an online Heaven on Earth webinar, and met with two members of The Alternative party in the Danish parliament.

Watch my interview with her here: tinyurl.com/HonEDenmark

In Austria, Elisabeth Ziegler has set up a Heaven on Earth Wiki in both German and English to showcase people and organizations that are Heaven Makers. She says, "It's very easy for me [to make Austria a Heaven on Earth country]. …Everyone deserves to live in Paradise." She is committed to doing this work for the rest of her life. In addition to Austria, she wants to also impact the rest of the world.

Watch my interview with her here: tinyurl.com/HonEAustria

In Mexico, Gabriel Nossovitch has set up a Facebook community, in Spanish, called El Cielo En La Tierra Para Mexico (Heaven on Earth for Mexico). In addition to the three Heaven on Earth questions, he's asking a fourth one:

"Imagine you have a magic wand and with it you can create Heaven on Earth for Mexico. What is Heaven on Earth for Mexico?"

You can join the conversation on Facebook here: tinyurl.com/HonEMexico

In Croatia, Sanja Plavljanic-Sirola, meets with a group regularly to make her country Heaven on Earth. She has a Facebook page: tinyurl.com/HonECroatiaA, as well as a website in Croatian: tinyurl.com/HonECroatiaB

There are also people doing the same for **Japan**, **Argentina**, **Hungary**, and **Kenya**.

Banti Tarifa

Banti is a hotel-bar-restaurant in Tarifa on the southernmost coast of Spain. Tarifa is the kitesurfing/windsurfing capital of Europe with ideal winds blowing all day long on the waters of the Mediterranean. Banti is a warm, relaxing, and welcoming spot. Their motto:

Banti = a meeting point for those who truly believe we are living in heaven on earth.

More information here: tinyurl.com/HonEBanti

The New Magna Carta Includes Heaven on Earth

In 1215 England's King John was forced by noblemen to sign the Magna Carta, transforming the country from an absolute monarchy into a democracy. 2015 marked the 800th anniversary of the document that changed the story of governance.

Dr. Nicholas Beecroft is a British psychiatrist who is deeply concerned with the future of western civilization. He conducted the "Future of Western Civilization" series of interviews with visionary leaders. I was honored to be one of those interviewed and that interview has become Nicholas's book *Creating Heaven on Earth: Taking Small Steps in the Right Direction*.

Nicholas thought the 800th anniversary would be a good time to revisit the Magna Carta and write a new version, which he's done in his book *New Magna Carta: A Psychiatrist's Prescription for Western Civilization*. The book offers a bold vision, along with a strategy, aimed at rejuvenating western civilization. Nicholas offers a clear image of who we are, what we believe, what we value, where we want to get to, and the necessary steps to get there. *New Magna Carta* is a living, evolving document that Nicholas sees being continuously improved.

He begins Chapter 5.11 with the three Heaven on Earth questions. He answers Question 2 — Imagine you have a magic wand and with it you can create Heaven on Earth. What is Heaven on Earth for you? — in great depth and clarity. His answer is extensive, detailed, and expansive.

Not getting caught up in the pessimistic cynicism of our time, *New Magna Carta* envisions a bright future. It invites us to rise to the challenges we face and harness the creative energy of every human being to create a new civilization that enables each one of us to fulfill our potential.

You can read Nicholas's Heaven on Earth answer in full and learn more about *New Magna Carta* here: tinyurl.com/HonEMagnaCarta

Heaven on Earth in a Dentist's Chair

Dr. Dana Colson is a dentist who leads a practice of several dentists and more than twenty team members in Toronto. She attended a workshop I gave and was very moved by the idea of making Heaven on Earth real. Wanting to introduce Heaven on Earth into her practice, she came up with an innovative way of doing it. Patients sit down in the dental chair in her office and are slowly tilted back until they're lying almost flat. When they look up at the ceiling, they see a sign that says "Heaven on Earth." If a patient asks what the sign is about, Dana asks them the 3 Heaven on Earth questions and talks about the exponential power of sharing. She says several people ask or comment about the sign every day.

"Heaven, I'm in Heaven"

David Sunfellow studies people who have had Near-Death Experiences (NDEs), people from all races, religions, and cultures who have died and then returned to life with fantastic stories about what they experienced while clinically dead. He has firsthand reports — audio, video, and written — from thousands of people.

David says we "systematically study, teach, and seek to embody the core truths presented by near-death experiences."

Imagine speaking to all these people, who come from different parts of the world, speak different languages, practice different religions, and don't know each other. Over time you'd start to see similarities. And then, what if you distilled those similarities down to their essential attributes?

Here are the twelve essential attributes that David describes in his "The Formula for Creating Heaven on Earth" chart and worksheet:

- Connect with God

- Feel God's Love for Us

- Love Others via Daily Acts of Kindness

- Monitor & Direct Inner Dialogue

- See, Speak, Live The Truth

- Discover & Manifest Our Unique Purpose

- Guidance from Spirit, Within & Without

- Shadow Work

- Body Care & Healthy Lifestyle

- Spend Time In Nature; Love the Earth

- Join Deeply with Other Human Beings

- Miracles: Master The World Through Love

More information here: www.the-formula.org/about/

A Christmas Inspiration

Patty O'Sullivan in Santa Fe, New Mexico, saw the Project Heaven on Earth presentation just before Christmas and had an idea. She asked forty of her extended family members to send her a very short description of what Heaven on Earth is for them. Thirty-three people responded and she combined them all into her Christmas letter, which she sent to all forty. Here are some of the responses she received:

- Having the family that I do. They're all so thoughtful. There isn't anything they wouldn't do for each other. (Mom)

- Being surrounded by my family and having such a wonderful family, including my children, their wives and husbands, grandchildren, and a great-grandchild. Being content with everything that has transpired in my life. I'm proud of my family and I'm at peace with the world. Heaven on Earth is, most of all, my wife, Ruth. (Dad)

- A newborn baby's smile. (Peg)

- Heaven on Earth is love at first sight…and the miracle of marriage. (Megan)

- Being with Patty and Buddy in our home. (Sam)

- The children of the world being loved, cared for and valued, and being a catalyst for that to happen. (Patty)

- Waking up to a bright morning sun, the smell of fresh sticky buns in the oven, and Claire's laugh. (Bill)

- World peace. People living full lives. No war. People loving life. (Terry O.)

- Remembering to feel the Divine connectedness in all moments, all things, and all people. Imagining a world where all people feel that connectedness and love the spark of beauty and uniqueness in each other, where each one lives and enjoys their own unique gifts passionately. Such a world will harbor no ill or anger or war. It will be a miraculous, beautiful symphony of differences. (Rosie)

- To be around my kids, especially when they start having families, and to be near family members. (Mar)

- The recognition of how blessed my life truly is. I feel so much gratitude for the gifts I've received — family, friends, and teachers. The only way to appreciate God's gifts is by giving back and living as compassionately and selflessly as I can. (Donna)

Heaven on Earth in Your Congregation

Bread of Life is a spiritual center offering programs in an economically depressed area of Sacramento, California. They offer:

- Spirit in the Arts programs: A free, self-directed open art studio that serves as their mission into the neighborhood.

- Formation Programs for Leaders: This includes a 3-year internship in the art of spiritual direction, contemplative dialogue trainings, and experiences in the ancient four-fold journey of Spirit and transformation called Quadratos.

- Spirit Print: A print shop offering basic print services to support the work of Bread of Life while mentoring local at-risk youth.

I gave a couple of Heaven on Earth presentations for them. Their co-director, Sandra Lommasson, felt that Heaven on Earth would be a wonderful program to offer in every congregation in the country. To have that happen she wrote a 28-page guide called *Co-Creating Heaven on Earth: A Resource Packet for Congregations*. It's available for free at tinyurl. com/ResourcePacket. Any donation to help with their work would be appreciated.

Ask Your Board

Ray Blanchard is the president of Blanchard Consulting Group, LLC, a training, development and consulting company with offices in San Antonio, Texas, and Burbank, California. I asked him the three Heaven on Earth questions and he loved them. A week later, he had a meeting of his company's Advisory Board, which was looking at the future of the business. He asked them the questions, and later told me they were actually crying, as they were so deeply in touch with Heaven on Earth for themselves and the company. Ray said, "Heaven on Earth put us back in touch with our passions for our work, and it set a powerful context for getting things done. We'll be using it again and again."

A Home for Everyone

Brenda MacKenzie, a real estate agent in Halifax, Canada, and I were having coffee one day and talking about Heaven on Earth. I asked her what world suffering upset her the most. Her face went pale as she said, "Homelessness." I asked her what Heaven on Earth would be for homelessness and she simply said, "A home for everyone."

Then she immediately went into how difficult that would be. "Martin, you don't understand. I'm a real estate agent, I work 60 hours a week, and I'm also in a relationship that takes time. How am I supposed to do all that and create a home for everyone?"

I responded by saying, "Brenda, put all your very real considerations aside for the moment. Now, how are you going to get this done?" — and that's when a light bulb went on for her.

She went back to her real estate agency, Domus Realty, and called an all-agents meeting. She told them she wanted to end homelessness, create a home for everyone, and she wanted it to be easy to do. Would they agree to have $100 taken out of their commission every time they sold a property, up to a maximum of $4,000 per year, and put into a special Domus Fund to end homelessness? They all agreed and set up "A Home for Everyone."

Each year they fund innovative programs that help end homelessness and ask for submissions from registered charities. There are six volunteer board members, all clients, who review the applications and choose what they feel is the best match for their criteria. Brenda chairs the board and reports back to the Domus agents. A Home for Everyone has made grants totaling $114,000 since its inception.

You can see a list of the yearly winners and read more about the program here: www.domusrealty.ca/questionnaire

A Theme Song for Singapore's Environment

The National Environment Agency of Singapore holds a contest every year in search of a new theme song for their "Clean and Green Singapore" campaign. The 2011 theme song was "Heaven on Earth," music and lyrics composed by Kathryn Cheng:

"This is our Singapore —
clean air & water, wide green spaces, and a diverse eco-system.
Let's cherish this beautiful environment and make it our Heaven on Earth
for future generations."

There's a beautiful video of the song here: tinyurl.com/KathrynCheng

IMAGINE…a Heaven on Earth

Catherine Burnett is an Associate Professor in the Department of Theatre and Film at the University of British Columbia in Vancouver. I shared the Heaven on Earth presentation and questions with her, and several weeks later she came up with an idea.

She gave her intermediate year Bachelor of Fine Arts (BFA) acting students the assignment of interviewing different people of different ages about heaven on earth by asking them the three Heaven on Earth questions. The students would then re-create these people on stage in monologues. The first-year BFA actors were given their own assignment of choreographing several musical pieces.

The show they created is called IMAGINE. It explores the concept of heaven on many levels, empowers individuals to create Heaven in their own lives, and affirms that now is the time to start.

The show includes music, dance, acting and visual imaging, and it brought together her students with outside professional artists. It opens with the Fred Astaire−Ginger Rogers dance number "Cheek to Cheek" (with the famous line "Heaven, I'm in Heaven…") and closes with a dance piece to "Your Love Lifts Me Higher." The show is infused with an art expression piece featuring a soprano, a tenor, a singer-songwriter, and a jazz artist. Also participating in the show were a whirling Sufi dancer, a local professional actress, and an African dancer.

Catherine and her fellow artists believe it's through the medium of the arts that the Heaven on Earth message has the most impact.

The Flowering of Heaven on Earth

Jocelyn Ann Flores is a young poet in Harrisburg, Pennsylvania. I discovered her poem from a Google Alert sent to me. I wrote asking for permission to publish it and she asked me why. I explained that her poem expresses the essence of what I've heard many people say Heaven on Earth is for them.

Heaven on Earth

I'm on a search for heaven
And at times I find it in the strangest places
In the flowers that bloom
And in children's smiling faces
I've witnessed a man stand up for what he believes in
I've witnessed the changing of the seasons
I've woken up with a smile on my face
And I've seen light shine down on the darkest of places
I've seen the hardest working people struggle for success
And I've seen them come home to three small smiling faces with no regrets
I've witnessed real love that a man has for his wife
And the joy of knowing he comes home to only her every night
I've seen leaves dance with the breeze
And I've seen a lake provide joy for entire families
I've felt the sun share its warmth during bone chilling days
And I've seen rain unselfishly shower flowers till the month of may
Generation after generation
In search for peace within yourself
You must look at the beauty around you
At times it seems as though heaven has found you

A Heart's Yearning

John E. Wade II, a businessman in New Orleans, Louisiana, felt a real heart's yearning for Heaven on Earth. Taking action on his yearning, he compiled and edited a significant book on the subject, *How to Achieve a Heaven on Earth: 101 insightful essays from the world's greatest thinkers, leaders, and writers*. John believes there are ten elements that are essential to do this: Peace, Security, Freedom, Democracies, Prosperity, Spiritual Harmony, Racial Harmony, Ecological Harmony, Health, and Moral Purpose and Meaning.

His book has contributions from both Barack Obama and George W. Bush, among many others. When I asked him why he'd included both of them, who are clearly from different ends of the political spectrum, he said, "If we're going to create Heaven on Earth, we'll need everyone."

John's next step was to ask four people, including myself, to co-author a new book with him, *Glimpses of Heaven on Earth: Inspiring Quotations and Insightful Essays*, published in 2014.

John continues writing and publishing on his heart's yearning, Heaven on Earth.

Visit John's website here: www.heavenonearth.org

❖

Prince Edward Island
Canada's First Heaven on Earth Province

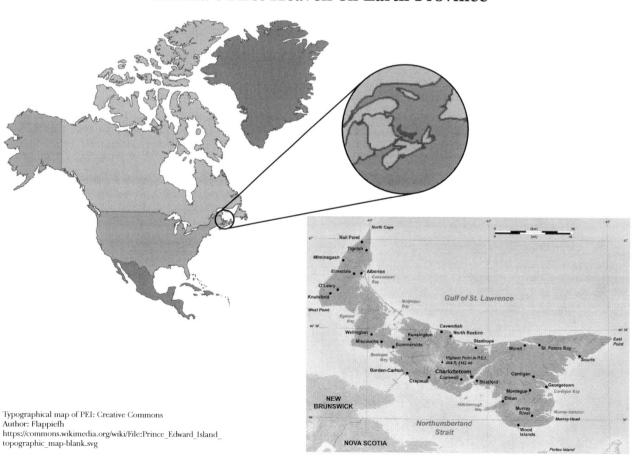

Typographical map of PEI: Creative Commons
Author: Flappiefh
https://commons.wikimedia.org/wiki/File:Prince_Edward_Island_
topographic_map-blank.svg

In the early 2000s, I gave a series of yearly Heaven on Earth workshops in the Canadian province of Prince Edward Island (PEI). Situated off the east coast, PEI is the birthplace of Canada and its smallest province.

One summer, during a workshop I was giving, a thought popped into my head, "PEI is Canada's first Heaven on Earth province." I dismissed the idea at first, but the more I thought about it the more I loved it. Since the way you start a new story is to start the story, I said the sentence out loud to the participants and it became a declaration. In the years since, it's continued to expand as others have joined in the same declaration.

Every summer, when I go back to the island, a group of us committed to this declaration explore it in more depth, discovering what we can do to expand and forward it. I especially want to thank Kele Redmond, Mark Belfry, Wendy Foster, Bob Mueller, Hannah Bell, Basil Hambly, Gail Lecky, and Amanda Gallant for their co-creative partnership.

Here are six projects and initiatives that continue coming out of a growing number of people committed to "PEI: Canada's First Heaven on Earth Province."

The Kiwanis Key Club Heaven on Earth Leadership Awards
The Key Club is one of the youth organizations within the worldwide Kiwanis Service Club. The Key Club at Colonel Gray High School in Charlottetown, PEI, has established the Heaven on Earth Leadership Awards. During the school year, students team up on projects that respond to the question, "Here is a magic wand and with it you can create Heaven on Earth. What is Heaven on Earth and what will you do to make it happen?"

The idea is to have members of the Key Club reflect on the kind of world they want, feel free to talk about it, and begin playing their part individually or in groups to make their dreams come true.

This initiative is a natural fit with the Kiwanis Key Club mandate, which provides members with opportunities to provide service, build character, and develop leadership. Their vision statement is, "We are caring and competent servant leaders transforming communities worldwide!"

Basil Hambly of the Kiwanis Club of Charlottetown is excited to see what the youth members create. "We answered this [Heaven on Earth] question at an international Kiwanis event we hosted recently, and it's a powerful individual and group experience," he said.

The youth leadership awards will recognize a Colonel Gray High School Key Club member or group of members who "demonstrate leadership qualities in planning and organizing one of the following: an event, project, website, YouTube video, newspaper editorial/column, advertising/marketing campaign, or other enterprise."

Suzanne Lee, teacher adviser for the Key Club, says, "This is a great initiative. I'd love to see Key Clubs worldwide be able to apply for this award."

Kiwanis has expanded the program to all 12 Island high schools and has made available $100 per High School. Heaven on Earth projects can be anything students choose that they believe will make a positive impact in their community.

A full description of the award, along with the application form and award criteria, is available here: tinyurl.com/HonEKiwanis

PEI Business Women's Association

Hannah Bell is the Executive Director of the PEI Business Women's Association — "We empower women in business through training, counseling, and networking opportunities."

I strongly believe in their mission and work. To support them, I offered Hannah and the organization a workshop on vision building as my gift. She was delighted and accepted.

A couple of weeks later we were having coffee to discuss the workshop, and she asked me what other projects I was involved in. I told her about Heaven on Earth. She sat bolt upright and said, "That's it, that's it — we need to do your workshop on Heaven on Earth!" Of course, I agreed. I led the workshop, the members loved it, and we did it again the next year.

The workshop title was:

A BOLD Tomorrow:

Co-Creating Heaven on Earth for Yourself, Your Work/Business, and PEI

The workshop "provides a process for you, your work, and your province to align with deeply held values and initiatives that enrich humanity. A BOLD Tomorrow for Islanders is motivated by a sentiment to do something, deep in our hearts, deep in our souls, which takes our province to its next evolutionary level. What we want is a new context, a new story for the Third Millennium — one that inspires us all.

"Come and hear what others are doing all around the world personally and in their workplaces to make meaningful change in unique and individual ways — and discover your contribution to your personal and professional growth and to a province and planet that works."

Lady Baker's Tea: Brewing Heaven on Earth

Katherine Burnett is a tea lover who has turned her passion into her business, running Lady Baker's Tea. She took one of my workshops and came up with the idea of blending a special mix for a Heaven on Earth tea. It is one of her signature blends.

The back of the package is reproduced in part here:

Heaven on Earth

Here are the earth's cultures harmonized in a tea blend where all the flavors marry and complement each other, not one overpowering another and each humbly living in equality.

The enclosed blend was inspired by many people's desire to have Prince Edward Island be Canada's first Heaven on Earth province. Blended with the tea varieties of Assam, Oolongs, Pai Mutan, and herbal Peppermint, are sweet rose petals from the south shore of PEI.

Please visit: **www.projectheavenonearth.com**

You can order the tea here: tinyurl.com/HeavenOnEarthT

A Heaven on Earth Vision for Anderson House

Anderson House in Charlottetown, PEI, is a provincial, 24-hour emergency shelter for women and their children victims of domestic abuse and violence. This short-term sanctuary offers a safe, secure environment for recovery and recuperation, while providing programs and services to enhance a family's quality of life and enable them to move forward with their lives.

As a non-profit, Anderson House relies on donations from community members and businesses. Amanda Gallant, a talented singer and event organizer, put together the PEI Heaven on Earth Extravaganza for Anderson House: "a night of wonderful music, terrific food, and a whole lot of laughter with a silent auction in support of Anderson House."

Amanda says, "I believe that Anderson House is a wonderful example of a dream to not only improve the lives of Islanders, but to give them hope. That is my vision of a PEI Heaven on Earth. A home filled with hope, where artists and businesses alike are free to express their highest and greatest vision for our Island family."

You can see the write-up here: tinyurl.com/HonEAndersonHouse

Beginning a New Story for Summerside

Wendy Foster took the PEI Business Women's course (A BOLD Tomorrow). Inspired by the workshop, the participant involvement and the energy in the room, she said publicly that she would create a similar event for her community of Summerside, PEI's second largest city. She also wanted to use it to officially launch her business, The Coaching Playground.

Wendy and her partner, Bob Mueller, blitzed the city. They brought me down a week before the workshop to do an intensive marketing campaign. We met with the Mayor, influential businesspeople, and people we met on the street that Wendy knew. Wendy and Bob put posters up all over the city. Heaven on Earth was everywhere. The workshop was a success.

Bob created a short video of the campaign and my workshop, which you can view here: tinyurl.com/HonESummerside

Along with Every Purchase...

Nessya Neemron owns Nessya's Gems and Jewels in Charlottetown, PEI, with one store downtown on Queen Street and the other at the cruise ship terminal. Along with every purchase, Nessya includes a card with the 3 Heaven on Earth questions on it, as well as an invitation to sign up for the free "One Week to Simply Begin Creating Heaven on Earth" course. (See page 245 to learn more about the course.)

A Heaven on Earth Coffee Blend

Also on Queen Street is The Kettle Black cafe. The owner, Mazen Aldossary, has created a Heaven on Earth coffee blend, a medium roast from Nicaragua and Guatemala. The back of the package says, "(Coffee is)...An idea that brings people together, a consortium of cultures and nations sharing their experience to create something new, something beautiful only possible by the partnership of so many people that it gives us our very first taste of Heaven on Earth."

tinyurl.com/HonEcoffeeblend

Facebook: PEI Heaven on Earth

There's a devoted Facebook page: PEI Heaven on Earth. The image at the top of the FB page is the current PEI license plate (we've just put in the 00-000 as a placeholder number). On the bottom of the real license plate are the words: "Birthplace of Confederation" (Canada is a confederation of provinces). We've changed those words to now say: The Heaven on Earth Province.

After reading the Heaven Maker examples in this chapter, please answer these questions:

• What are the characteristics of a Heaven Maker for you?

• Who would you say is a Heaven Maker? Why?

• Did any of the Heaven Makers spark any ideas in you? If so, list your ideas here.

_____

_____

_____

_____

_____

_____

_____

_____

_____

_____

_____

Heaven Making

Several years ago my wife, Maida, and I were talking about Heaven on Earth. She said that what she wanted to do to help co-create Heaven on Earth was so very, very different than what I wanted to do. She liked volunteering for a program called "Many Mothers." It helps mothers who have a newborn in any way they want and need. Maida would, once or twice a week for three hours at a time, visit with the new mother and do whatever was asked: look after the baby so the mother could get some rest, do the laundry, play with the other kids so the mother could be alone with the newborn, or anything else the mother wanted.

As we were talking, Maida said, "But you're bringing the idea of Heaven on Earth into the world and I'm only helping a new mother." Then both of us "got" that there was no difference between her contribution and mine. Both of us were contributing to co-creating Heaven on Earth in the ways that felt right for us and addressed a need we saw in the world.

I realized that what's important is making the contribution to Heaven on Earth that only you can make.

Other Ways Heaven on Earth Is Showing Up Globally

Google:

I wanted to see how many times the phrase "Heaven on Earth" has been referenced on Google, so I typed in: World searches for Heaven on Earth, (the numerical year). For example: World searches for Heaven on Earth, 2016.

In 2006 there were 1,560,000 results. In 2017 there were 9,330,000.

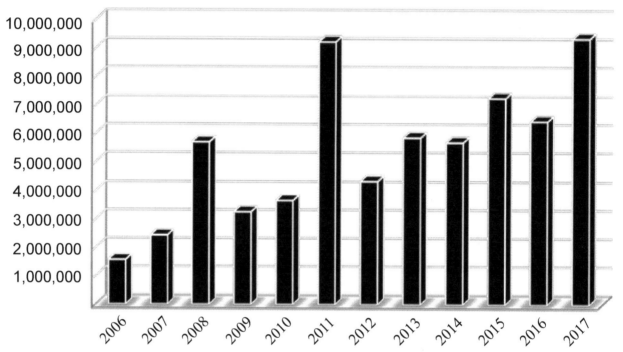

Books:

A Jan. 2018 search on Amazon returned over 2,000 books with Heaven on Earth in the title.

Music:

Here are some of the artists who sing about Heaven on Earth: Britney Spears, Belinda Carlisle, Melissa Etheridge, Asia, ABBA, The Del-Vikings, Gene Pitney, Maria Muldaur, The Platters, and Sonny James.

TV:

Britain's Channel 5 network has a show called "Holiday Heaven on Earth," which takes viewers to vacation spots all around the world.

Newspapers:

The Wall Street Journal, in a column about the 2012 presidential race, said: "Americans want a President to describe how to create a little bit of heaven on Earth, not to lecture them about their failures in getting there."

Google Alerts:

Go to www.google.com/alerts and enter the phrase "Heaven on Earth," and you'll receive daily, for free, a listing of blogs, videos, articles, and websites talking about Heaven on Earth.

BENEFITS OF HAVING YOUR OWN HEAVEN ON EARTH PROJECT

In this chapter you've read many examples of people who've discovered what their Heaven on Earth project is and are taking simple actions to make it happen.

Over the years of working with people helping them discover their project and then supporting them in taking easy actions to make it real, here's what I've discovered:

- Most projects are simple for the person doing it. You have to find what's "simple" for you, what's easy for you. I remember speaking to a woman in Austria, Elisabeth, who said she wanted to make her country a Heaven on Earth Nation. I asked her why and she said, "Because it's simple."

  Another woman, Susan in Hawaii, added her definition of Heaven on Earth to the end of her e-mails. Why? Because it was simple.

  It's what's simple to you that will be where you gladly and freely put your energy.

- The project is obvious to you. It's what you know has to be done and you know you're the person to do it.

- You feel a sense of empowerment. Your project lets you clearly know: "I am making a difference."

- You are not defined by what you see and feel is *not* working in the world. You've chosen to not be a victim. Instead, you're defined by the actions you're taking to contribute to Heaven on Earth.

- Doing your Heaven on Earth project gives you an increasing sense of self-confidence, of "I am doing this!"

- When you're doing your Heaven on Earth project, you are realizing that your dream for the kind of world you want has begun. You see tangible results beginning to show up and grow in momentum…and this gives you a deep sense of pleasure and accomplishment.

In the next chapter, you'll begin discovering the Gateways into Heaven on Earth. You'll see the eight major doorways in — one or more of them will directly appeal to you — and you'll discover your own Heaven on Earth project.

"Catalytic projects are those that unleash the human spirit…."

John Coonrod
The Hunger Project

"Heaven on Earth is...

not focusing on why things don't work and who's to blame;
it's focusing on making things work
and celebrating our accomplishments."

David Christel
Author, Editor
USA

"Finding your passion is largely about finding out who you are.
Living your passion is a choice to offer who you are to the world."

Oriah Mountain Dreamer

Chapter 8

The Heaven on Earth Gateways

Creating Heaven on Earth asks you to begin by discovering and exploring the Gateways that help unlock Heaven on Earth for you and the world.

I've asked thousands of people what Heaven on Earth is for them, and what I've learned is that their answers fall into distinct categories: Gateways. Gateways are action/service doorways, ways of moving from feeling and thinking into direct action. They're portals to help us realize Humanity's new story.

By discovering, opening and stepping through these Gateways, your creative juices begin flowing as new opportunities and more ways to participate and make a positive difference appear. You enter Heaven on Earth and Heaven on Earth enters you.

For some people, the Gateway to Heaven on Earth is realized within themselves. They say, *"As I experience more Heaven on Earth internally, the outer world will reflect that."* Chapter 9, "Your Inner World," focuses on this.

For other people, it's all about relationships — with themselves, others, and The Divine. Chapter 10, "Relationships – Co-creating Heaven on Earth" unifies these three aspects. Relationships bridge the Inner and Outer Worlds.

Chapter 11 also bridges the Inner and Outer Worlds. This Gateway, "Living Your Global Values," centers on those values you cherish and want to see lived by Humanity now and far into the future.

Then there are those people for whom Heaven on Earth has to be real in the outer world. They say, *"We will have Heaven on Earth when it exists in the outer world."* Chapters 12–14 focus on the three Gateways of Your Outer World:

- Chapter 12, "Ending the World's Major Sufferings"
- Chapter 13, "Our Institutions Taking Their Rightful Place in Co-Creating Heaven on Earth"
- Chapter 14, "Co-Creating Heaven on Earth Nation(s)"

And finally, some people want to engage with the Gateway of "Heaven on Earth This-Here-Now," which is the focus of Chapter 15.

The following two pages are an overview of the Gateways.

The Heaven on Earth Gateways

▷ **Your Inner World (Chapter 9)**
- ➤ Working on Yourself
- ➤ Living Your Personal Values
- ➤ Discovering and Living Your Life's Purpose and Vision
- ➤ Expressing Your Essence Word
- ➤ Expressing Your Artistry
- ➤ Discovering and Giving Your Gift
- ➤ Enlivening Affirmations
- ➤ Experiencing The Divine

▷ **Relationships – Co-Creating Heaven on Earth (Chapter 10)**
- ➤ With Yourself
- ➤ With Others
- ➤ With God/The Divine

▷ **Living Your Global Values (Chapter 11)**

▷ **Your Outer World (Chapters 12 – 14)**
- ▶ **Ending the World's Major Sufferings (Chapter 12)**
  - ➤ Hunger and Malnutrition
  - ➤ Disease
  - ➤ Lack of Adequate Shelter
  - ➤ War, Genocide, Refugees, & Weapons Proliferation
  - ➤ Illiteracy
  - ➤ Poverty, No Access to Opportunity
  - ➤ Lack of Clean Water and Sanitation
  - ➤ Environmental Pollution and Degradation
  - ➤ Lack of Freedom: Tyranny, Repression
  - ➤ Lack of Meaning and Purpose

▶ **Ending the World's Major Sufferings** *(cont'd)*
  ➤ Crime, Violence, and Terrorism
  ➤ Prejudice, Hatred, and Discrimination
  ➤ Torture, Slavery, Human Rights Abuse, Child Labor, Violence Against Women/Children
  ➤ Sexual Abuse
  ➤ Bad Governance, Corruption, and Poor Management
  ➤ Overpopulation
  ➤ Animal Abuse and Species Extinction
  ➤ Spiritual Malnourishment

▶ **Our Institutions Taking Their Rightful Place in Co-Creating Heaven on Earth (Chapter 13)**
  ➤ Education
  ➤ Culture: Arts, Media, Sports
  ➤ Health Care & Medicine
  ➤ Commerce: Business, Industry, Labor
  ➤ Resources: Agriculture, Fisheries, Forestry, Mining
  ➤ Law
  ➤ Government
  ➤ Religion
  ➤ Science & Technology
  ➤ Civic Organizations
  ➤ International Intergovernmental Organizations
  ➤ The Military

▶ **Co-Creating Heaven on Earth Nation(s) (Chapter 14)**
  ➤ Uniting a Nation to Resolve an Issue
  ➤ Uniting a Nation to Co-Create Heaven on Earth for that Nation
  ➤ Uniting Nations to Resolve an Issue
  ➤ Uniting All Nations to Co-Create Heaven on Earth

▷ **Heaven on Earth This-Here-Now (Chapter 15)**

"Heaven on Earth is...

Instead of always talking about 'Hell on Earth'
and how we can't do anything about it,
I think it's now time to talk about Heaven on Earth
and what we can do about it."

Gurucharan Singh Khalsa
Teacher, Psychologist, Writer
USA

"Give me a lever and a fulcrum,
and I will raise the world."
Archimedes

Getting Started

Whether it's the Inner World, Relationships, Global Values, the Outer World or This-Here-Now, find the Gateway or Gateways you connect and resonate with, and begin using that Gateway(s) as your entryway into creating Heaven on Earth. Each of the Gateways to Heaven on Earth can be viewed as a goal that then elicits a process for accomplishing it, as a process that then leads to the goal, or as both.

What will count is the unique contribution that only you can make. Working on Heaven on Earth from your deep truth, your deep longing, is where your contribution will be made. All contributions, assuming your intention is to contribute and be of service to the greater good, are valuable and necessary.

What is created when you multiply your contribution with the rest of Humanity's contributions is a powerful, energizing movement that continues building and expanding.

Let's explore each Gateway and discover which one(s) is uniquely yours.

"Heaven on Earth is...

with /in you."

Randy Austill
Computer Programmer, Musician, and Integral Coach
USA

"Hidden in the very essence of who we are — in the distant echoes of forgotten dreams
and in the remote yearnings of our hearts — are the keys to our true identity
and to the enduring contributions we can make to society…
(Our job is to) come face to face with that which calls to us from the deepest parts
of ourselves, encouraging us to discover and fulfill a higher purpose with our lives."

Laurel Airica

Chapter 9

▷ **Your Inner World**

> ➤ Working on Yourself
> ➤ Living Your Personal Values
> ➤ Discovering and Living Your Life's Purpose
>   and Vision
> ➤ Expressing Your Essence Word
> ➤ Expressing Your Artistry
> ➤ Discovering and Giving Your Gift
> ➤ Enlivening Affirmations
> ➤ Experiencing The Divine

Let's begin our exploration of the Gateways with "Your Inner World." You may be someone who believes that the way to create Heaven on Earth is to create it within yourself: *"As I experience more Heaven on Earth internally, the outer world will reflect that."* For you, the more Heaven on Earth within, the more it will show up out in the world. The outer world is a reflection, a mirror, of your inner world.

Working on your inner world helps you create Heaven on Earth in two ways:

1. It removes the inner blocks to Heaven on Earth.

2. It lets more of the Heaven on Earth already within you shine out into the world.

This chapter offers eight different avenues to enter into the Gateway of "Your Inner World." As you explore each one in depth, see which one(s) resonates the most with you.

➤ WORKING ON YOURSELF

Discovering and expressing Heaven on Earth in your inner world requires working on yourself to clean house and let more of your light shine. It means doing those things that:

• Clear out the blockages in you, such as misperceptions, fears, insecurities, etc.

• Resolve old hurts, angers, and resentments.

• Give you new insights into your sense of self, and your life purpose and vision.

• Give you new energy, creativity, and resolve.

Some possible ways of working on yourself include:

- Taking self-development courses.

- Having a regular meditation practice.

- Realizing how you project your fears and insecurities onto others and life.

- Cleaning up incompletions in your life.

- Stopping an addictive behavior.

- Setting and accomplishing objectives.

- Observing what shows up in the outer world that reflects your inner world.

Working on yourself is an ongoing process, not in the sense of a never-ending burden, but as a continual process of deepening self-discovery. The more you discover of yourself, the more you realize an unending expansiveness and awe. You let the Heaven on Earth already within you work through you and out into the world. Both "who you are" and "what you do" make a greater contribution.

"Heaven on Earth is...

when one's personality is an agent of one's soul."

Kerry Cochrane
Lecturer, University of Sydney
Australia

➤ LIVING YOUR PERSONAL VALUES

Each of us has values we consider essential to our lives. These values provide the internal directional guidance that keep us on course and allow us to be true to ourselves. Our values permeate what we do and what we express. We live by our values. They are the motivating foundation influencing every aspect of our lives.

Discovering your values at a deeper, clearer level can be your Gateway, your contribution, to creating Heaven on Earth.

On the next page in alphabetical order is a list of values. Check the ones you feel are the most vital to you. There may be additional values not on this list that you feel should be included. Please add them. Ask your family, friends, and colleagues which of these values best describe you.

After you've clarified which values are important, observe how living these values contributes to helping create Heaven on Earth.

- Authenticity
- Beauty
- Being/Doing Good
- Belonging
- Clarity
- Communication
- Compassion
- Courage
- Creativity
- Dignity
- Efficiency
- Encouragement
- Excellence
- Faith
- Family
- Forgiveness
- Friendship
- Generosity
- Graciousness
- Growth
- Harmony
- Health
- Honesty
- Honor
- Hope
- Humility
- Inspiration
- Integrity
- Joy
- Justice
- Kindness
- Leadership
- Love
- Making a Difference
- Meaning
- Moral Courage
- Order
- Peace
- Perseverance
- Play
- Productivity
- Quality
- Reliability
- Respect
- Responsibility
- Results-focused
- Risk-taking
- Safety
- Security
- Self-discipline
- Teamwork
- Tolerance
- Tradition
- Wisdom

"Heaven on Earth is...
joy, and joy for me is a sense of contentment
that comes from my value system being directly in line
with how I'm living my life.
There is no dishonesty. There's no untruth."

Pat Gierschick
Director of Financial Planning
USA

➤ DISCOVERING AND LIVING
YOUR LIFE'S PURPOSE AND VISION

Your Life's Purpose

Purpose answers the question "Why?" It gives you direction. It's your guiding light. It's your reason for existence. It gives you ongoing motivation when the going gets rough. Purpose answers "Why am I here? Why was I born? Why did I come to Earth? What is my assignment, my job, my contribution?"

You *do* have a specific contribution to make. It's why you're here.

Keep digging, keep asking "Why?" until you feel you've truly discovered your purpose in life. If you get discouraged or frustrated, don't stop the process until you've come up with the bottom line of why you're here. Commit to discovering and living your life's purpose!

My life's purpose is: _____

_____

Your Life's Vision

Vision answers the question "What?" What do you want to be, to do, to have? What do you want for yourself, your family, your relationships, your work, your community, your nation, and the world?

Here's a simple tool that will help clarify your vision. Suppose you have a magic wand and can create anything you want with it. A magic wand relieves you of the necessity of knowing how something will be achieved because that's its job. You don't have to be constrained by knowing how something will get done. This gives you tremendous freedom. You can let your imagination take flight. You can discover deeper levels of your heart's desire.

Imagine you have this magic wand in your hand right now and simply answer the question "What do I want?"

Using your magic wand, describe your life's vision.

_____

_____

_____

_____

_____

Please take the time now to answer the purpose and visions questions. Your answers can literally transform your life. Re-visit your answers periodically to see if they are still accurate and true for you.

"Heaven on Earth is...
people in touch with their own magnificence
as the springboard for possibility."

Christine Barnes
Seeker
Canada/USA

➤ EXPRESSING YOUR ESSENCE WORD

Your Inner Gateway may be the discovery and living of your essence word, the one word that describes who and what your Soul is at its deepest, core level.

My essence word is "Harmony." It resonates in my very being like a tuning fork tuned to the specific frequency of my Soul. Whenever I hear "Harmony," a shudder of deep recognition and peace surges through me.

What's your essence word? What's the one word that profoundly resonates in you?

My essence word is: _____

Once you've discovered it, print it out and put it in different places in your life so you regularly see it to remind yourself of who you are.

"Heaven on Earth is...
the power of one."

Irving Warhaftig
Therapist
USA

➤ EXPRESSING YOUR ARTISTRY

The universal Life Force flows through us and desires expression. One means of that expression is the arts. Whether through music, art, writing, photography, dance or any other form, you can paint Heaven on Earth, dance Heaven on Earth, or compose and play the music of Heaven on Earth.

If artistic expression is your Inner Gateway, make your artistry known. My artistry is:

_____

_____

"Heaven on Earth is...

the most real expressions of our life and our lives."

Steve Hinkle
Founder & Executive Director
The Perryman Institute
USA

➤ DISCOVERING AND GIVING YOUR GIFT

You have a gift within you that you were born to give, to share with the world. Deep within you, you know what your gift is, that it is to be given, and that sharing it will be a contribution toward building a better future — Heaven on Earth. Your job is to discover your gift and give it. The world needs the unique gift that only you have to give.

Here are some questions to help you discover your gift:

- What talent or skill do I have to give to the world?

- How will discovering and giving my gift create a difference in my life and others' lives?

- How will the future be better because I am giving my gift?

- What do I deeply know that needs to be achieved?

- How will my gift build a stronger sense of community, locally and/or globally?

- How can my gift help toward ending a suffering or pain in the world?

- How will giving my gift give me a sense of meaning and accomplishment?

- How will my gift make the world a better place and help co-create Heaven on Earth?

- What simple step will I now take to give my gift to the world?

My gift is: _____

I will give my gift by doing the following:_____

_____

"Heaven on Earth is...

consciously expressing what's Heavening you."

Bonnie Bond
Businesswoman/Designer
USA/Canada

➤ ENLIVENING AFFIRMATIONS

An affirmation is a phrase repeated over and over again. It's a very simple, powerful tool that can be used to focus more intently on something and develop greater awareness of it, affirm your desired outcome, and create a state of greater intention.

Here are some Heaven on Earth affirmations. Choose one that feels right for you or make up your own, and keep affirming it.

- "This is Heaven on Earth."
- "Heaven on Earth is showing up."
- "Now is the time for Heaven on Earth."

- "I am co-creating Heaven on Earth."
- "I ask for God's help in having Heaven on Earth."

The process of repetition may bring up obstacles or challenges within you. Whatever thoughts, emotions or physical sensations arise, whether negative or positive, just notice them and return to repeating your affirmation.

Create an affirmation that feels right for you and then keep affirming it. Experience the affirmation in your body and with all your senses and emotions. Say it to yourself silently, under your breath, or out loud. Print it and put it on your desk or on your refrigerator. Make it a screen saver on your computer. Do what works to keep it in your awareness as a Gateway to Heaven on Earth.

"I live in a world of infinite possibility.
Within this world I have freedom of choice.
Through my thinking, I create heaven on earth."

Affirmation for the week of
December 29, 2002
Church of Religious Science
Santa Rosa, CA

My Heaven on Earth affirmation is: _____

_____

_____

➤ EXPERIENCING THE DIVINE

You may be a deeply religious or spiritual person for whom experiencing Heaven on Earth involves your religious or spiritual practice and obligations. Here are three possible avenues:

- **Experiencing The Divine**
  Recall a time when you felt connected to The Divine, to God. For me, I experience what I can only describe as "sweetness." It's beyond words and outside of time. It is these moments that remind me of my Divine connection, of being in and with God. For many people, it is this deep experience they are seeking, a time of Heaven on Earth. Take time to experience your connection to The Divine.

- **Praying**
  You can pray daily. I once read a story about a Sister living in a convent who was in her nineties. Her assignment was to pray 4–5 hours every day for others.

  What is prayer for you? Who and what would you pray for? How would you deepen your prayer? Your prayer can be as short as a single breath or as long as an entire day.

- **Feeling Blessed**
  Feeling blessed is experiencing awareness of the fullness of the moment, gratitude for everything that fills it, and a deep sense of peace and serenity. Gift yourself with the time to feel blessed every day.

"Heaven on Earth is...
the interpenetration of ourselves
with the Heart and Mind of God."

Anglican Bishop Henry Hill
Canada

YOUR OWN UNIQUE EXPRESSION

There might be other Gateways to your inner world that I've not mentioned. If so, please add it or them to your list.

The objective of all the inner Gateways is to remove any obstacles and let your essence shine — to allow the Heaven on Earth within to flower and flourish.

One small step every day grows and expands our new story and keeps it moving forward. And when we seek and get support from others, when we unite with others helping to co-create Heaven on Earth, our actions build an unstoppable momentum. Heaven on Earth builds in size, velocity, and impact.

"Heaven on Earth is...
owning the Glory."

Joe Mittiga
Speaker, Author
USA

▷ Your Inner World

- ➤ Working on Yourself
- ➤ Living Your Personal Values
- ➤ Discovering and Living Your Life's Purpose and Vision
- ➤ Expressing Your Essence Word
- ➤ Expressing Your Artistry
- ➤ Discovering and Giving Your Gift
- ➤ Enlivening Affirmations
- ➤ Experiencing The Divine

Do any of these avenues in the Inner Gateway resonate with you? Are any of them your Gateway? If so, which one(s) is it? What simple, easy, concrete step(s) will you take in the next 24 hours to make it happen? Write your answers here:

_____

_____

_____

_____

_____

_____

_____

"Heaven on Earth is...

realized to the extent

that one accepts the state of Heaven within themselves."

Jeffrey Milburn
Artist, Founder of Omni Art
USA

"Heaven on Earth is...

*the time when my young daughter, Sylvia, fell asleep in my bed
and I then moved her to her crib. In my exhausted state,
I climbed into my bed and the warmth of where her body had been
enveloped me."*

Cathy Driscoll
Mother
Canada

"The more each person approaches the universe,
the more he communicates himself to others,
and the more perfectly do they become one; none is conscious of himself alone,
but each is simultaneously conscious of the other. They are no longer merely people,
but also humanity; going out beyond themselves, triumphing over themselves,
they are on the way to true immortality and eternity."
Friedrich Schleiermacher

Chapter 10

▷ **Relationships – Co-Creating Heaven on Earth**
➤ With Yourself
➤ With Others
➤ With God/The Divine

Relationships are a Gateway into Heaven on Earth. Each day, our experience is filled with relationships: with ourselves, with others, with The Divine. Relationships link our inner and outer worlds. They are an essential part of co-creating the new story of what it means to be a human and what it means to be Humanity.

Heaven on Earth relationships contain qualities that are deeply satisfying and pleasurable for ourselves and others:

- honesty and authenticity
- deepening awe
- boundless energy
- being present
- never-ending creativity
- efficient effectiveness
- nurturing
- compassionate caring
- emanating harmony
- generous hospitality

- quiet peacefulness
- radiant
- spontaneous thankfulness
- co-ownership
- purposeful direction
- respectful regard
- richly connected
- magnetic vitality
- patience and flexibility
- serene integrity

- timeless wisdom
- joyous love
- adventurous
- consistent accountability
- overflowing laughter
- making a difference
- lightness of being
- deep joy
- all-embracing
- unconditionally giving

As these and other similar qualities are expressed over time, they become an ever-expanding treasure chest engaging us in that which is larger than ourselves.

For me, at a deeply personal level, the Heaven on Earth purpose of relationships is to continue experiencing evermore profound aspects of The Divine. For others, the purpose could be discovering avenues of greater expression, building networks of interaction for conscious commerce, or creating communities of more profound connection. Heaven on Earth relationships allow us to experience increasing clarity about the greater reality of ourselves, others, our world, and The Divine.

Let's begin by exploring the three dimensions of relationship...

- **With Yourself**
  There are parts of your relationship with yourself that work and parts that don't, parts that are hellish and parts that are heavenly. Acknowledge and resolve the parts that

block your increased expression of Heaven on Earth and nourish those parts that are already heavenly.

Becoming more aware of yourself in this way opens you more deeply to your relationship...

- **With Others**
  These include your spouse, children, parents, extended family, friends, acquaintances, strangers, people at work, members of your community, your city, your nation, and our entire global family. Here, too, clean up the parts that block your increased expression of Heaven on Earth and nourish those parts that are already heavenly.

  Your relationships with others extend the boundaries of your capacity, your creativity, and your compassion. Your relationships support you in being present with those who hold differing values, beliefs, and desires. Your sense of self expands as you appreciate other people and groups of people in a larger context of interconnectedness...

- **With God/The Divine**
  A deepening relationship with The Divine moves you into a deepening appreciation of The Divine in all, as each person is a spark of The Divine. You appreciate that all existence offers infinite value to your own life and to all of life. Through this relationship, you can experience awe, humility, compassion, gratitude, and peace.

"Heaven on Earth is...
the moments I am not sensing time.
I am fully present to another, to myself,
to a situation or experience. I am who I truly am.
I want for nothing.
There is no sense of any kind of separation in life or in me."

Debra Reynolds
Writer/Teacher
USA

Your Relationships: Hell on Earth or Heaven on Earth?

What does it take to transform a relationship from one that isn't working to one in which you experience Heaven on Earth?

"The major cause of divorce is
the inability to communicate in conflict situations."
Howard Markman & Scott Stanley

When a relationship isn't working, it's easy to jump to the negative: to blame, get angry, be resentful, make the other person responsible and at fault. You move into a defensive position. You close down. The result is physical, emotional, mental, and spiritual separation. In short, you're in the hell of relationships.

It's easy to blame others, but that doesn't give you any ongoing satisfaction or deep pleasure. All it gives is the momentary gratification of being right. But being right doesn't enter into your Soul, doesn't give you and the other person the experience of Heaven on Earth in the relationship.

What it takes to transform a Hell on Earth relationship into a Heaven on Earth one is you being responsible for the relationship working.

Notice those relationships where you are willing to be responsible up to a certain degree, but no further. Look at those relationships in your life where you've drawn the line: "I *won't* be responsible for my relationship with that person. I've done everything I can. They have to come to me and make it work."

Why are we willing to be responsible for certain relationships and not others? Why do we limit our responsibility when we know that the benefits we get from a relationship that *does* work is expanded pleasure and joy? It's because our belief structures tell us that there are certain relationships we are not and cannot be responsible for. "I'm not responsible for the fighting between the Palestinians and the Israelis." "I'm not responsible for the relationship between North Korea and the U.S." "I'm not responsible for making a relationship that hasn't been working with someone dear to me work." Why do we draw a line where our responsibility ends, especially if we want to see these relationships resolved and heavenly?

Take some time to look at your life, at the relationships you're not willing to be responsible for. Where do you draw the line?

People are also unwilling to be responsible because responsibility is often associated with blame, shame, guilt, or burden. This leads to feeling apprehensive, frightened, or overwhelmed. And why would you want more of that in your life?

Operating from "I am not responsible," you are at the effect of life — you feel life happens to you, that you have to defend and protect yourself. Events and people's actions toward you can't be fully controlled. You feel like a victim, you experience worry, anxiety, and fear. The result is you miss out on the joy, pleasure, contentment, and peace that life offers.

If each of the more than seven billion people in our world think they are not responsible for making relationships work, then we have a global mindset that will at best only produce interim solutions to selected relationships. We won't have a global mindset that is committed to being responsible for making relationships work. Imagine all seven billion of us actually being responsible for transforming relationships that don't work into ones that do. How long do you think the proliferation of war would last? How long do you think hunger and homelessness would last? Yet, isn't that exactly the thinking, perspective, and commitment we need to help co-create Heaven on Earth?

Let me ask the question again: How can you transform a Hell on Earth relationship into a Heaven on Earth one?

Start by looking at specific problem relationships in your life or at problems common to many of your relationships — problems you are not willing to be responsible for. Notice any persistent patterns. Notice where you consistently step away. What reasons do you give yourself, what justifications? Doing this will give you some perspective. And from this new point of view, ask yourself if you're at least willing to be responsible for making it work. If the answer is yes, then you can begin creating a bridge to being responsible. Simply being *willing* to be responsible for ensuring that a relationship that isn't working *will work* is the key that opens the door.

Living from "I am responsible" is living life as cause. You're centered in your power and creativity, making the kind of difference in the world that gives you the pleasure of accomplishment. You're moving to a higher perspective of observation, which gives you more options. You're being responsible and noticing that it feels good. Your relationships and your life start to work beyond what you believe is possible. Being responsible gives you freedom to act — it gives you the full capacity to be response-able (able to choose your response instead of unthinkingly reacting).

Here's a personal story to illustrate this:

> Years ago, my wife, Maida, and I were living in Toronto and we had just bought our first home. The nearest bank was a block and a half away, so we opened our accounts there. Whenever we went to the bank, we noticed how consistently unfriendly the staff was. We began wanting to avoid banking there, but the next nearest bank was much further away.
>
> At the time, I was teaching a personal development course and one of the issues we examined in depth was being responsible for relationships we thought could not work. During one particular seminar, I had an insight. I realized that I was letting the bank dictate my relationship with it and that our relationship wasn't working. In that moment, I made a commitment to be responsible for the relationship working. I would be responsible for producing satisfying relationships for myself and the entire bank staff.
>
> How was I going to do this? I had no idea. A part of me questioned whether it could really happen. But I'd already made the commitment, so I began looking at what I could do.
>
> The first thing I did was bring the tellers candy. Then I brought them flowers. I enrolled my assistant, Larry, who was having the same experiences at the bank, in the same adventure. He brought his own creativity, including writing funny personal notes to the staff.
>
> Within a very short time our relationships with the bank staff completely transformed for the better. Things turned around so much that I can remember many times even being allowed to go behind the counter to speak to staff.
>
> Several years later Maida and I decided to move about 40 miles away to another town that had a branch of the same bank. I went to our bank manager and told

him we were going to move, but not to worry because we were going to stay with the same bank, just a different branch. He looked at me and simply said, "No." Our relationship meant so much to him that he didn't want us to leave. I burst out laughing and said, "Okay," and we kept our account at that bank branch for more than 40 years.

Experiencing Heaven on Earth Relationships

What is a Heaven on Earth relationship?

Recall a time when you experienced a Heaven on Earth moment in a relationship. What was it like? What were its qualities? What was present?

Do you have a Heaven on Earth relationship in your life now? What's it like? What are its qualities? What's present?

When I look at Heaven on Earth relationships, mine and others, these are some of the qualities I experience. Allow them to further open the Heaven on Earth Relationships Gateway for you.

• Connection	• Ease	• Gratefulness	• Joy
• Pleasure	• Authenticity	• Celebration	• Laughter
• Generosity	• Being present	• Nurturance	• Playfulness

What Heaven on Earth Relationship qualities would you add?

_____   _____   _____

_____   _____   _____

_____   _____   _____

When you're in a Heaven on Earth relationship, there is a connection, a *communion* that is open, sparkling, and loving — there's laughter, generosity, an easy flow.

And when Heaven on Earth is present in one relationship, you can start reaching out and being responsible for having it in more of your relationships. You begin experiencing and living in the commitment that relationships are an expression of Heaven on Earth.

Imagine these two circles represent two people, each separate, whole, and complete. When they come together, a new forum is brought into existence, an overlapping area common to both known as the mandorla, Italian for almond (its shape). Notice that each circle is still unique *and* a relationship has been created. The mandorla is a communion, an arena of co-creation, symbolizing the merging of Heaven and Earth through which life itself originates.

How You Can Co-create Heaven on Earth Relationships

A Hell on Earth relationship is created when an issue remains unresolved. Another way of saying this is that when a relationship doesn't work an incompletion is present.

Incompletions can exist in three dimensions of relationship:

1) Incompletions with Yourself

2) Incompletions with Others

3) Incompletions with God/The Divine

Let's explore what the incompletions are in each dimension and how to complete them.

1) INCOMPLETIONS WITH YOURSELF

- **Broken Agreement**
  You made an agreement with yourself and you didn't keep it.

  To Complete This: Acknowledge that you didn't keep the agreement, forgive yourself, and see if you'd like to make the agreement again or not.

- **Completed Agreement not Acknowledged**
  You made an agreement with yourself and you did complete it, but you didn't acknowledge yourself for completing it.

  To Complete This: Take the time to stop and acknowledge yourself.

- **Not Committed**
  1. There were times when you didn't want to make a commitment to yourself, but you did. You felt forced into it in some way.

  To Complete This: Acknowledge that you didn't want to make the commitment, notice any emotional and mental attachments, and then release them. Re-evaluate the benefits of the commitment and choose to either make it or not.

  2. There were times when you didn't make a commitment to yourself and now is the time.

  To Complete This: Make the commitment.

2) INCOMPLETIONS WITH OTHERS

- **Telling a Lie**
  Lying to someone, whether or not they know, clearly creates an incompletion.

- **Breaking an Agreement**
  Telling someone you'll do something and not doing it.

- **Withheld Communication (negative or positive)**
  Not communicating something negative or not communicating something positive.

- **Damage Done by Word or Deed**
  Saying or doing something damaging or hurtful to another person. Similarly, not saying or doing something can cause damage or hurt to another person.

- **Non-acknowledged Acknowledgment**
  Not responding when someone acknowledges or recognizes you in some way, or gives you a gift.

- **The Commitment Doesn't Match the Relationship**
  Being in a relationship, but (1) the commitment isn't there for one or both of you; (2) the commitment is less than the current form of the relationship, e.g., you're a member of an organization whose functions you don't enjoy attending; or (3) the commitment is greater than the current form of the relationship, e.g., you're happily living together, want to be married, but neither of you has proposed marriage.

How You Can Complete Incompletions with Others

How do you complete a relationship incompletion? Communicate.

First, communicate with yourself. Do what is necessary and appropriate for you to be complete within yourself. That could be meditating, contemplating, journaling, taking a step back to gain a greater perspective of the situation, talking with someone else, or getting some coaching or therapy.

Then, focus your intention on completing with the other person. Begin by asking if they would be willing to listen to something you'd like to say to them. Tell them that the purpose of your communication is to resolve an issue(s) and strengthen your relationship.

If they refuse, gently ask them again. If the answer is still no, tell them you're available to speak whenever they'd like. For the moment, you've done your best.

If they do agree to speak with you, there are three possible ways to tell them what the issue is. It's critical to be aware of how you state the issue and its effect on them.

1. You can dump what you have to say on them like a dump truck. While you've technically communicated the issue, the result is the other person feels dumped on, attacked, and defensive.

2. The second way is to communicate in a neutral tone. Communicating in this way doesn't leave the other person feeling attacked, diminished, or defensive. They feel open and can more easily respond to you.

3. The third way, the Heaven on Earth way, is for you to first set the context. "Bill, I want to tell you something that is unpleasant for me to tell you, but the reason I want to do this is because it's bothering me and I want to resolve it. Can I do this?" Once Bill has agreed, begin by saying, "Would you also not say anything until I've finished, then please say whatever you'd like and I'll completely listen to you."

Once he's agreed, continue by saying, "Our relationship hasn't been working for me lately and I'd like to clean it up. I'd like to take a step toward improving our relationship. I'm 100% responsible for this situation being the way it is, and I'm totally committed to doing whatever it takes to resolve it." Then tell Bill whatever you have to say in a respectful, gentle, and non-attacking/non-threatening manner.

Once you've said what you have to say, be silent for a moment. Then ask Bill to tell you what he heard you say so you're sure he's heard exactly what you want him to hear. If it's not completely accurate, clarify the inaccurate parts. Once you feel completely heard and understood, thank him, wait a moment, and then ask him if there's anything he'd like to say. Let him speak without interrupting, then tell him what you've heard him say so that he knows you've heard and understood him. Keep doing this process until both of you feel complete.

Make sure you both acknowledge what's just happened so that you realize you're *both* now co-creating a Heaven on Earth relationship.

When you initiate this process by choosing to be 100% responsible for making your relationship work, it opens the opportunity for the other person to also be 100% responsible for making your relationship work. This is co-creation. (This process also works with a group. Make sure that you and everyone else are heard and are complete.)

Being complete with people clears up old hurts, anger, and resentments. It brings a new sparkle, a new lightness, a new joy to your relationships. From this point on, make it your intention and commitment to create more Heaven on Earth relationships in your life.

3) INCOMPLETIONS WITH GOD/THE DIVINE

- **Anger**
  You're mad at God/The Divine for something done or not done.

- **Out of Relationship**
  You feel out of relationship with God/The Divine and want to be back in relationship.

- **Deciding Against God's Presence**
  You've decided to not include the presence of God/The Divine in your life.

How You Can Complete Incompletions with God/The Divine

Sit down and be with God. You can do this by praying, writing a letter to God, or talking directly to God. "Listen" for any response you feel in your heart or experience intuitively.

I do all of these and I also journal — I write a dialogue between myself and God using one color of ink for my voice and another color for God's "reply." I find this process to be very powerful because of the depth of new understanding, appreciation, and clarity that emerges.

Whatever method you choose, keep going until you feel complete and experience your renewed relationship.

Completing an incompletion can involve some level of fear or anxiety. It's seems easier and more comfortable to just let things slide and not be complete. But it doesn't open up a new clearing, a new excitement, a new sparkling brilliance in your relationship.

What you're doing when you complete an incompletion, especially if it's an uncomfortable one, is co-creating more Heaven on Earth. And the only way to do it…is to do it. Over time you begin to understand what it takes to be complete. It may or may not get easier — that's not the point. The point is to complete the incompletion. Go over the list of the three relationship dimensions (You, Others, and God/The Divine) again and write down any incompletions that exist for you. Which ones will you commit to being responsible for completing and by when?

Incompletions I Commit to Completing	Completion Date

Be willing to operate as though you are responsible for co-creating Heaven on Earth for all relationships. The outcome is growth in courage, inner strength, compassion, and integrity. The experience is joy, pleasure, excitement, and love.

"Heaven on Earth is…
every human being feeling they are perfectly complete
or completely perfect."

Friederike Scheu
Body Therapist &
Health Management Institute Owner
Germany

"Heaven on Earth is...

*for me, the feeling that family, friends, co-workers, and
people on the street are just extended family.
It's about growing this warm, loving family.
This is what I'm going for."*

Dorman Woodall
Learning Consultant for Internet-Delivered Training
Author, Trainer & Workshop Leader
USA

"If we could only perceive each other like works of art...
we would then see life as heaven on earth."
Karen Chastain-Haughey

And remember to…

Celebrate
the Heaven on Earth relationships
you do have.

Look for and acknowledge the Heaven on Earth relationships that are already in your personal life and those you see being expressed in the world. Be aware of the qualities and feelings that are present. Celebrate these relationships. Use them as models and inspiration for transforming those that aren't, so that you're continuously expanding the number of Heaven on Earth relationships in your life and in the world.

"Heaven on Earth is…

the journey from one to oneness."

Barbara Curl
Founder & President
Kaua`i Aloha Foundation
USA

▷ Relationships – Co-Creating Heaven on Earth
➤ With Yourself
➤ With Others
➤ With God/The Divine

"Heaven on Earth is…

being fully present in our relationships,

and with that, making the right choices becomes organic."

Lori Knutson
Nurse
USA

"Heaven on Earth is...

the expectation we have of ourselves."

Yuko Yamaguchi
Realistic Visionary
Japan

"We are at the dawn of an age in which extreme political concepts and dogmas
may cease to dominate human affairs. We must use this historic opportunity
to replace them with universal human and spiritual values
and ensure that these values become the fiber of the global family which is emerging."

His Holiness the Dalai Lama

Chapter 11

▷ **Living Your Global Values**

I once heard a young woman talk about volunteering in a hospice where she worked with people nearing death. What stood out for her was how important values were to them. They wanted to pass on and entrust a vital appreciation of their values to family, friends, the broader world, and future generations.

What is it about values that would make someone want to devote the very last moments of their life to ensuring they were passed on? On their deathbeds, with their last breaths, they want to make an impact, they want to contribute to making the world a much better place, and they see values as fundamental to achieving that.

In Chapter 9, we looked at how "Living Your Personal Values" could be a contribution to Heaven on Earth. In this chapter we'll look at how you can make a contribution through living your Global Values — those values you want to see lived by Humanity now and long into the future.

Public discussion and agreement about what our global human values are and how we should live by them is rare. Commonly held global values aren't the subject of ongoing public conversation. They're not engaged with, deepened, or collectively agreed upon and practiced. As the human family, we haven't consciously, openly, and visibly chosen the collective, global values we want to live by.

Yet as the world moves more and more into living together as one global family, having and living global values becomes even more necessary for effectively addressing our planetary problems.

There are, of course, occasional times when we do see and feel life-nourishing global human values being concretely lived. For example:

- The summer and winter Olympic Games
  (Peaceful competition, friendship, excellence, striving to be the best)

- The annual awarding of the Nobel prizes
  (Contributions to academic, cultural and scientific advances, as well as the well-being of Humanity)

- The great artistic expressions in music, literature, film, art, and dance
  (Creativity, beauty, dedication, mastery)

Notice how you feel when you see these kinds of life-affirming global values being lived in the world. There's a feeling that we are clearly expressing the essence of our Humanity. There's the knowing that we're expressing our authentic collective self, and in doing so we and these global values blossom. We see our global values alive, positively impacting the world now and for generations to come.

Global human values are a lens through which our essence shines out into the world like a beacon. They are also a global touchstone for others to live by. Living our global human values has an effect greater than each of our individual contributions. A new communal field of good comes into existence that uplifts our individual and collective Soul. We touch that which is larger than our personal selves, experiencing the magnificence of our entire human family as we venture into the transcendent.

Deep within, we know what would happen when one or more of our global values are publicly lived by Humanity — another Heaven on Earth Gateway opens.

What Is a Global Value & Why Is it Valuable?

"A person's principles or standards of [global] behavior; one's judgment of what is important in life."

OxfordDictionaries.com

"A value is an idea which serves as a ground for choosing between possibilities."

Philip Allott
Eunomia: New Order for a New World

A global value is the specific way you act in the present moment on behalf of the world based on what is deeply important to you. It's also what you hold as fundamental and essential for the world's ongoing evolution. A global value is your compass, your glide path, an internal guiding star setting a true direction for our global family.

Why is a global value that you value valuable? It's your Soul's desire for the world. It is, as practical philosopher Gordon Allan says, "Your relationship with Creation." Deep down, it's the way you'd like your life and the lives of others to be lived. If a global human value you hold dear is lived, your Soul knows. If a global human value you hold dear is not lived, your Soul knows.

A global value isn't physical and yet it's very real. It belongs not to the material world, but to the transcendent, spiritual, Soul world. A global value allows us to access that world and live vibrantly in and from it.

Mis-beliefs about Global Values

Sometimes when people think about the possibility of their global values actually being lived in the world, thoughts may arise such as:

- I can't impose my values on anyone else.

- How can I, one person, be responsible for a global value that the entire world lives by?

- I'm responsible for myself, not for anyone else, and certainly not for the values every other human being lives by.

- What difference can I, one person, make in this world?

Thoughts like these make it seem impossible to have the world live by consciously chosen global values. "Impossibility" arises from the conclusions we've made about what happened and didn't happen in the past, about what's been done and not been done before. And over time these conclusions become beliefs.

By being attached to these beliefs, we're allowing the past to determine the future. Yet many things long thought impossible — human spaceflight, open-heart surgery, nanotechnology — are commonplace realities today. Impossible only exists if we believe it does. Mike Norton said, "Human beings are limited only by what we allow ourselves to be limited by." Instead of being limited by impossibilities, let's be unlimited with possibilities.

Imagine what would happen if people were publicly living their global values. Imagine what would happen if our world, rather than limping along with values not consciously chosen — with values that aren't moving us, as one, towards more Heaven on Earth — was more and more defined by collectively agreed upon, chosen, and lived values. Wouldn't the collective sufferings we face today (poverty, transnational epidemics, homelessness, etc.) be much more easily solved by people sharing life-affirming, Heaven on Earth, global human values, and working together to end the world's sufferings?

Let's be defined by the public expression of the world we deeply long for and our commitment to the kind of world we want. Let's be defined by living global values that are working, growing and flourishing, creating more and more Heaven on Earth.

Discovering Your Global Values

Begin discovering what your global values are by looking at some of the global values you do *not* want to see lived and sustained in the world. Here are some possibilities. Check off the ones you don't want and add any of your own on the blank lines at the end of the list.

- ❑ Terrorism masquerading as religious idealism

- ❑ Environmental degradation

- ❑ Narcissism and selfishness

- ❑ Wars bring peace

- ❑ Life without the spiritual, transcendent, or religious

- ❑ The suppression of women
- ❑ Moral corruption
- ❑ Racism
- ❑ Pettiness
- ❑ Cynicism and pessimism
- ❑ Greed, miserliness, and hoarding
- ❑ This is not Heaven on Earth and we can never have Heaven on Earth
- ❑ _____
- ❑ _____
- ❑ _____
- ❑ _____
- ❑ _____

Review the boxes you've checked:

- What did you notice as you went over the list?

- Do any of these global values stand out for you as ones you especially do not want?

- Do you notice any underlying pattern with the ones you've checked?

- Be aware of your thoughts and feelings when you consider which of these values you don't want and why.

- Having done this exercise, what has become clearer for you?

Now that you know there are global values you *don't* want, let's look at those you *do* want: Heaven on Earth global values — life-nourishing, life-sustaining, life-affirming.

The following are some suggestions for global values you'd like to see lived and sustained. Read over the list. Check off the ones that deeply resonate with you. If there are values you feel aren't included, please add them on the blank lines at the end of the list.

Values are usually written in a one-word format: Hope, Peace, Love, etc. I describe global values in a way that makes them much more alive and inspiring. I use a format I call "Living Global Values," which adds vibrant descriptors to each of them. For example, instead of just Hope, a living global value would be "Optimistic hope blooming."

Begin reading this list by saying out loud:

For Humanity, I value a world filled with...

- ❑ Ethics in action, seen and felt
- ❑ Wisdom being expressed
- ❑ Economic opportunity and prosperity flourishing
- ❑ Relationships thriving
- ❑ The living presence of ecological sustainability
- ❑ The flowering of peace and security
- ❑ The exciting freedom of exploring and expressing our full potential
- ❑ Democracy thriving
- ❑ Transparency dissolving corruption
- ❑ A free press informing, inspiring, engaging, and activating
- ❑ Justice seen and felt
- ❑ Moral courage being expressed
- ❑ People feeling powerfully linked to others through our shared Humanity
- ❑ An epidemic of health
- ❑ Optimistic hope blooming
- ❑ Truth spoken, written, and adored
- ❑ Multiple, daily, micro-acts of caring
- ❑ The feeling that the Human Family is my family
- ❑ A culture of service
- ❑ Unending generosity
- ❑ Unrequested kindness
- ❑ Respect respected
- ❑ The giving of love, feeling loved, being love
- ❑ Protection of the Earth
- ❑ People welcoming strangers
- ❑ Doing and seeing what is good and what is right
- ❑ All children being protected and safe

- ❑ People bringing their light into the world
- ❑ Respectful free speech
- ❑ Felt autonomy and embracing community
- ❑ Freedom of religion
- ❑ The promotion of the welfare of society as a whole
- ❑ Holiness honored
- ❑ Ongoing learning being prized
- ❑ Knowledge freely and happily shared
- ❑ Vibrantly healthy communities
- ❑ Laughter and well-being
- ❑ Heartfelt compassion
- ❑ Forgiveness and being forgiven
- ❑ Daily acts of philanthropy
- ❑ Personal accountability
- ❑ Collective social responsibility
- ❑ Enlightening beauty
- ❑ Spiritual clarity and boldness
- ❑ An ongoing progression of successes
- ❑ Authenticity reigning
- ❑ Daily acts of charity
- ❑ Safety all around
- ❑ Mental, emotional, physical, and spiritual well-being
- ❑ Expressing our global citizenship
- ❑ Humanity moving in the right direction
- ❑ People holding steady for the world working, for Heaven on Earth
- ❑ _____
- ❑ _____
- ❑ _____
- ❑ _____
- ❑ _____

Review the boxes you've checked:

- Which global values resonate with you?
- Do you notice any underlying pattern with the ones you've checked?
- Which ones are essential for you?
- Be aware of your thoughts and feelings when you consider which of these values you do want and why.
- Having done this exercise, what has become clearer for you?
- Circle the values you are committed to living.

How to Live Your Global Value(s)

Within you *right now* is the potential to initiate, promote, and instill the global values you want to see present in the world. To release this potential:

1. Consciously choose the global values you want.

2. Declare to yourself and the world:

   "_____, _____, _____ are the Global Values I stand for."
   (Insert your Global Values)

   (If you have additional values, create a list that includes them all.)

3. Commit to enlivening your values.

4. Live your life expressing your global values, making them clearly visible, felt, and flourishing in the world.

5. Enroll others in discovering and living their global values.

6. Join together in ever-expanding communities of shared global values.

After you've consciously chosen your global values and lived them over time, they move beyond choice. You embody them, you act from them spontaneously, without thought.

You become a person who has as your moral center, as your gyroscope, the global values you're committed to. You make your choices in life from your values, not in reaction to what life presents. You're effective, you're inspiring.

As a role model you encourage others to live their global values and in this way bring more Heaven on Earth into our world. Your heart's desire for the world you want becomes real.

How to Enroll Someone in Living Their Global Values

Enrollment involves speaking with others about what their global values are and asking them if they choose to live those values in the world. This is not about manipulating, imposing, or proselytizing. Instead, you're supporting them in discovering and living the global values that are true for them. Here's how to enroll someone:

- Ask them if they'd be willing to have a conversation about global values. (If they say no, thank them and talk about something else of mutual interest.)

- If they say yes, ask them what their global values are. If they don't know, ask what they value for the world now and into the future.

- Ask them what simple, easy, concrete thing(s) they will do every day to move their global values forward.

- Thank them for being willing to live their global values and ask what support you could give them.

- If you're willing, let them know what they could do to support you in living your global values.

- Talk about how both of you could support an expansion of global values.

- After some time has passed, check back with them to see how they're doing. Ask again if they'd like support from you, and if you're willing, ask them for the specific support you'd like.

What Global Values Can Do for Us as Humanity and You as a Human

Lived global values unite us across cultures, religions, economic and political viewpoints, and nations.

In order to solve the major sufferings affecting our world, we need to be acting together much more effectively and efficiently. The Internet and other global-reaching technologies already give us an avenue for doing this. Living our global values by leveraging these technologies gives us a more powerful vehicle for the implementation and accomplishment of Heaven on Earth.

As Peter H. Diamandis and Steven Kotler say in their book *Bold: How to Go Big, Create Wealth and Impact the World*, "Exponential technology allows us to scale up like never before. Small groups can have huge impacts. A team of passionate innovators can alter the lives of a billion people in an eye blink. To say that this kind of impact is unfathomable is putting it mildly."

What's being birthed now is the power of you, individually and in groups, to positively impact the world.

Living our global values helps reveal the next chapter of Humanity's story. This is where you come in. Living and honoring your global values can be your contribution to co-creating Heaven on Earth.

"Heaven on Earth is...

*when I know that I'm part of something
bigger than me."*

Charles Bower
Entrepreneur
Canada

"For the first time in human history, a global consensus on universal societal values
may be capable of being formed.... We would in essence be agreeing upon
the collective wisdom of humankind at this point in our evolution."

David Woolfson

How a Simple Photo Can Change the World

by Natalie Alexia

Love is the True Black™ (LTB) is a photographic movement rooted in social change. I was inspired to create this project while working with Jack Canfield, of the *Chicken Soup for the Soul* book series, in a year-long training in 2014. I was so moved by the 80 participants in the program that I was determined to find a way to create a lasting memory of and for each of them. And so LTB was born — a project that is both personally empowering and globally encompassing.

The origins of LTB actually began when I was a child. I grew up in five countries on three continents and went to eleven schools. There were different norms, fashions, and senses of humor. The overwhelming feeling I got from so much travel and cultural diversity at such a young age was that we are all different yet somehow all the same, all connected. I developed a deep sense of empathy because I was always "new" in a group. I imagined a world with greater love, compassion, and empathy. Rather than separate, alone and fearful, everyone would feel safe to be themselves, yet also a part of something, connected.

It's time for us to stop looking for what makes people different from us, what keeps us separate, and start to look for the similarities, for what connects us. LTB initiates that shift.

The LTB process begins with my asking you: *"If you had an opportunity to share a message with the world and knew that everyone would hear and understand it, what would you share?"*

The next step is the scariest, yet most exhilarating. It involves writing your message on your arm — in just five words. The magic of this is that it requires you to crystalize and encapsulate your guiding beliefs and values in five words or less. It takes courage to own your values, write them on your skin, and then have them photographed so that they become part of something much bigger than yourself — letting the world really see you and what you stand for. It's extraordinarily empowering to be seen and heard from the core of your being.

Guiding people through this process, I've experienced the raw emotion, excitement, and power that wearing your "inside" on your "outside" creates. My greatest joy lies in witnessing a more expansive and embracing awareness emerge in each person and to see their greatness blossom.

At the end of each workshop, I present a slideshow. When participants see their message alongside all the other members of the group, they are astonished and captivated! Every slideshow has received a standing ovation. People cry, hug, laugh, and the entire group bonds to the depths of their hearts and being through their shared experience. This sense of community from the heart is exactly what I know Love is the True Black will create on a global scale.

I've now taken LTB to many groups, ranging from The Transformational Leadership Council to charity workshops with homeless foster kids. Wherever I take LTB and pose this one question, no matter who people are, where they come from, how much success they've achieved or how hard their lives have been, their answers always reflect the same desire found within each of us: to live in a world of greater love, truth, and compassion.

LTB's vision is to have millions of people discover and share their guiding values through their photo. We can show in an instant that somehow at the heart of the heart — when you strip away all the philosophy about why and how — we're all the same, we're all connected.

Our Mission is to start a global conversation about love and values, to lift up and celebrate our differences, and to grow empathy. We want to highlight how connected we are as a human race…with a simple photo.

tinyurl.com/HonELove

Natalie Alexia

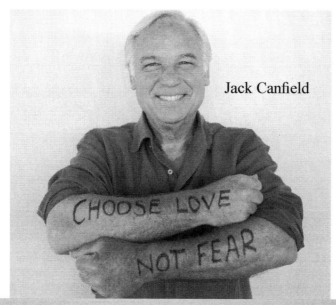

Jack Canfield

Dr. Sue Morter

Raymond Aaron

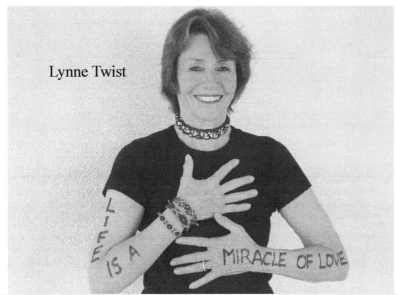

Lynne Twist

Gabriel Nossovitch

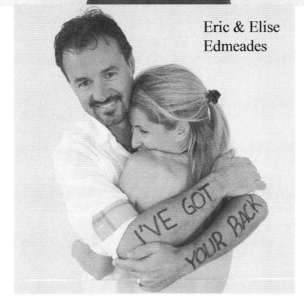

Eric & Elise
Edmeades

Living Your Global Values

Arielle Ford

Sonia Choquette

Carter Phipps

Janet Bray Attwood

Martin Rutte

"Heaven on Earth is...

the end of suffering."

Norma Kipnis Wilson
Financial Advisor
USA

"Between April 6, 1994, and the middle of July, some 800,000 Rwandans
died in a genocide that saw them hacked and butchered to death....
The slaughter was unimaginable. Overwhelmingly, ethnic Hutus killing ethnic Tutus.
Families, friends, children, entire villages were wiped off the face of the map.
The physical and sexual violence against women was of biblical proportions;
rape, gang rape, mass rape was everywhere, was a weapon of war.
Children were never spared. Indeed, children were targeted.
If you're going to exterminate a people you try to exterminate its future."

Stephen Lewis
Former Canadian Ambassador to the United Nations
Member of the International Panel of Eminent Personalities

Chapter 12

▷ **Your Outer World**

▶ **Ending the World's Major Sufferings**

- ➤ Hunger and Malnutrition
- ➤ Disease
- ➤ Lack of Adequate Shelter
- ➤ War, Genocide, Refugees, & Weapons Proliferation
- ➤ Illiteracy
- ➤ Poverty, No Access to Opportunity
- ➤ Lack of Clean Water and Sanitation
- ➤ Environmental Pollution and Degradation
- ➤ Lack of Freedom: Tyranny, Repression
- ➤ Lack of Meaning and Purpose
- ➤ Crime, Violence, and Terrorism
- ➤ Prejudice, Hatred, and Discrimination
- ➤ Torture, Slavery, Human Rights Abuse, Child Labor, Violence Against Women/Children
- ➤ Sexual Abuse
- ➤ Bad Governance, Corruption, and Poor Management
- ➤ Overpopulation
- ➤ Animal Abuse and Species Extinction
- ➤ Spiritual Malnourishment

Throughout history, Humanity has suffered in innumerable ways: hunger, disease, poverty, crime, homelessness, corruption, slavery. The list is long. Human suffering is occurring around the globe as you read this, and it continues. And it's not only in other countries — poverty and malnutrition exist in your own community. Isn't it time we begin saying, "Enough"? Enough war, enough illiteracy, enough poverty and malnutrition. Enough of the immoral, unnecessary, and recurring sufferings we've been putting up with. Project Heaven on Earth says, "Yes, enough! We are going to end the world's major sufferings once and for all!" That clearly and specifically is the commitment.

Since the world's sufferings are interrelated and impact each other, every contribution to ending a suffering has a ripple effect. Your contribution does matter and is needed now.

In this chapter, I cast a light on some of the world's major sufferings. If one or more of them speaks directly to you, I invite you to become part of the individual and collective commitment and responsibility to end it. From this moment on, we need to engage our individual and collective power to responsibly end the world's major sufferings. We need this purposeful commitment evident and clearly felt the world over.

And the commitment to ending the world's major sufferings has already begun:

- The organization, Free the Slaves, says: "Our mission is to end slavery worldwide. We believe that ending slavery is an ambitious — and realizable — goal."

- In an important step towards a polio-free world, the Global Commission for the Certification of Poliomyelitis Eradication (GCC) concluded on Sept. 20, 2015 that wild poliovirus type 2 (WPV2) has been eradicated worldwide.

- *The End of Poverty* by Dr. Jeffrey Sachs, Professor of Economics, Director of The Earth Institute at Columbia University and Special Advisor to the United Nations Secretary-General on the Millennium Development Goals.

- *The End of Illness* by Dr. David. B. Agus, Professor of Medicine & Engineering at the University of Southern California's Keck School of Medicine and Viterbi School of Engineering.

- *The End of War* by John Horgan. Reviewer Tyler Volk says of the book, "In the end, though, war is an invention, a social technology. And that means, thankfully, it can be un-invented, dismantled, and made obsolete with more advanced social inventions, such as better mechanisms for creating and maintaining peace, which…not only should become a global, collective goal, but also is achievable."

- *The Responsibility to Protect: Ending Mass Atrocity Crimes Once and For All* by Gareth Evans, president and CEO of the International Crisis Group since 2000 and foreign minister of Australia from 1988 to 1996. Co-chair of the International Commission on Intervention and State Sovereignty (2000-01), which initiated the Responsibility to Protect concept.

- *Apocalypse Never: Forging the Path of a Nuclear Weapon-Free World* by Tad Daley who directs the Project on Abolishing War www.abolishingwar.org, at the Center for War/Peace Studies in New York.

- *I BELIEVE IN ZERO: Learning from The World's Children: Zero Hunger, Zero Poverty, Zero Disease* by Caryl M. Stern President and CEO of the U.S. Fund for UNICEF. The book reflects her — and UNICEF's — mission to reduce the number of preventable deaths of children under the age of five from 19,000 each day to zero.

We'll begin by exploring ten major sufferings giving some facts and statistics about each one. I'll then define its Heaven on Earth Result, offer an opportunity for you to describe what simple actions you'll take to end the suffering and then support you with resources, an uplifting story, and several inspiring quotes. The chapter concludes with eight additional sufferings in an abbreviated format. (If I've left out a suffering close to your heart, use one I've already listed to inspire you.)

In this chapter, I want to make it easier for you to get your arms around a suffering. I'm doing this so that instead of you being overwhelmed by the suffering, which does nobody any good, you can make your unique contribution to ending it if you choose.

The sufferings may at first seem daunting in their scope and magnitude. As you read through them, allow whatever feelings or thoughts you're having to just be: whether it's overwhelm, hopelessness, sadness, repugnance, disinterest, challenge, or excitement. It's important to allow, acknowledge, and honor your thoughts and feelings.

At the same time, notice if you feel drawn to end any particular suffering(s). What simple, easy, concrete steps will you take to end it?

To make it very easy for you to discover what part you can play in ending a suffering, I have designed this chapter with a simple template. Each suffering covers two pages. The left hand page (see Example A below) begins with the name of the specific suffering ❶ and The Heaven on Earth Result ❷ for when it is ended. Below this is an inspiring story of someone playing their part in eliminating the suffering ❸. Below the story are one or two quotes ❹ to inspire you to end the suffering.

On the right hand page of Example A is the Eye Openers section ❺, which contains facts and statistics about the suffering. (The data for each Eye Opener is current as of the writing of this book. If in reading through this chapter you discover one particular suffering that is yours to end, please Google the most current data for it.) To the right of that is a request to have you look at what simple, easy, concrete step(s) you will take to help end this suffering by filling in your answers in the space provided ❻.

At the bottom right of the right hand page are a list of Resources to help you learn more and support you in taking action ❼.

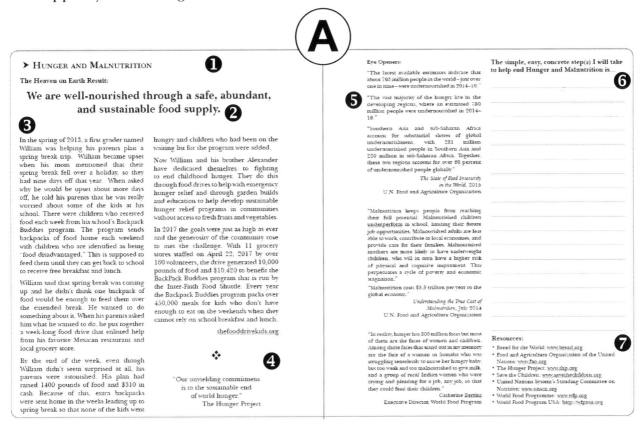

Because of the number of sufferings, I've templated the initial ten like Example A and an additional eight in a contracted format (Example B) using all of the same components as Example A, except for not including a story, ❸.

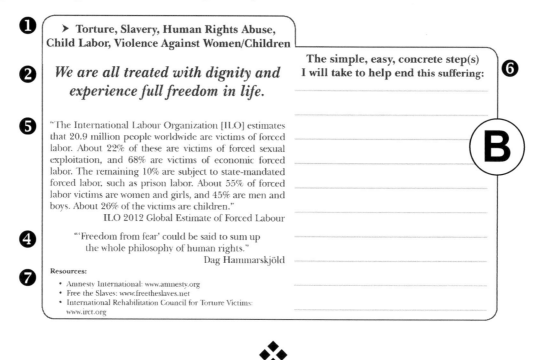

❶ ➤ **Torture, Slavery, Human Rights Abuse, Child Labor, Violence Against Women/Children**

❻ The simple, easy, concrete step(s) I will take to help end this suffering:

❷ *We are all treated with dignity and experience full freedom in life.*

❺ "The International Labour Organization [ILO] estimates that 20.9 million people worldwide are victims of forced labor. About 22% of these are victims of forced sexual exploitation, and 68% are victims of economic forced labor. The remaining 10% are subject to state-mandated forced labor, such as prison labor. About 55% of forced labor victims are women and girls, and 45% are men and boys. About 26% of the victims are children."
ILO 2012 Global Estimate of Forced Labour

❹ "'Freedom from fear' could be said to sum up the whole philosophy of human rights."
Dag Hammarskjöld

❼ Resources:
- Amnesty International: www.amnesty.org
- Free the Slaves: www.freetheslaves.net
- International Rehabilitation Council for Torture Victims: www.irct.org

B

❖

The Heaven on Earth Goal for each suffering is to end it.

Just because we've always had a particular suffering does not mean it has to continue. While we've certainly made considerable progress on many sufferings, the fact is — the major sufferings are still here.

Seven billion people all thinking a suffering *can't* be ended results in a mindset that has the suffering stay in place. But the more people who are committed to and responsible for ending a suffering, the more possibilities there will be created and actions taken resulting in its ending.

We can no longer afford the indulgence of being overwhelmed when we confront a specific suffering, nor of thinking there's nothing we as individuals can do. Being overwhelmed puts the focus on you, not on the suffering. While you're spending time feeling overwhelmed, the suffering continues in the world.

A more powerful response in the face of overwhelm is to re-ask Question 3 focused on a suffering: What simple, easy, concrete step(s) will I take in the next 24 hours to help end this suffering?

Seven billion people all *now* taking simple, easy, concrete steps to end a suffering builds unstoppable momentum.

As you read this chapter, please put your attention on the simple, easy, concrete steps you can take to end a suffering(s).

Now, LET'S END THESE SUFFERINGS!

"Heaven on Earth is...

consciously taking action
for a future you would prefer to live into
and doing it with others."

Tom Feldman
Life Coach
USA

"Whatever you can do or dream you can, begin it.
Boldness has genius, power and magic in it."

Johann Wolfgang von Goethe

➤ HUNGER AND MALNUTRITION

The Heaven on Earth Result:

We are well-nourished through a safe, abundant, and sustainable food supply.

In the spring of 2013, a first grader named William was helping his parents plan a spring break trip. William became upset when his mom mentioned that their spring break fell over a holiday, so they had nine days off that year. When asked why he would be upset about more days off, he told his parents that he was really worried about some of the kids at his school. There were children who received food each week from his school's Backpack Buddies program. The program sends backpacks of food home each weekend with children who are identified as being "food disadvantaged." This is supposed to feed them until they can get back to school to receive free breakfast and lunch.

William said that spring break was coming up and he didn't think one backpack of food would be enough to feed them over the extended break. He wanted to do something about it. When his parents asked him what he wanted to do, he put together a week-long food drive that enlisted help from his favorite Mexican restaurant and local grocery store.

By the end of the week, even though William didn't seem surprised at all, his parents were astonished. His plan had raised 1400 pounds of food and $310 in cash. Because of this, extra backpacks were sent home in the weeks leading up to spring break so that none of the kids went hungry and children who had been on the waiting list for the program were added.

Now William and his brother Alexander have dedicated themelves to fighting to end childhood hunger. They do this through food drives to help with emergency hunger relief and through garden builds and education to help develop sustainable hunger relief programs in communities without access to fresh fruits and vegetables.

In 2017 the goals were just as high as ever and the generosity of the community rose to met the challenge. With 11 grocery stores staffed on April 22, 2017 by over 160 volunteers, the drive generated 10,000 pounds of food and $10,420 to benefit the BackPack Buddies program that is run by the Inter-Faith Food Shuttle. Every year the Backpack Buddies program packs over 450,000 meals for kids who don't have enough to eat on the weekends when they cannot rely on school breakfast and lunch.

thefooddrivekids.org

"Our unyielding commitment
is to the sustainable end
of world hunger."
The Hunger Project

Eye Openers:

"The latest available estimates indicate that about 795 million people in the world – just over one in nine – were undernourished in 2014–16."

"The vast majority of the hungry live in the developing regions, where an estimated 780 million people were undernourished in 2014–16."

"Southern Asia and sub-Saharan Africa account for substantial shares of global undernourishment, with 281 million undernourished people in Southern Asia and 220 million in sub-Saharan Africa. Together, these two regions account for over 60 percent of undernourished people globally."

The State of Food Insecurity
in the World, 2015
U.N. Food and Agriculture Organization

"Malnutrition keeps people from reaching their full potential. Malnourished children underperform in school, limiting their future job opportunities. Malnourished adults are less able to work, contribute to local economies, and provide care for their families. Malnourished mothers are more likely to have underweight children, who will in turn have a higher risk of physical and cognitive impairment. This perpetuates a cycle of poverty and economic stagnation."

"Malnutrition costs $3.5 trillion per year to the global economy."

Understanding the True Cost of
Malnutrition, July 2014
U.N. Food and Agriculture Organization

"In reality, hunger has 800 million faces but most of them are the faces of women and children. Among those faces that stand out in my memory are the face of a woman in Somalia who was struggling senselessly to nurse her hungry baby, but too weak and too malnourished to give milk, and a group of rural Indian women who were crying and pleading for a job, any job, so that they could feed their children."

Catherine Bertini
Executive Director, World Food Program

The simple, easy, concrete step(s) I will take to help end Hunger and Malnutrition is...

Resources:
- Bread for the World: www.bread.org
- Food and Agriculture Organization of the United Nations: www.fao.org
- The Hunger Project: www.thp.org
- Save the Children: www.savethechildren.org
- United Nations System's Standing Committee on Nutrition: www.unscn.org
- World Food Programme: www.wfp.org
- World Food Program USA: http://wfpusa.org

➤ DISEASE

The Heaven on Earth Result:

We are healthy and there is affordable, quality care for all.

Helping cure, prevent, or manage all diseases in our children's lifetime.

Researchers, doctors, and entrepreneurs are working tirelessly to expand our understanding of the human body and disease. Husband and wife team, Priscilla Chan and Mark Zuckerberg, have launched the Chan–Zuckerberg Initiative, which backs leaders in building cutting-edge tools and technologies to foster collaborations seeking to end all disease by the end of the century.

Their first investment is the Chan–Zuckerberg Biohub, an independent research center that brings together physician-scientists, engineers and faculty from the University of California, Berkeley, University of California, San Francisco, and Stanford University to tackle today's biggest scientific challenges.

Their focus is on making long-term investments over 25 – 100 years and understanding that the greatest challenges require very long-time horizons and cannot be solved by short-term thinking. "We must take risks today to learn lessons for tomorrow."

"This is about the future we all want for our children. If there is even a chance we can cure disease in our children's lifetime,

we're going to do our part." said Mark Zuckerberg.

"...we are at the limit of what we understand about the human body and disease, the science of medicine, the limit of disease and suffering," Chan said. "We want to push back that boundary."

tinyurl.com/HonENoDisease

"Making Cancer History®"
M.D. Anderson
Cancer Center

"Healthy citizens are the greatest asset any country can have."
Winston Churchill

Eye Openers:

Listed are the number of people dying from infectious diseases for the most recent year available. I have equated that number to the population of two representative cities in the same year.

Air Pollution
   Seven million people died as a result of air pollution in 2012, the equivalent of:
   Greater Kuala Lumpur, Malaysia **or**
   Hong Kong
Diarrheal Diseases
   1.5 million died in 2012
   Auckland, New Zealand **or**
   Philadelphia, Pennsylvania, USA
Tuberculosis
   1.5 million died in 2014
   Cordoba, Argentina **or**
   Kampala, Uganda
AIDS
   1.2 million died in 2014
   Prague, Czech Republic **or**
   Dallas, Texas, USA
Malaria
   438,000 died in 2015
   Sochi, Russia **or**
   Santa Barbara, California, USA

"More than half (52%) of all deaths in low-income countries in 2015 were caused by the so-called "Group I" conditions, which include communicable diseases, maternal causes, conditions arising during pregnancy and childbirth, and nutritional deficiencies.

"All but 1 of the 10 leading causes of death in high-income countries were NCDs [noncommunicable diseases]."
World Health Organization, 2015

"As of 2015, an estimated 13.4 million [11.4 – 15.7 million] children worldwide had lost one or both parents to AIDS. More than 80 percent of these children (10.9 million) live in sub-Saharan Africa."
Protection, Care and Support for Children Affected by HIV and AIDS, 2016
UNICEF

The simple, easy, concrete step(s) I will take to help end Disease is...

Resources:
- The End of Polio: www.theendofpolio.com
- The Carter Center's Health Programs: www.cartercenter.org/health/index.html
- Centers for Disease Control and Prevention: www.cdc.gov
- PATH: www.path.org
- World Health Organization: www.who.int

➤ Lack of Adequate Shelter

The Heaven on Earth Result:

We have safe, ample, and affordable housing for everyone.

Nearly two-dozen college students earn a degree by digging in the earth and finding or buying whatever building materials they can — from hay bales to used tires — to construct homes, repair structures, and bring a sense of community to a place some considered lost.

Their inspiration? A scruffy-looking, bearded man, Samuel "Sambo" Mockbee, a professor, counselor, friend and mentor but mostly, an educator, to the students who live and work at the Auburn University College of Architecture, Design & Construction's Rural Studio and the West Alabama people whose lives are changed by the work he and the students do.

Students come away having learned about architecture and about life. One of the greatest lessons Mockbee teaches is that as soon-to-be-architects, they are responsible for more than just the building they design. He's passionate about teaching students the how-to of architecture while instilling in them social responsibility as architects.

Students have built homes for the elderly, made repairs to hundreds of homes for safer living conditions, built playgrounds and designed and built a chapel from stucco-covered recycled tires. They have used hay bales for insulation, corrugated-metal siding, fragmented curbstones, colored-glass bottles, and milled timber to complete structures.

"He motivated us to do our best and to find the ultimate answer," says former student Ruard Veltman. "He would guide, not lead."

"Mockbee ushers his students into a world without subdivisions and Wal-Marts, exposing them to a reality that, despite its financial despair, has all the qualities of individuality, family, and community they hope for in their own lives," says Bruce Lanier.

"The goal is not only to have a warm, dry house, but to have a warm, dry house with a spirit to it," Mockbee says. "What we build are shelters for the soul as well as homes for bodies."

tinyurl.com/HonEShelter

"...homelessness is a problem that's solvable."
Roseanne Haggerty
Common Ground

"Home is a pleasant word."
Scottish Proverb

Eye Openers:

For the U.S.

"2.5 million children in America – one in every 30 children – go to sleep without a home of their own each year."

America's Youngest Outcasts, 2014
The National Center on Family Homelessness

"There are 10.3 million extremely low income renter households in the U.S., many of whom lack affordable, safe, and well-maintained housing. Three in four (75%) extremely low income renters spend more than 50% of their income on housing costs, leaving these 7.8 million households with little left over to meet other basic needs."

Out of Reach 2013
National Low Income Housing Coalition

For the World

"Slums feature the most deplorable living and environmental conditions and are characterized by inadequate water supply, poor sanitation, overcrowded and dilapidated housing, hazardous locations, insecurity of tenure and vulnerability to serious health risks – all of which have major implications for quality of life. Slums are also known for their atmosphere of fear and the social and economic exclusion of their residents. Slum dwellers are often stigmatized on account of their location and are often discriminated against in terms of access to public and social services, as well as employment."

State of the World's Cities 2012/2013
UN-Habitat

"One billion people are currently living in slums – that's one in six of us. Unless urgent action is taken, 1.4 billion people will be living in slums by 2020."

Reall (Real Equity For All), 2016

"Fifty-five million new slum dwellers have been added to the global population since 2000. Sub-Saharan Africa has a slum population of 199.5 million, South Asia 190.7 million, East Asia 189.6 million, Latin America and the Caribbean 110.7 million, Southeast Asia 88.9 million, West Asia 35 million and North Africa 11.8 million."

UN-Habitat, 2016

The simple, easy, concrete step(s) I will take to help end Lack of Adequate Shelter is...

Resources:

- Domus Realty – A Home for Everyone: tinyurl.com/HomeforEveryone
- Habitat for Humanity: www.habitat.org/
- The Rural Studio: www.ruralstudio.org
- UN-Habitat: www.unhabitat.org

➤ **WAR, GENOCIDE, REFUGEES, & WEAPONS PROLIFERATION**

The Heaven on Earth Result:

We have global peace, stability, and reverence for the life of every human being.

Is there a more urgent problem in the world today than war?

[First]…war exacerbates or perpetuates our other problems, either directly or by draining precious resources away from their solution. War subverts democracy and promotes tyranny and fanaticism; kills and sickens and impoverishes people; ravages nature. War is a keystone problem, the eradication of which would make our other social problems much more tractable.

Second, war is more readily solvable than many other human afflictions. War is not like a hurricane, earthquake or Ebola plague, a natural disaster foisted on us by forces beyond our control. War is entirely our creation, the product of human choices. War could end tomorrow if a relatively small group of people around the world chose to end it.

Third, more than any of our other problems, war represents a horrific moral crime. We cannot claim to be civilized as long as war or even the threat of war persists.

Yes, annual war casualties have declined sharply since the cataclysmic first half of the 20th century. But in our heavily — and nuclear — armed world, war is a few decisions away from becoming exponentially more destructive.

Our biggest challenge is making the transition from our world, which is still armed and dangerous, to a world in which war and even the threat of war have vanished.

…nations and other groups should act in a manner consistent with the ultimate goal of eradicating war once and for all. This is what I call the "end-of-war rule."

According to surveys I've carried out for more than a decade, the overwhelming majority of people view war as inevitable, a permanent feature of human existence. This fatalistic outlook is wrong, both empirically and morally. Empirically because it contradicts what science and history tell us about war. Morally because it perpetuates war by discouraging us from seeking solutions.

If we all join together in pursuing the end of war, we will surely succeed, not in some hazy, distant future but soon.

John Horgan, Science Journalist
Author, *The End of War*
tinyurl.com/HonEEndofWar

"Only Peace, No War."
Muhamed Fejzic (Bosnia/USA)

Eye Openers:

"In the 10-year period 2004-13 there were 74 active state-based conflicts, including 33 that were active in 2013; 238 non-state conflicts, including 48 that were active in 2013; and 116 actors recorded as carrying out one-sided violence, including 25 in 2013.

"…World military expenditure was estimated at $1776 billion in 2014, representing 2.3 percent of global gross domestic product or $245 per person."

*SIPRI Yearbook 2015: Armaments,
Disarmament and International Security*
Stockholm International Peace
Research Institute

Genocides (number of people killed)
- Armenia: 1,000,000 from 1915-23
- Rwanda: 1,000,000 in 1994
- Cambodia: 1,600,000 1975-78
- Holocaust: 5,700,000 1933-45
- USSR under Stalin: 20,000,000
- China under Mao: 58,000,000

Detailed Death Tolls for Man-made
Multicides throughout History

"The number of refugees of concern to UNHCR in mid-2014 stood at 13 million, up from a year earlier. A further 5.1 million registered refugees are looked after in some 60 camps in the Middle East…."

UN High Commissioner for Refugees

"There are women, girls, as young as five and as old as 80, who have been systematically raped several times, tortured and injured by firearms. We have never come across as many victims of rape in a conflict situation."

Christiane Berthiaume, 2003
World Food Programme, speaking about
eastern Democratic Republic of Congo

"There are an estimated 875 million small arms in circulation worldwide…the Small Arms Survey estimates that their annual authorized trade exceeds $8.5 billion."

Small Arms Survey

The simple, easy, concrete step(s) I will take to help end War, Weapons Proliferation, Genocide, and Refugees is…

Resources:
- Global Action to Prevent War and Armed Conflict: www.globalactionpw.org
- Stockholm International Peace Research Institute: www.sipri.org/
- Prevent Genocide International: www.preventgenocide.org
- U.S. Department of State's Bureau of Population, Refugees, and Migration: www.state.gov/j/prm/index.htm
- Office of the United Nations High Commissioner for Refugees: www.unhcr.org
- United Nations Institute for Disarmament Research: www.unidir.org
- U.S. Department of State – World Military Expenditures and Arms Transfers reports: tinyurl.com/MilitaryArms
- Organisation for the Prohibition of Chemical Weapons: www.opcw.org
- International Action Network on Small Arms: www.iansa.org

➤ ILLITERACY

The Heaven on Earth Result:

We are literate, educated, and empowered in making our contributions.

Meet Earl Mills. Earl is all too familiar with the shame and embarrassment of being illiterate. At 45 years old, Earl was married with five children, owned his own home, and worked for 25 years at the same company. Yet he had a secret that few others knew: he could not read.

His lack of reading skill was exposed when he was put on the spot at church one night when he was asked to read a Bible passage. The problem was that at 44 years old, he couldn't read. No one knew except his wife. Earl says, "When you can't read, you keep it under a lock and a key and you let hardly anyone inside of that part of your life."

Earl sought the assistance of the Craven Literacy Council. When he went to them they assessed him at a second-grade reading level. He had trouble spelling words like girl and bird. With sheer determination he embarked on a three-year process of learning how to read. In addition to improving his literacy skills, Mills developed his ability to capture the frustrations and triumphs through his poetry. Today, he has published several books of poetry, including *From Illiterate to Poet* and *From Illiterate to Author*.

Earl is now a passionate advocate for adult literacy. He recently attended the National ProLiteracy Conference on Adult Literacy in Charleston, South Carolina where he was asked to read a few of his inspiring poems to the audience of 500 adult literacy professionals. ProLiteracy is a national nonprofit whose mission is to help adults learn to read by developing materials and programs for over 1,000 literacy member programs across the country. When adults learn to read and write, they have the power to change their lives and their communities.

tinyurl.com/HonENoUneducated

"Literacy is much more than an educational priority – it is the ultimate investment in the future and the first step towards all the new forms of literacy required in the twenty-first century. We wish to see a century where every child is able to read and to use this skill to gain autonomy."
Irina Bokova
Director-General, UNESCO

"Elimination of illiteracy is as serious an issue to our history as the abolition of slavery."
Maya Angelou

Eye Openers:

"More than 773 million young people and adults around the world cannot read this message. …Two out of three are women.…"

"…Worldwide, at least 250 million children of primary school age cannot read, write, or count. Half of these girls and boys never make it to school or are pushed out before their fourth year."

> UN Secretary-General Ban Ki-moon's
> message for World Literacy Day 2013

"Three-quarters of the global illiterate population live in only two regions: South and West Asia, with 407 million or more than one-half of all illiterate adults worldwide, and sub-Saharan Africa, with 182 million illiterate adults.…"

> *Adult and Youth Literacy: National, Regional*
> *and Global Trends, 1985-2015*
> UNESCO Institute for Statistics

"For the school year ending in 2013, 124 million children and young adolescents, roughly between the ages of 6 and 15 years, have either never been to school or dropped out, compared to 122 million in 2011."

> UNESCO Institute for Statistics, 2015

"An estimated 90% of children with disabilities in the developing world do not go to school."

> *Global Initiative on*
> *Out-of-School Children*, 2014
> UNICEF

"…many classrooms in developing countries continue to face real resource constraints. Average pupil-teacher ratios in Malawi, Chad and Rwanda were at least 60:1, while Pakistan, Cambodia, Uganda, Tanzania, Burkina Faso all had ratios over 40:1.…"

> Isaac M. Mbiti
> "The Need for Accountability in
> Education in Developing Countries"
> *Journal of Economic Perspectives*—Volume 30,
> Number 3—Summer 2016—Pages 109–132

The simple, easy, concrete step(s) I will take to help end Illiteracy is…

Resources:

- Curious Learning: www.curiouslearning.org
- Literacy and Education at SIL International: www.sil.org/literacy
- National Center for Families Learning: www.familieslearning.org
- United Nations Educational, Scientific and Cultural Organization (UNESCO): www.unesco.org

➤ POVERTY, NO ACCESS TO OPPORTUNITY

The Heaven on Earth Result:

We have abundant income and an empowering livelihood.

Maria Tuesta Pizango remembers that she always wanted to escape the life she had in Nueva Luz, Peru, because of a lack of economic and educational opportunity. She married, had three kids at age 15, then separated from her husband due to his alcoholism.

Maria began knitting clothing and selling artisanal products in order to support her children's health and education. After a few years, the district mayor invited Maria to participate in a contest with her products. She won a cash reward, which inspired her to keep working passionately. Because of her success, the district mayor also took her to the cities of Iquitos and Moyobamba, where she presented her products, allowing her and her work to gain prestige.

Maria used the money they awarded her to plant crops and continue to educate her children. Seeing Maria's success, other women began promoting their own knitting and artisanal products.

Maria says that The Hunger Project trainings in her community have changed her life, teaching her the best farming and livestock-raising practices. Maria is overjoyed by the impact she notices herself making on other women in the community who are now knitting, creating artisanal products, planting vegetables, and attending trainings.

"The truth is that I feel very happy because it is not only me who is advancing and getting better, it is also my neighbors and the families of other communities…when we have the will and we dream of doing it, we make it into a reality."

tinyurl.com/HonENoPoverty

"No society can rise higher than its poorest citizens."
Dr. Oscar Arias

"The poverty of the world is entirely man-made and is wholly unnecessary."
Swami Agnivesh

"The time has come for us to civilize ourselves by the total, direct, and immediate abolition of poverty."
Martin Luther King, Jr.

Eye Openers:

"...more than 3 billion people — live on less than $2.50 a day. More than 1.3 billion live in extreme poverty — less than $1.25 a day. 2.1 billion children worldwide are living in poverty. According to UNICEF, 22,000 children die each day due to poverty."

DoSomething.org

"More than 880 million people are estimated to be living in slums today, compared to 792 million in 2000 and 689 million in 1990."

United Nations Millennium Development Goals and Beyond 2015

"Median per-capita incomes in the top 10 wealthiest populations are more than 50 times those in the 10 poorest populations, all of which are in sub-Saharan Africa."

Gallup World Poll 2013

"...growth tends to be faster in countries with a more even income distribution. Inequality slows growth – because it can generate political instability, and because much of the nation's talent goes to waste. How many potential Bill Gateses are trapped among India's 300 million illiterates?"

John McMillan

"...the top 0.7 percent of the global population holds 44 percent of global wealth, whereas the bottom 69.8 percent holds 2.9 percent of global wealth."

Global Wealth Report 2014
Credit Suisse Research Institute

"In developed and developing countries alike, the poorest half of the population often controls less than 10% of its wealth."

Outlook on the Global Agenda 2015
World Economic Forum

"Income disparities have become so pronounced that America's top 10 percent now average nearly nine times as much income as the bottom 90 percent. Americans in the top 1 percent tower stunningly higher, averaging over 38 times more income than the bottom 90 percent. ...the nation's top 0.1 percent... are taking in over 184 times the income of the bottom 90 percent."

Inequality Data and Statistics, 2014
Inequality.org

The simple, easy, concrete step(s) I will take to help end Poverty, No Access to Opportunity is…

Resources:

- Aid to Artisans: www.aidtoartisans.org
- Center for International Development at Harvard University: www.hks.harvard.edu/centers/cid
- Development Gateway: www.developmentgateway.org
- Foundation for International Community Assistance (FINCA): www.finca.org
- Global Giving: www.globalgiving.org
- Grameen Bank: www.grameen-info.org
- Kiva: www.kiva.org
- NOVICA: www.novica.com
- Practical Action: http://practicalaction.org
- ReliefWeb: www.reliefweb.int
- Trickle Up: www.trickleup.org
- The World Bank: www.worldbank.org
- United Nations Development Programme: tinyurl.com/UNDevelopment

➤ LACK OF CLEAN WATER AND SANITATION

The Heaven on Earth Result:

We have a sustainable supply of clean, drinkable water, and world-class sanitation facilities.

The WAV Packet – Make WAVes for Action!

Water Action Volunteers (WAV) is a statewide program for Wisconsin citizens who want to learn about and improve the quality of Wisconsin's streams and rivers.

Citizens, civic groups, 4-H clubs, students and other volunteer groups participate.

The WAV resource program includes eight action-oriented activities. These projects promote good environmental stewardship through a solid educational framework. Volunteers learn about water quality issues, and then choose activities that promote a positive learning experience while benefiting a community's water resources.

The WAV packet is free (tinyurl.com/WAVPacket), and no training is necessary to use the materials. Each activity is very affordable and provides background information, extra fact sheets, and step-by-step directions.

Units included in the packet:

- Stream Walk Survey: Gather information about a waterway.

- Watershed in a Box: Build a simple watershed model to show runoff pollution.

- Stream or River Cleanup: Organize a waterway clean up.

- Erosion in a Bottle: Create a model that demonstrates the principles of soil erosion.

- Urban Runoff Model: Build a model that demonstrates the dynamics of storm water runoff.

- Critter Search: Learn how to collect aquatic insects and animals from a stream to assess water quality.

- Storm Drain Stenciling: Stencil the message, "Dump No Waste – Drains to Stream (or River or Lake)" next to storm drains.

- Human Watershed: Compare the similarities between the human circulatory system and streams and rivers.

"No innovation in the past 200 years has done more to save lives and improve health than the sanitation revolution triggered by invention of the toilet. But it did not go far enough. It only reached one-third of the world."
Sylvia Mathews Burwell

"We envision the day when everyone in the world can take a safe drink of water."
Water Partners International

Eye Openers:

"More than a quarter of the world's population – 2.4 billion people – live without adequate sanitation, and 664 million lack access to safe drinking water."

USAID

"Diarrheal deaths among children under five… [were] 622,000 in 2012. Inadequate water, sanitation and hygiene accounts for 361,000 of those deaths, or over 1,000 child deaths per day."

Preventing diarrhoea through better water, sanitation and hygiene, 2014
World Health Organization

"748 million people lack access to improved drinking water and it is estimated that 1.8 billion people use a source of drinking water that is fecally contaminated."

UN-Water Global Analysis and Assessment of Sanitation and Drinking-Water (GLAAS) 2014 Report
World Health Organization & UN-Water

"Worldwide, 1 in 3 people, or 2.4 billion, are still without sanitation facilities – including 946 million people who defecate in the open."

Progress on Sanitation and Drinking Water, 2015
World Health Organization

"Nearly three quarters (or around 1.8 billion) of the 2.5 billion people around the world who still have no access to improved sanitation live in rural areas."

The State of the World's Children 2015
UNICEF

"Neglected tropical diseases (NTDs) are a diverse group of communicable diseases that prevail in tropical and subtropical conditions in 149 countries and affect more than one billion people, costing developing economies billions of dollars every year. They mainly affect populations living in poverty, without adequate sanitation and in close contact with infectious vectors and domestic animals and livestock."

World Health Organization, 2015

The simple, easy, concrete step(s) I will take to help end Lack of Clean Water and Sanitation is...

Resources:

- Global Water Partnership: www.gwpforum.org
- United Nations Convention to Combat Desertification: www.unccd.int
- UNICEF Water, Sanitation and Hygiene: www.unicef.org/wash
- Water.org: www.water.org
- The Water Supply and Sanitation Collaborative Council: www.wsscc.org
- World Water Council: www.worldwatercouncil.org

➤ **ENVIRONMENTAL POLLUTION AND DEGRADATION**

The Heaven on Earth Result:

We have a healthy and sustainable environment.

Moms Clean Air Force is a community of over 1,000,000 moms and dads united against air pollution—including the urgent crisis of our changing climate — to protect our children's health. We arm members with reliable information and solutions through online resources, articles, action tools, and on-the-ground events. We work across the US on national and local policy issues, through a vibrant network of state-based field teams. Our moms meet with lawmakers at every level of government to build support for commonsense solutions to pollution.

We believe that protecting children's health is a non-partisan issue. In fact, we think of ourselves as "Mompartisan." We meet with members of Congress on both sides of the aisle to let them know that votes for clean air and a stable climate are urgently important to us. Moms have passion and power — an unbeatable combination. We are harnessing the strength of mother love to fight back against polluters.

Moms will do everything we can to keep our children safe and sound. That's why we are uniting to ensure that our children have clean air right now, and for their future.

At Moms Clean Air Force, we make it easy and fast for busy parents to make their voices heard — while baby naps.

Because sometimes, being a good mom means being an active citizen.

momscleanairforce.org

"Every time I have some moment on a seashore, or in the mountains, or sometimes in a quiet forest, I think this is why the environment has to be preserved."
Bill Bradley

"Sustainable development is the pathway to the future we want for all. It offers a framework to generate economic growth, achieve social justice, exercise environmental stewardship and strengthen governance."
Ban Ki-moon

"A civilization flourishes when people plant trees under which they will never sit."
Greek Proverb

Eye Openers:

"…as long as we're emitting CO2, it continues to build up in the atmosphere…. …Rising concentrations mean rising temperatures. The WMO has confirmed that 2011-2015 was the hottest five-year period on record and it expects 2016 to be the hotter…. This will mean 16 of the 17 warmest years on record will have been since 2000.

"Averaged over the last decade, emissions from fossil fuels and industry account for 91% of human-caused CO2 emissions, with 9% coming from land use change.

"Of the 9.9bn tonnes of carbon in the form of CO2 emitted from fossil fuels in 2015, 41% came from coal, 34% from oil, 19% from gas, 5.6% from cement production and 0.7% from flaring."

Roz Pidcock
Analysis: What global emissions in 2016 mean for climate change goals, CarbonBrief *2016*

"Some 129 million hectares of forest — an area almost equivalent in size to South Africa — have been lost since 1990."

The Global Forest Resources Assessment 2015
U.N. Food and Agriculture Organization

"The United States alone has lost about half of the 220 million acres of wetlands that once swathed the lower 48 states."

International Business Times, 2016

"Some 4.3 million premature deaths were attributable to household air pollution in 2012 [in developing countries]. Ambient (outdoor air pollution) in both cities and rural areas was estimated to cause 3.7 million premature deaths worldwide in 2012."

World Health Organization, 2016

"Marine litter is the largest downstream cost of plastic pollution[;] plastic waste causes damage of at least $13 billion to marine ecosystems each year and this figure is likely a significant underestimate."

Valuing Plastic
Plastic Disclosure Project (PDP) and Trucost
UN Environment Programme 2014

The simple, easy, concrete step(s) I will take to help end Environmental Pollution and Degradation is…

Resources:

- Earth Charter Initiative: www.earthcharter.org
- Zero Emissions Research & Initiatives: www.zeri.org
- Earth Day Network: www.earthday.org
- Greenpeace: www.greenpeace.org
- Natural Resources Defense Council: www.nrdc.org
- The Natural Step: www.naturalstep.com
- Pachamama Alliance: www.pachamama.org
- Sierra Club: www.sierraclub.org
- United Nations Environment Programme, World Conservation Monitoring Center: www.unep-wcmc.org
- World Resources Institute: www.wri.org
- Worldwatch Institute: www.worldwatch.org

→ LACK OF FREEDOM: TYRANNY, REPRESSION

The Heaven on Earth Result:

We are free and have self-determination.

Peter Benenson, the founder of Amnesty International and a barrister in London, was reading his newspaper in 1960. He read about two Portuguese students being sentenced to seven years' imprisonment for raising their glasses in a toast to freedom. He was outraged, went to a church, and sat for three-quarters of an hour and thought.

"I went in to see what could really be done effectively, to mobilize world opinion. It was necessary to think of a larger group which would harness the enthusiasm of people all over the world who were anxious to see a wider respect for human rights."

Within months, he launched his Appeal for Amnesty with a front page article in *The Observer* newspaper. Benenson's idea was simple: a network of letter writers would inundate governments with individual appeals on behalf of prisoners jailed and ill-treated in violation of the Universal Declaration of Human Rights.

The response was overwhelming. Newspapers in over a dozen countries picked up the appeal. Over a thousand letters poured in within the first six months.

Benenson left behind him a world changed. Nearly a hundred human rights treaties and other legal instruments are now in force internationally. Over ninety percent of the world's countries are now party to the most comprehensive of these, the twin international covenants on civil/political and economic/social rights. Almost all of those states have now formally given the right to their citizens to make international complaints.

The rights of women, children, minorities, workers, disabled persons — all of these have been codified and strengthened by successive declarations, conventions and acts of national legislation. Torturers have become international outlaws. As we enter the 21st Century, more than half the countries of the world have rejected the death penalty, either by abolishing it altogether or ceasing to carry out executions.

Peter Benenson left his indelible mark. Today there are well over a thousand domestic and regional organizations working to protect human rights. Among them, his brainchild Amnesty International, has almost 2 million members, subscribers, and supporters in more than 64 countries and territories.

Adapted from *Peter Benenson Remembered* by Richard Reoch

tinyurl.com/HonENoTyranny

"Voting is a civic sacrament."
Theodore M. Hesburgh

Eye Openers:

"Asia and the Pacific still has the largest numbers [of child labour] (almost 78 million or 9.3% of child population), but Sub-Saharan Africa continues to be the region with the highest incidence of child labour (59 million, over 21%)."

Marking Progress Against Child Labour, Global Estimates and Trends 2000-2012
International Labour Organization

"Violence against women is rampant in all corners of the world...including: violence against women in custody; acid burning and dowry deaths; 'honor' killings; domestic violence; female genital mutilation; human rights violations based on actual or perceived sexual identity; gender based asylum; the problem of impunity."

Violence Against Women: A Fact Sheet, 2005
Amnesty International

"Yodok is one of six known political prison camps in North Korea. Men, women and children in the camp face forced hard labour, inadequate food, beatings, totally inadequate medical care, and unhygienic living conditions. ...Around 50,000 people are held in Yodok, and most are imprisoned without trial or following grossly unfair trials on the basis of 'confessions' obtained through torture. There are two zones in Yodok. Prisoners in the 'Revolutionary Zone' are released after serving sentences lasting from a few months to ten years. Prisoners in the 'Total-Control Zone' are never released."

Yodok, North Korean – Write for Rights 2011
Amnesty International

"These crimes – of expressing 'blasphemy' or offending religious feelings – are still a crime in 55 countries, can mean prison in 39 of those countries, and are punishable by death in six countries."

Freedom of Thought 2013
International Humanist and Ethical Union

The 10 Most Censored Countries:
"1. Eritrea; 2. North Korea; 3. Saudi Arabia; 4. Ethiopia; 5. Azerbaijan; 6. Vietnam; 7. Iran; 8. China; 9. Myanmar; 10. Cuba."

Committee to Protect Journalists, 2015

The simple, easy, concrete step(s) I will take to help end Lack of Freedom: Tyranny, Repression is…

Resources:

- Amnesty International: www.amnesty.org/
- Community of Democracies: www.community-democracies.org/
- Human Rights Watch: www.hrw.org/
- International Programme on the Elimination of Child Labour: www.ilo.org/ipec
- The Greenleaf Center for Servant Leadership: www.greenleaf.org

➤ LACK OF MEANING AND PURPOSE

The Heaven on Earth Result:

We experience meaning, community, and the transcendent.

It is April, 1993, I am in a refugee camp in Split, Croatia, in what had been Yugoslavia, looking at a small blond girl with sorrowful blue eyes staring disconsolately at the floor. I ask her, "What is your name?" In a weary voice, she answers, "Nada." Suddenly I am flooded with 50-year-old memories.

It is 1948, a dark-eyed, dark-haired girl with deep circles under her eyes is thrust forward to meet me. "This is Nada," my father says. I ask my father. "What kind of name is Nada?" I know that in Spanish, Nada means "nothing." He answers, "In her language, Nada means hope."

Now, as I look through my tears at the little refugee girl in front of me, I realize that my childhood meeting with the earlier Nada was a first step on my lifelong mission of bringing hope to people caught in war and intolerance. I reach out my hand and give her a smile. I know that hope is the one thing my fledgling organization, Global Children's Organization, and I can offer children who once again are the youngest and saddest victims of genocide in Europe.

I keep thinking, "They have lost their childhoods, they need a respite from war. Why not do a summer camp, and call it 'Island to Island?" As a child, I loved going to camp and still remember the songs I learned and the friends I made.

How much more memorable a camp experience would be for children who have lost everything. On my long flight home, I reflect on the beliefs I so strongly hold

that each of us must repair the shattered fragments of the world and try to make it whole with compassionate action. Then I recall the words of Rabbi Hillel, "If not now? When?" I know I have been called, that I must answer the call and acting as one person, I can make a difference for children in this war.

I share my home, money, heart, soul, spirit, energy, and my love with many children. My parents' example of doing one's part to "mend the world" has taken root in me. My life is filled with purpose, creativity, wonder, hard work, challenge, adventure, joy, and love. The volunteers, of all ages, nationalities, professions and backgrounds, are caring people who experience the personal transformation and fulfillment that comes from truly sharing one's self with another — making a difference in the world, one child at a time.

Judith Jenya

judithjenyaarts.blogspot.mx

"To give life meaning one must have a purpose larger than one's self."
Will Durant

Eye Openers:

"A nationwide survey of youth grades 9-12 in public and private schools in the U.S. found that 16% of students reported seriously considering suicide, 13% reported creating a plan, and 8% reporting trying to take their own life in the 12 months preceding the survey."

Suicide Prevention, 2015
Injury Prevention & Control

"Over 800,000 people die due to suicide every year and it is the second leading cause of death in 15-29-year-olds. There are indications that for each adult who died of suicide there may have been more than 20 others attempting suicide."

Preventing suicide: A global imperative
World Health Organization, 2014

"The use of antidepressants increased nearly 400 percent between 1988 and 2008, mostly among women between the ages of 40 and 59. Today about 10.4 percent of Americans take antidepressants, compared to 6.5 percent in 1999. ...the number of people taking antidepressants long-term – more than 24 months – has doubled, from 3 percent to more than 6 percent."

"Are Antidepressants Overprescribed?"
Berkeley Wellness, 2015

"Global sales of antidepressants, stimulants, antianxiety and antipsychotic drugs have reached more than $76 billion a year."

Psychiatry: Hooking Your World on Drugs
Citizens Commission on Human Rights, 2017

"Worldwide, 3.3 million deaths every year result from harmful use of alcohol. This represents 5.9% of all deaths."

Alcohol Fact Sheet
World Health Organization, 2015

"Estimated annual value of global criminal markets in the 2000s: $88 billion (cocaine) and $65 billion (opiates). Criminal firearms markets = $1 billion, [cocaine and opiates are] 153 times bigger than the criminal firearms trade."

Cocaine, Heroine, Cannabis, Ecstasy:
How Big is the Global Drug Trade? 2014
Global Research News

The simple, easy, concrete step(s) I will take to help end Lack of Meaning and Purpose is…

Resources:

- The Passion Test: http://thepassiontest.com/
- Wisdom Quotes: Meaning: www.wisdomquotes.com/topics/meaning
- Wisdom Quotes: Purpose: www.wisdomquotes.com/topics/purpose
- The Wisdom Page: http://wisdompage.com
- YES! Magazine: www.yesmagazine.org
- Metanexus Institute: www.metanexus.net
- We, The World: www.we.net

More sufferings (abbreviated)

The simple, easy, concrete step(s) I will take to help end this suffering:

_____
_____
_____
_____
_____
_____
_____
_____
_____
_____

> ➤ **Crime, Violence, and Terrorism**

We have safety and security for everyone.

"One person is killed by a firearm every 17 minutes, 87 people are killed during an average day, and 609 are killed every week. …Between 2000 and 2010, a total of 335,609 people died from guns — more than the population of St. Louis, Mo. (318,069)."

"Just the facts: Gun violence in America"
NBC News, 2013

"To make peace with an enemy
one must work with that enemy,
and the enemy must become one's partner."

Nelson Mandela

Resources:
- Alternatives to Violence Project: www.avpusa.org
- The Center for Nonviolent Communication: www.cnvc.org
- Cutting Edge Law: http://cuttingedgelaw.com
- Transforming Violence: www.transformingviolence.org

The simple, easy, concrete step(s) I will take to help end this suffering:

_____
_____
_____
_____
_____
_____
_____
_____
_____
_____

> ➤ **Prejudice, Hatred, and Discrimination**

We express love and compassion. We have equality among all people.

"There are increasing concerns across Europe that what was once considered far-right and racist is moving toward mainstream political thought. Anti-immigration agendas have led to increased worry from immigrant communities across the European Union. In recent weeks, a new study has shown that at the same time, concerns among Jews of a resurgence of anti-Semitism are strong and growing."

McClatchy Newspapers
"Far-right hate crimes creep back into German society"
Dec. 24, 2013

"After all, there is but one race — humanity."

George Moore

Resources:
- Beyond Intractability: www.beyondintractability.org
- Hope in the Cities: http://us.iofc.org/hope-in-cities-iofc
- Understanding Prejudice: www.understandingprejudice.org

➤ Torture, Slavery, Human Rights Abuse, Child Labor, Violence Against Women/Children

We are all treated with dignity and experience full freedom.

"…we estimate that 45.8 million people are in some form of modern slavery in 167 countries."

The Global Slavery Index, 2016
Global Slavery Index

"'Freedom from fear' could be said to sum up
the whole philosophy of human rights."
Dag Hammarskjöld

Resources:

- Amnesty International: www.amnesty.org
- Free the Slaves: www.freetheslaves.net
- The Global Slavery Index: www.globalslaveryindex.org/
- International Rehabilitation Council for Torture Victims: www.irct.org

**The simple, easy, concrete step(s)
I will take to help end this suffering:**

➤ Sexual Abuse

We have esteem and respect for ourselves and others.

"In 2014, 205,438 children reported sexual abuse."
National Statistics on Child Abuse
National Children's Alliance (US)

"…in my wildest, most indulgent dreams,
we only hear about sexual assault & abuse
in history books."
Lisa Factora-Borchers
Dear Sister: Letters From Survivors of Sexual Violence

Resources:

- Legal Resources for Victims of Sexual Abuse: www.smith-lawfirm.com/resources.html
- Mothers Against Sexual Abuse: http://againstsexualabuse.org
- Rape, Abuse & Incest National Network: www.rainn.org
- UNESCO, Gender-based Violence: tinyurl.com/GenderViolence

**The simple, easy, concrete step(s)
I will take to help end this suffering:**

The simple, easy, concrete step(s) I will take to help end this suffering:

_____

_____

_____

_____

_____

_____

_____

_____

_____

_____

➤ **Bad Governance, Corruption, and Poor Management**

We have wise government that we are proud of.

"Corruption destroys lives and communities, and undermines countries and institutions. It generates popular anger that threatens to further destabilize societies and exacerbate violent conflicts. ...It leads to failure in the delivery of basic services like education or healthcare. It derails the building of essential infrastructure...."

Transparency International, 2012

"Go to people, live with them, love them, learn from them. Start with what they know, build with what they have, and work with the best leaders, so when the work is done, people can say, 'We did this ourselves.'"

Lao Tzu

Resources:

- Financial Accounting Standards Board: www.fasb.org
- Group of States Against Corruption: www.coe.int/greco
- Transparency International: www.transparency.org
- The World Bank: http://go.worldbank.org/KUDGZ5E6P0

The simple, easy, concrete step(s) I will take to help end this suffering:

_____

_____

_____

_____

_____

_____

_____

_____

_____

➤ **Overpopulation**

We are a globally sustainable population.

"In 2015, the world has around 7.3 billion inhabitants. We have added one billion people since 2003 and two billion since 1990. By 2030, we expect that the world will have around 8.5 billion people, and around 9.7 billion by 2050. ...our medium-variant projection foresees a world population of around 11.2 billion people in 2100."

World Population Prospects: The 2015 Revision
Department of Economic and Social Affairs
United Nations

"Live simply so that others can simply live."

Mahatma Ghandi

Resources:

- Facing the Future: www.facingthefuture.org
- World Overpopulation Awareness: www.overpopulation.org

Project Heaven on Earth

➤ Animal Abuse and Species Extinction

We honor and preserve all species.

The simple, easy, concrete step(s) I will take to help end this suffering:

- The global Living Planet Index (LPI) shows an overall decline [in biodiversity] of 52% between 1970 and 2010.

- Falling by 76%, populations of freshwater species declined more rapidly than marine (39%) and terrestrial (39%) populations.

Living Planet Report 2014
World Wildlife Fund

"Kindness and compassion towards all living things is a mark of a civilized society."

César Chávez

Resources:

- Bagheera: www.bagheera.com
- The Current Mass Extinction: www.mysterium.com/extinction.html
- Illegal Wildlife Trade: www.wildaid.org
- International Union for Conservation of Nature: www.iucn.org/what/biodiversity

➤ Spiritual Malnourishment

We are consciously connected to our spiritual Source.

The simple, easy, concrete step(s) I will take to help end this suffering:

"In our increasingly materialistic world, we are driven by a seemingly insatiable desire for power and possessions. Yet in this vain striving, we wander ever further from inner peace and mental happiness. Despite our pleasant material surroundings, many people today experience dissatisfaction, fear, anxiety, and a sense of insecurity. There seems to be something lacking within our hearts. What we seem to be missing is a proper sense of human spirituality."

The Dalai Lama

"People are like stained glass windows.
They sparkle and shine when the sun is out,
but when the darkness sets in, their true beauty
is revealed only if there is a light from within."

Elisabeth Kübler-Ross

Resources:

- Matthew Fox and Creation Spirituality: http://matthewfox.org
- Institute of Noetic Sciences: www.noetic.org
- Miriam's Well: www.miriamswell.org
- Museum of World Religions: www.mwr.org.tw/index_en.aspx

▷ Your Outer World
▶ Ending the World's Major Sufferings
- ➤ Hunger and Malnutrition
- ➤ Disease
- ➤ Lack of Adequate Shelter
- ➤ War, Genocide, Refugees, & Weapons Proliferation
- ➤ Illiteracy
- ➤ Poverty, No Access to Opportunity
- ➤ Lack of Clean Water and Sanitation
- ➤ Environmental Pollution and Degradation
- ➤ Lack of Freedom: Tyranny, Repression
- ➤ Lack of Meaning and Purpose
- ➤ Crime, Violence, and Terrorism
- ➤ Prejudice, Hatred, and Discrimination
- ➤ Torture, Slavery, Human Rights Abuse, Child Labor, Violence Against Women/Children
- ➤ Sexual Abuse
- ➤ Bad Governance, Corruption, and Poor Management
- ➤ Overpopulation
- ➤ Animal Abuse and Species Extinction
- ➤ Spiritual Malnourishment

As you explored the sufferings, did any one in particular jump out at you? Many people have one suffering that affects them more than others. They feel more pain, heartache, and sadness about it. This is the primary suffering for them, the one they most want to eliminate.

I call it the "Keystone Suffering." A keystone is the wedge-shaped stone at the apex of a stone arch. It is the final piece placed during construction and locks all the other stones into place. If the keystone is removed, the arch collapses. In the same way, people feel that once their Keystone Suffering is removed, all the other sufferings will collapse.

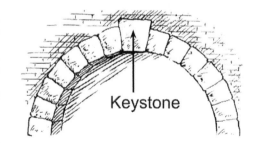

I invite you to find your Keystone Suffering and begin the process of ending it.

Feeling Overwhelmed:

You may be feeling overwhelmed at the thought of ending a particular suffering. You deeply want your Keystone Suffering to cease to exist, to simply end, but the thought of doing that overwhelms you. It's just too big. And so…you stop…you wait for the overwhelm to no longer be there before taking any action.

But, if we truly want the world to work, we can't let this state of mind incapacitate us and stop us from getting into action.

If the majority of the seven billion people in the world feel overwhelmed at the thought of their actually ending a suffering, then the context we have is called, "I want to end it, but I'm overwhelmed." This results in the suffering continuing while we indulge ourselves in feeling overwhelmed.

All you get out of feeling overwhelmed is the empty victory of being right…meanwhile, the suffering continues.

Here's what you can do with overwhelm: just let it be there…you don't have to do a thing about it…and begin — take one simple, easy, concrete action and start your journey of ending the suffering. Taking tiny steps causes big differences over time. Before you know it, you'll find you're moving forward, you're accomplishing.

You can either feel overwhelmed and stop, or feel overwhelmed and get on with helping create Heaven on Earth. It's really that simple.

My invitation to you: Jump in! Begin.

**When we as Humanity
eliminate these unnecessary sufferings**

— and we will —

**we will have turned a seemingly impossible dream
into an accomplished reality.**

"Heaven on Earth is...

*organizations that empower everyone
to continue to use all their gifts, talents, and wisdom
from the very first moment they join the organization."*

Susan E. Greene
Catalyst, Author, Consultant
USA

"...we judge institutions productive, efficient and rational
not only to the extent that they maximize wealth and power
but also to the extent that they maximize our capacities
to be caring, ecologically aware, ethically and spiritually sensitive,
and capable of responding to the universe with awe, wonder and
radical amazement at the grandeur of creation."

Rabbi Michael Lerner

Chapter 13

▷ Your Outer World

▶ Our Institutions Taking Their Rightful Place in Co-Creating Heaven on Earth

- ➤ Education
- ➤ Culture: Arts, Media, Sports
- ➤ Health Care & Medicine
- ➤ Commerce: Business, Industry, Labor
- ➤ Resources: Agriculture, Fisheries, Forestry, Mining
- ➤ Law
- ➤ Government
- ➤ Religion
- ➤ Science & Technology
- ➤ Civic Organizations
- ➤ International Intergovernmental Organizations
- ➤ The Military

Institutions exist to serve all of us. They are a collective intention whose expression impacts our world. They participate in and share a leadership role in the creation of something larger and better. They organize, focus effort, and coordinate and mobilize resources to carry out and accomplish results.

In this chapter I want to focus on the collective power for good expressed through our institutions. When institutions are doing great and noble work, their collective highest values and ideals are effectively expressed. When the people of an institution are aligned and focused in this way, their positive impact is enormous.

However, when these values and ideals are not expressed, the results are ineffective and inefficient — at worst, they are debilitating and disastrous. People become enmeshed in and victim to politics, bureaucracy, procrastination, sluggishness, and pettiness. At a deeper level, they can feel they're losing part of their Soul.

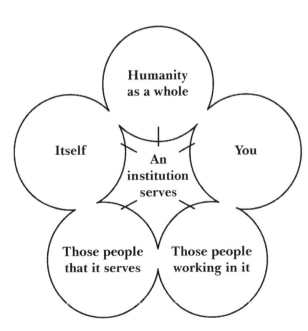

When institutional unworkability becomes endemic in society, we automatically blame the institution. We make them the target of our anger and the butt of our jokes. We complain that they are not living up to our expectations, aren't doing their job: government is wasteful, slow, and too bureaucratic; education is turning out graduates who can't read; law enforcement is powerless against drugs and crime; the media focuses on the lowest common denominators of violence and sensationalism; religion is no longer relevant. We become stuck in resignation, thinking that nothing can be done, that we're powerless to change them, that that's just the way institutions are.

In the context of Heaven on Earth, this kind of giving up is no longer effective or useful. In the context of Heaven on Earth, people working in institutions express more of their Soul. In the context of Heaven on Earth, institutions enliven and ennoble — those who work in them, those they serve, and the world at large. Institutions become efficient, inspiring, and consistently of high service. They take their rightful place in helping co-create Heaven on Earth.

Imagine what it would be like to be immersed in an institution operating in this way? Imagine being inside the great and ennobling experience of a lawyer who is at trial for a case of great moral importance; a scientist seeing pictures from a distant galaxy for the first time; a politician who has just passed a bill that will aid deserving people; a peacekeeping force establishing and maintaining peace between two groups of enemy combatants; a rabbi, priest, or imam who has just discovered some new and wondrous insight from their religion.

I remember being a young 20 year old working for the Canadian federal government. One day a mid-level manager, Lavada Pinder, took me aside and said, "Martin, you now work for the 'Public Service' and both words count." She said this with deep sincerity and great conviction. She felt it was her job to pass on the purpose of this institution to me and ensure that I continued to live and foster it.

We've got to break the hypnotic trance of thinking there's nothing one individual can do to have our institutions be great agents of Heaven on Earth. We can no longer afford being overwhelmed, thinking one individual can't make a difference. We can no longer indulge in our misbelief that one individual can't change an institution. And we can no longer let our institutions operate at their current levels — there is so much more potential just waiting to be unleashed.

It's no longer acceptable to say, "I don't like gays, I don't like Jews, I don't like women." These remarks are homophobic, anti-Semitic, and sexist. Yet we're allowed to say the same kinds of derogatory things about our institutions: government is corrupt and inefficient, business is only about the bottom line, academia is divorced from the real world. These declarations only serve to blame, make wrong, insult, and diminish. What they don't do is empower.

The potential for consistent greatness already resides in our institutions. We know it during those rare instances when we experience the highest caliber of that greatness, and we know it by the frustration and anger we feel when our institutions don't live up to their potential. Our job now is to begin the inquiry into what it will actually take to have the institutions of our society live their full potential.

Let's shift from blaming our institutions to supporting them in discovering the ways and means of expressing their greatness. Let's unleash the full potential of our institutions so that we experience Heaven on Earth when we work in them and when they serve us. Let's be willing to be responsible for our institutions really working. Let's have them be shining examples of collective purpose, service, and results.

What can you do to produce the experience that our institutions *are* working for us, that we are proud of them, that we are inspired by them? What would it take for you to be proud of your government? Would you be willing to take on your own religion and make it work? What about the media, science, law, or any of the other institutions of society — would you be willing to be responsible for helping one of them take their rightful place in co-creating Heaven on Earth?

Imagine having a magic wand and with it having an institution actually begin the process of heavening itself and those it serves. What's the institution? What's Heaven on Earth for this institution? What simple, easy, concrete steps can you take to begin moving in this direction?

"…we need to transform our institutions
into entities capable of sustaining our common life,
to provide a structure for individual liberty and interdependence."

Robert H. Bellah, Professor of Sociology
University of California, Berkeley
and Chris Adams, Director, Center for Ethics and Social Policy
The Graduate Theological Union, Berkeley

"Heaven on Earth is…

an issue of public policy."

Claudio Ruben
Human Being
USA

"Heaven on Earth is...

using our collective goodwill to build it,
make it real, and sustain it."

Chris Caton
Retired Insurance Executive &
Workplace Chaplain
Canada

"...great institutions...must begin to put as a purpose
central to their policies and actions,
the creation of a world of democracy, peace, and prosperity."

Nelson Mandela

To make it easy for you to understand an institution's potential for co-creating Heaven on Earth, and to help jump-start you in this Gateway, I've designed this chapter with another simple template. Each of the twelve institutions we'll be looking at has two pages devoted to it. The left-hand page (see example below) begins with the name of the institution ❶ and what its Heaven on Earth purpose is ❷. (If you disagree with the purpose for the institution, please write in your own.) Below these two elements is a Heaven on Earth quote for the institution ❸, and to the right of that, still on the left page, are a series of inspiring quotes designed to give you a deeper appreciation of what Heaven on Earth could be for this institution ❹.

At the top of the right-hand page is a request ❺ to have you look at what simple, easy, concrete steps you'll take to have that institution take its rightful place in co-creating Heaven on Earth. Please fill in your answers in the space provided.

Finally, on the bottom right of the right-hand page are a series of quotes designed to encourage and support you in taking action ❻.

Note: Each of the twelve institutions covered in this chapter are self-evident except for Civic Organizations and International Intergovernmental Organizations.

"Civic Organizations" refers to voluntary, non-governmental associations such as service clubs, youth groups, cultural associations, philanthropic organizations, and advocacy groups that foster responsible citizenship.

"International Intergovernmental Organizations" refers to globe-spanning organizations such as the United Nations, the International Monetary Fund, and the World Bank. These organizations deal with issues affecting all nations, all of Humanity.

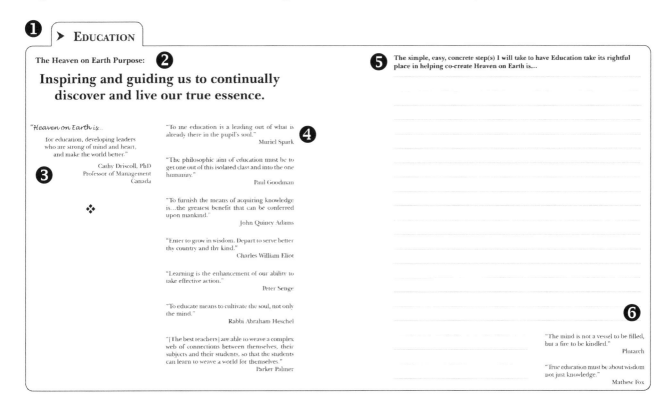

❶ ➤ EDUCATION

The Heaven on Earth Purpose: ❷

Inspiring and guiding us to continually discover and live our true essence.

"Heaven on Earth is…
for education, developing leaders who are strong of mind and heart, and make the world better."

Cathy Driscoll, PhD
Professor of Management
Canada

❸

❖

"To me education is a leading out of what is already there in the pupil's soul." ❹
Muriel Spark

"The philosophic aim of education must be to get one out of this isolated class and into the one humanity."
Paul Goodman

"To furnish the means of acquiring knowledge is…the greatest benefit that can be conferred upon mankind."
John Quincy Adams

"Enter to grow in wisdom. Depart to serve better thy country and thy kind."
Charles William Eliot

"Learning is the enhancement of our ability to take effective action."
Peter Senge

"To educate means to cultivate the soul, not only the mind."
Rabbi Abraham Heschel

"[The best teachers] are able to weave a complex web of connections between themselves, their subjects and their students, so that the students can learn to weave a world for themselves."
Parker Palmer

❺ The simple, easy, concrete step(s) I will take to have Education take its rightful place in helping co-create Heaven on Earth is…

❻

"The mind is not a vessel to be filled, but a fire to be kindled."
Plutarch

"True education must be about wisdom not just knowledge."
Mathew Fox

The Heaven on Earth Purpose:

Inspiring and guiding us to continually discover and live our true essence.

"Heaven on Earth is...

for education, developing leaders who are strong of mind and heart, and make the world better."

Cathy Driscoll, PhD
Professor of Management
Canada

"To me education is a leading out of what is already there in the pupil's soul."

Muriel Spark

"The philosophic aim of education must be to get one out of this isolated class and into the one humanity."

Paul Goodman

"To furnish the means of acquiring knowledge is...the greatest benefit that can be conferred upon mankind."

John Quincy Adams

"Enter to grow in wisdom. Depart to serve better thy country and thy kind."

Charles William Eliot

"Learning is the enhancement of our ability to take effective action."

Peter Senge

"To educate means to cultivate the soul, not only the mind."

Rabbi Abraham Heschel

"[The best teachers] are able to weave a complex web of connections between themselves, their subjects and their students, so that the students can learn to weave a world for themselves."

Parker Palmer

The simple, easy, concrete step(s) I will take to have Education take its rightful place in helping co-create Heaven on Earth is…

"The mind is not a vessel to be filled, but a fire to be kindled."

Plutarch

"True education must be about wisdom not just knowledge."

Mathew Fox

➤ CULTURE

(ARTS, MEDIA, SPORTS)

The Heaven on Earth Purpose:

Expanding possibility, exemplifying what works, confronting what doesn't work, and contributing to the flourishing of joy.

"Heaven on Earth is...

a continually evolving global culture that is developing in healthier and healthier ways."

Carter Phipps
Author, *The Evolutionaries*
USA

"My role is to bring as much joy to the world as I can."

Dizzy Gillespie

"New artists must break a hole in the subconscious and go fishing there."

Robert Beverly Hale

"...architecture cannot always be reduced to matters of image and style. It is the art of extracting marvels out of the void."

Herbert Muschamp

"The purpose of my painting is to illuminate and illustrate the life current and the glory of the human spirit. It is my passion to serve humanity by creating art that functions as a transformational tool: to bring joy and celebration to our hearts and to awaken us to our spiritedness, our unlimited potential."

Linda Naiman

"A transformed media sends out the good news of innovations and inspiring stories about our victories over hunger, disease, homelessness, and illiteracy. This mobilizes others into action and ignites a chain reaction of service and support."

Carolyn Anderson

The simple, easy, concrete step(s) I will take to have Culture (Arts, Media, Sports) take its rightful place in helping co-create Heaven on Earth is...

"Beauty of whatever kind, in its supreme development, invariably excites the sensitive soul to tears."
Edgar Allan Poe

"We need images of social wellness to attract us forward. We need a mass media to communicate our evolutionary potentials."
Barbara Marx Hubbard

➤ HEALTH CARE & MEDICINE

The Heaven on Earth Purpose:

Experiencing being Whole.

"Heaven on Earth is...

for health care and medicine,
where these values are shared by all:
Excellence fostering the best possible
combination of art and science;
Integrity engendering trust and
encouraging authenticity;
Respect for individuals and their differences;
Caring which is empathetic and
compassionate and emphasizes
personal responsibility;
Community honoring diversity
and inclusiveness;
Open-mindedness promoting a spirit
of inquiry and creativity; and
Collegiality promoting personal
and professional growth."

Valerie Ulstad, MD
Clinical Associate Professor of Medicine &
Cardiologist
USA
&
Kathleen Ogle, MD
Oncologist
USA

"Health is my expected heaven."
John Keats

"The first wealth is health."
Ralph Waldo Emerson

"The human body is the best picture of the human soul."
Ludwig Wittgenstein

"A sad soul can kill you quicker than a germ."
John Steinbeck

"Love cures people — both the ones who give it and the ones who receive it."
Dr. Karl Menninger

"Health is the first of all liberties...."
Henri Amiel

"When health is absent, wisdom cannot reveal itself, art cannot manifest, strength cannot fight, wealth becomes useless, and intelligence cannot be applied."
Herophilus

"...health care is not an industry but a sacred ministry."
Carl Hammershlag, MD

The simple, easy, concrete step(s) I will take to have Health Care & Medicine take its rightful place in helping co-create Heaven on Earth is...

"The Global Eradication of Polio."
The World Health Assembly
(Governing body of the
World Health Organization)

"We believe good health is a basic human right."
The Carter Center

COMMERCE

(BUSINESS, INDUSTRY, LABOR)

The Heaven on Earth Purpose:

Experiencing creation as service.

"Heaven on Earth is...

companies leading with their humanity,
while generating profits."

Elsie Maio
Management consultant
in brand strategy
USA

"Work puts the autograph of my soul on the development of the world."

Sister Joan Chittister, O.S.B.

"Let us choose to unite the power of markets with the authority of universal ideals. Let us choose to reconcile the creative forces of private entrepreneurship with the needs of the disadvantaged and the requirements of future generations."

Kofi Annan
Former United Nations Secretary-General

"Your work is to discover your work, and then with all your heart to give yourself to it."

Buddha

"Blessed is he who has found his work.
Let him ask no other blessedness.
He has a work, a life purpose.
He has found it and will follow it."

Thomas Carlyle

"If we are serious about our work, we tend to find ourselves apprenticed to something much larger than we expected, something that calls on more of our essence than we previously imagined."

David Whyte

"Great work is done by people who are not afraid to be great."

Fernando Flores

The simple, easy, concrete step(s) I will take to have Commerce (Business, Industry, Labor) take its rightful place in helping co-create Heaven on Earth is...

"All labor that uplifts humanity has dignity and importance and should be undertaken with painstaking excellence."

Martin Luther King, Jr.

"Business has become...the most powerful institution on the planet. The dominant institution in any society needs to take responsibility for the whole.... So business has to adopt a tradition it has never had throughout the entire story of capitalism: to share responsibility for the whole. Every decision that is made, every action that is taken, must be viewed in the light of that kind of responsibility."

Willis Harman
Co-founder of
The World Business Academy

➤ RESOURCES

(AGRICULTURE, FISHERIES, FORESTRY, MINING)

The Heaven on Earth Purpose:

Cultivating and nurturing our sustainable future.

"Heaven on Earth is...

the agricultural sector feeling respected
and being compensated fairly
and having the world fed."

Michael Sandeson
Farmer
Canada

"How we eat determines to a considerable extent how the world is used."

Wendell Berry

"Let's make places where there are fishing communities, fishing boats and fresh, locally-caught fish in markets and restaurants, where the waters support diverse native populations of marine life, where fishing men and women work together with those exploring the ocean's mysteries, a place where our children and their children's children can find happiness, solace and a connection with nature."

Pietro Parravano
President, Institute for Fisheries Resources

"Responsible forest management means forests are managed in a way that protects water, soil and wildlife. It means communities, Indigenous Peoples, forest workers, industry, forest owners — anyone who is affected by what happens to forests — agree how the forest will be managed. And it means people can continue to work, live and earn an income from the forest."

The Forest Stewardship Council

"If the minerals sector is to contribute positively to sustainable development, it needs to demonstrate continuous improvement of its social, economic, and environmental contribution, with new and evolving governance systems."

Breaking New Ground
The Report of the Mining, Minerals and
Sustainable Development Project

The simple, easy, concrete step(s) I will take to have Resources (Agriculture, Fisheries, Forestry, Mining) take its rightful place in helping co-create Heaven on Earth is...

"The earth is mother of all."
Ugandan Proverb

"Sustainability is not just about wise use of resources; it is about the cultural, political, and spiritual footprint we leave on the planet."
David Bolling

➤ LAW

The Heaven on Earth Purpose:

Experiencing equity and healing.

"Heaven on Earth is...

when formalized laws and legal institutions are no longer necessary because we have all internalized spiritual laws and principles and no longer need outside authorities to prescribe the ways in which we interact with others.

"Until that time, as long as we continue to have a need for formal legal institutions, heaven on earth in law occurs when:

- people who participate in the legal system are treated with dignity and respect;
- interactions within the legal system lead to transformation and healing resulting in people feeling more whole and integrated rather than fragmented and alienated; and
- the legal system elicits the best in people and fosters unity and connection rather than widening the separation between the parties."

> Donna Boris
> Attorney
> USA

"The entire legal profession — lawyers, judges, law teachers — have become so mesmerized with the stimulation of the courtroom contest that we tend to forget that we ought to be healers... healers of conflicts. ...Should lawyers not be healers? Healers, not warriors? Healers, not procurers? Healers, not hired guns?"

> Warren Burger
> Former Chief Justice, U.S. Supreme Court,
> in his State of the Judiciary Address
> to the American Bar Association

"Justice is truth in action."

> Joseph Joubert

"It was the boast of Augustus that he found Rome of brick and left it of marble. But how much nobler will be the sovereign's boast when he shall have it to say that he found law...a sealed book and left it a living letter; found it the patrimony of the rich and left it the inheritance of the poor; found it the two-edged sword of craft and oppression and left it the staff of honesty and the shield of innocence."

> Henry Brougham

"In civilized life, law floats in a sea of ethics."
> Earl Warren
> Former Chief Justice, U.S. Supreme Court

"The law is the witness and external deposit of our moral life. Its history is the history of the moral development of the race."

> Oliver Wendell Holmes

The simple, easy, concrete step(s) I will take to have Law take its rightful place in helping co-create Heaven on Earth is...

"Law should express 'our values and aspirations for our society.'"
Former Senator Joseph Lieberman

"Seven hours to law, to soothing slumber seven, Ten to the world allot, and all to Heaven."
Sir William Jones

➤ GOVERNMENT

The Heaven on Earth Purpose:

Having the profound intention of the People realized.

"Heaven on Earth is...

Enabled Democracy."

Richard Porter
Consultant
Canada/Ecuador

"...[the] six dimensions of governance:
• Voice and Accountability
• Political Stability and Absence of Violence
• Government Effectiveness
• Regulatory Quality
• Rule of Law
• Control of Corruption

World Bank Institute

"We find that a country improving its quality of governance from a low level to an average level can in the long term quadruple the income per capita of its population, and similarly reduce infant mortality and illiteracy."

Daniel Kaufmann
World Bank Institute

"The day will come when the progress of nations will be judged not by their military or economic strength, nor by the splendour of their capital cities and public buildings, but by the well-being of their peoples: by their levels of health, nutrition and education; by their opportunities to earn a fair reward for their labours; by their ability to participate in the decisions that affect their lives; by the respect that is shown for their civil and political liberties; by the provision that is made for those who are vulnerable and disadvantaged; and by the protection that is afforded to the growing minds and bodies of their children."

UNICEF
Preamble to the annual
Progress of Nations report

The simple, easy, concrete step(s) I will take to have Government take its rightful place in helping co-create Heaven on Earth is…

"Let's build a new relationship between the authorities and society: a government that fulfills its responsibility, and a society that evaluates and participates."

Vicente Fox
Former President of Mexico

"The test of political institutions is the condition of the country whose future they regulate."

Benjamin Disraeli

The Heaven on Earth Purpose:

Providing the ongoing experience of being One with The Source.

"Heaven on Earth is...

thousands of religious and spiritual leaders
publicly affirming that the commonalities
that unite them are more profound
and more important than the differences
that divide them.
What is more,
they are working together productively
to use their conjoint moral authority
to take on public issues."

Robert K. C. Forman, Ph.D.
Executive Director, The Forge Institute;
Founding Executive Editor,
Journal of Consciousness Studies;
Associate Professor of Religion, CUNY
USA

"The true purpose of religion, from a Jewish perspective, is not to focus on the world the way it is, but rather on the way it ought to be, and to inspire humanity to realize that vision."

Rabbi Shmuley Boteach

"The enemy of a religion cannot be another religion. The enemies of religions are poverty, injustice, illiteracy, exploitation, discrimination and all that subverts the spiritual goal of fullness of life for all people. ...The good news is that in religion, when it is understood and practiced according to the scriptural ideals, we have a mighty weapon to defeat the forces of oppression and exploitation and to usher in a new heaven and a new earth."

Swami Agnivesh

"The purpose of religion is for you to find the one that best serves your path to God."

Maida Rogerson

"Nextgen worship is the voice of a movement whose purpose is to empower generations to carry heaven and shift culture. As sons of God, we bear the responsibility to import heavens heart and mind culture into the earth in such a way that it causes societal transformation. We believe that the ecosystem we are creating as sons and daughters of God is going to build in momentum resulting in a stronghold of heaven on earth that cannot be undone."

Nextgen Worship

The simple, easy, concrete step(s) I will take to have Religion take its rightful place in helping co-create Heaven on Earth is...

"...the ideals that could rally theists and non-theists alike, ideals that could unite our modernity with a new power and purpose, lie in the ancient major religions of the world. The retrieval and re-articulation of these ideals would seem to be the most important challenge for religious thinkers today."
Daniel Maguire

"...work together with other religions to resolve issues affecting humanity."
From the Soka Gakkai
International Charter

The Heaven on Earth Purpose:

The use of awe in the service of Humanity.

"Heaven on Earth is...

the fundamental operating system."

Dr. David Miller
Poet/Chiropractor
USA

"Our quest is a vision for humanity which integrates science and spirit and illuminates our connectedness to each other, to the Earth, and most particularly to our inner self."

Vision Statement of the
Institute of Noetic Sciences

"Green chemistry in essence looks at finding ways to create products that do little or no harm in manufacture or use. It attempts to develop materials that can be recycled into new products and used again and again. Green chemistry starts from the moral and ethical premise of not harming the producer, the user, or the environment."

John Todd, President
Ocean Arks International

"Because of what you have done, the heavens have become a part of man's world, and as you talk to us from the Sea of Tranquility, it inspires us to redouble our efforts to bring peace and tranquility to earth."

Former President Richard M. Nixon
to Neil Armstrong on the moon

"The fairest thing we can experience is the mysterious. It is the fundamental emotion which stands at the cradle of true science. ...The true scientist never loses the faculty of amazement. It is the essence of his being."

Dr. Hans Selye

The simple, easy, concrete step(s) I will take to have Science & Technology take its rightful place in helping co-create Heaven on Earth is...

"Technology guided by conscious evolution would be used to restore the Earth, to free people from hunger and disease, to emancipate human creativity, and to explore the universe in which we dwell. Technology itself will mature and become ever more like nature — miniaturized, nonpolluting, regenerating."

Barbara Marx Hubbard

"It will free man from his remaining chains, the chains of gravity which still tie him to this planet. It will open to him the gates of heaven."

Dr. Wernher von Braun
on the meaning of space travel

The Heaven on Earth Purpose:

Participating in collective service.

"Heaven on Earth is...

participating in creating public good."

Brian Donst
Minister
Canada

"Civil society has come to mean the network of voluntary, non-governmental associations — clubs, youth groups, sports and service groups, professional organizations, trade unions, cultural alliances, independent political parties, philanthropic funds, advocacy centers, community coalitions — that provide the fertile soil in which an expansive, responsible citizenship takes root and flourishes."

A Call to Our Guiding Institutions
Council for a Parliament of the
World's Religions

"The best way to find yourself, is to lose yourself in the service of others."

Mahatma Gandhi

"I don't know what your destiny will be, but one thing I do know: The only ones among you who will be really happy are those who have sought and found how to serve."

Albert Schweitzer

"Everyone who receives the protection of society owes a return for the benefit."

John Stuart Mill

"I slept and dreamt that life was joy. I awoke and saw that life was service. I acted and behold, service was joy."

Rabindranath Tagore

* "Civic Organizations" refers to voluntary, non-governmental associations such as service clubs, youth groups, cultural associations, philanthropic organizations, and advocacy groups that foster responsible citizenship.

The simple, easy, concrete step(s) I will take to have Civic Organizations take their rightful place in helping co-create Heaven on Earth is...

"You cannot hope to build a better world without improving the individuals. To that end each of us must work for his own improvement, and at the same time share a general responsibility for all humanity, our particular duty being to aid those to whom we think we can be most useful."

Marie Curie

"In every community, there is work to be done. In every nation, there are wounds to heal. In every heart, there is the power to do it."

Marianne Williamson

➤ INTERNATIONAL INTERGOVERNMENTAL ORGANIZATIONS

The Heaven on Earth Purpose:

Experiencing community and cooperation working globally.

"Heaven on Earth is...

TRUE Community."

Andrew Cox and Martin Rutte
Human Beings
South Africa/Canada/USA

"...we do need...a world system of institutions and cooperative arrangements through which we can attempt to manage systemic forces that cannot be managed within the confines of a single nation."

Maurice Strong

"On our increasingly small and interconnected planet...global problems cannot be solved within any one nation-state. They call for collective and collaborative action...."

Jean-François Rischard
Vice President for Europe, the World Bank

"We want it (the United Nations) to take a greater part in handling crises before they occur through the implementation of what is known as preemptive diplomacy...."

His Royal Highness, Prince Saud al-Faisal
Foreign Minister
Kingdom of Saudi Arabia

"The growing body of humankind is in need of a center, which is more centered than the UN of our days. If synergy is to arise on a planetary level, the UN has to be structurally and ideologically renewed. ...For the UN to become what is expected of it, namely to warrant peace and justice worldwide, it has to become a center which offers guidance and help to humankind."

Institute for the Development of
Spiritual-Political Consciousness

The simple, easy, concrete step(s) I will take to have International Intergovernmental Organizations take their rightful place in helping co-create Heaven on Earth is...

-

"The purpose of International Intergovernmental Organizations is to midwife the emergence of higher level worldviews."
Gordon Allan

"A reasonable number of non-economic and internationally binding treaties based on the primacy of ethics and the public good have begun to take form: the Ottawa treaty against land mines, the International Criminal Court, the Kyoto accord against global warming. They represent the beginnings of an attempt at an international balance in which the prism of civilization is neither naïve market economics nor national selfishness."
John Ralston Saul

→ THE MILITARY

The Heaven on Earth Purpose:

Establishing permanent peace.

"Heaven on Earth is...

"the world's militaries being of global service by first tending to the planetary commons — the soil, the forests, the seas, and the atmosphere. Then they all team up to tackle the problems of the world. Our military men and women feel proud because these are the kinds of operations at the heart of real military service."

Jim Channon
Consultant and Colonel (Ret.), U.S. Army
USA

"...along with the ability to attack and kill, soldiers must learn peacekeeping, negotiation, and human rights preservation."
Terry J. Allen, writing about General Romeo Dallaire's beliefs about the military

"Let us invoke the blessings of peace. And, as we build an international capacity to keep peace, let us join in dismantling the national capacity to wage war."

John F. Kennedy

"We cannot have sustainable development, or respect for human rights, or good national development and stability, if we're being robbed of the best of our life and our economy through conflict. Our primary focus needs to be on developing ways of preventing conflict, dealing with its causes, helping to develop the attitudes and cultures that permit people to understand why differences can often lead to conflict, and learning how to mitigate or manage differences before they erupt into conflict."

Maurice Strong

"The way to win an atomic war is to make certain it never starts."

General Omar N. Bradley

"Though force can protect in emergency, only justice, fairness, consideration and cooperation can finally lead men to the dawn of eternal peace."

Dwight D. Eisenhower

The simple, easy, concrete step(s) I will take to have The Military take its rightful place in helping co-create Heaven on Earth is…

"The Peace-keeping forces of the United Nations have, under extremely difficult conditions, contributed to reducing tensions where an armistice has been negotiated but a peace treaty has yet to be established. In situations of this kind, the UN forces represent the manifest will of the community of nations to achieve peace through negotiations, and the forces have, by their presence, made a decisive contribution towards the initiation of actual peace negotiations."

From the citation awarding the 1988 Nobel Peace Prize to the Peacekeeping Forces of the United Nations

Inspiring Institutional Examples

Here are some examples of institutions working in innovative ways to help co-create Heaven on Earth.

University for Peace

The mission of the University for Peace is "to provide humanity with an international institution of higher education for peace and with the aim of promoting among all human beings the spirit of understanding, tolerance and peaceful coexistence, to stimulate cooperation among peoples and to help lessen obstacles and threats to world peace and progress, in keeping with the noble aspirations proclaimed in the Charter of the United Nations."

"At our main campus near San José, Costa Rica, we are teaching international groups of students from all over the world in specific fields critical to the prevention of conflict and the building of sustainable peace."

The University for Peace consists of these departments: Peace Education, Natural Resources and Peace, International Law and Human Rights, Gender and Peace, and Human Security.

www.upeace.org

Garbage & Values

Ogunquit, Maine, is a seaside vacation destination. It has a walkway called the Marginal Way, which hugs the coastline for over a mile just south of the Village Center. The Board of Selectmen, i.e., the City Council, came up with a creative way to keep litter at a minimum, keep beauty intact, and keep human values at the forefront. They painted their trash collection cans black, and on each one, in large white letters, painted a value, such as Love, Integrity, or Harmony.

Even garbage collection can contribute to Heaven on Earth.

www.townofogunquit.org

Journalism's New Story

"Journalism That Matters is a nonprofit that convenes conversations to foster collaboration, innovation, and action so that a diverse news and information ecosystem supports communities to thrive. We believe journalism matters most when it is of, by, and for the people.

"Since 2001, the organization has hosted unconferences that have inspired hundreds of varied media initiatives around the nation. JTM has a proven track record catalyzing disruptive innovation and fostering new collaborations within the news industry.

"Journalism That Matters believes that when communities and news organizations create meaningful connections, it leads to:

- More relevant stories told by both professionals and community members

- Greater involvement in civic life by an increasingly diverse mix of the community

- Innovative solutions to community challenges, inspired by stories that highlight possible solutions and a more engaged public

- Mutual trust and respect between institutions and community members

- Greater public support for news gathering and quality journalism

- Stronger economic well-being for the community and for news organizations.

"Through our initiatives we are involved with news organizations that are engaging their communities. We work across these organizations to extend the impact of their work by developing the means to:

- Connect news organizations in a learning community for journalism innovation and engagement

- Chronicle what we and participating organizations are learning

- Share learning and resources widely

- Build capacity to extend engagement work to news organizations of all types and sizes."

www.journalismthatmatters.org

Go WEST Young Woman

Most scientists, men and women, are trained for academic careers and receive little or no exposure to small-business career development during their formal schooling. Up until now no organization focused on developing the entrepreneurial talents of women with substantial training in science and technology. Women have not played a significant entrepreneurial role in advanced technology industries. This is beginning to change.

WEST, Women Entrepreneurs in Science and Technology, is a non-profit organization whose value proposition is to "…provide a powerful and challenging forum for women to engage with peers and learn from leaders who drive innovation in science and technology. Our programs are designed to enhance skills, develop professional relationships, and provide inspiration, empowering women to achieve their full leadership potential."

WEST gives women the opportunity to explore innovative opportunities in entrepreneurship and intrapreneurship; to initiate and cultivate professional and strategic relationships with successful entrepreneurs/intrapreneurs and the larger business community; and to encourage innovative thinking, risk taking, and professional agility.

www.westorg.org

"Heaven on Earth is...

institutions
that enhance the quality of life,
create meaningful work and benefit,
as well as build society."

Janice Fiovaranti
Organizational Capability Architect
Canada

"Organizations...should provide a way for people to overcome isolation,
to connect with others and participate in something larger than themselves."

Rick Lash

If having an institution take its rightful place in co-creating Heaven on Earth is a Gateway for you, here are three ways to get involved:

1. **Engage with one particular institution and make it work.**

2. **Engage one institution in interacting with another institution and be responsible for having the interaction work.** In the matrix below, put an "X" in the intersecting square that you feel is your responsibility or where your heart is drawn (e.g., Religion & Commerce, or Government & Education).

As an example, the World Bank (Intergovernmental) and the Anglican Church (Religion) are working together to reduce poverty. There would be an "X" where Intergovernmental and Religion intersect. Another example might be someone wanting to create a program where student lawyers (Law) help lower-income patients in a medical clinic (Medicine). They would put an "X" where Law and Medicine intersect.

Once you've put your "X" in a square, write down some simple, easy, concrete steps on the lines below the matrix that will get you started.

	Education	Culture	Health Care	Commerce	Resources	Law	Government	Religion	Science & Tech.	Civic Organizations	Intergovernmental	The Military
Education												
Culture												
Health Care												
Commerce												
Resources												
Law												
Government												
Religion												
Science & Tech.												
Civic Organizations												
Intergovernmental												
The Military												

_____

_____

_____

_____

3. **Engage with all our institutions.** You can do your part to have the institutions, as a collective body, play their rightful role in creating Heaven on Earth. If you find this possibility intriguing and want to address it, you could write an article, develop a course, do research, create a seminar, write a book, or hold a conference, etc. For example, Janice Fiovoranti, an organizational consultant, is researching how to transform the negative and disempowering beliefs people hold about institutions.

Are you willing to be responsible for any of the institutions below to play their rightful, integral, and noble role in helping co-create Heaven on Earth? If so, what is your contribution, role, or task? (If there is an institution I haven't listed, please list it and describe what your contribution will be.) The simple, easy, concrete steps I will take are:

_____

_____

_____

_____

▷ Your Outer World
▶ Our Institutions Taking Their Rightful Place in Co-Creating Heaven on Earth
> ➤ Education
> ➤ Culture: Arts, Media, Sports
> ➤ Health Care & Medicine
> ➤ Commerce: Business, Industry, Labor
> ➤ Resources: Agriculture, Fisheries, Forestry, Mining
> ➤ Law
> ➤ Government
> ➤ Religion
> ➤ Science & Technology
> ➤ Civic Organizations
> ➤ International Intergovernmental Organizations
> ➤ The Military

*"Guided by a vision of the world as it might be,
with deep concern for the well-being
of the Earth, its people, and all life,
the Council for a Parliament of the World's Religions
respectfully calls upon the world's guiding institutions
to reassess and redefine their roles in order
to assure a just, peaceful, and sustainable future.
We invite these institutions to join with each other
in a process of creative engagement to address
the critical issues that face the world."*

Council for a Parliament of
the World's Religions

"Heaven on Earth is...

organizations that empower everyone
to continue to use all their gifts, talents, and wisdom
from the very first moment they join the organization."

Susan E. Greene
Catalyst, Author, Consultant
USA

"Humanity is at the threshold of nothing short of a profound change
in the evolution of consciousness:
the possibility of creating new societal structures and processes
to facilitate a social spiritual awakening
beyond anything previously experienced in history."
Alex Kochkin

My business travels take me to many cities and many different hotels. One hotel I stayed at stands out as an example of how simple, easy, and inexpensive it can be to create a Heaven on Earth experience.

The hotel is the Holiday Inn in Sheridan, Wyoming. I'd flown from Santa Fe to Denver and then on to Sheridan. The flights, each an hour and a half long, were on small 19-seater prop planes. The flight from Denver to Sheridan was particularly bumpy. I was tired and grumpy. When I got to my hotel room, I found sitting on the bed a 6x8-inch laminated card that completely shifted my mood and gave me a Heaven on Earth experience:

To Our Guests

In ancient times there was a prayer for
"The Stranger within our gates."
Because this hotel is a human institution to serve people,
and not solely a money making organization,
we hope that God will grant you peace and rest
while you are under our roof.

May this suite and hotel be your "second" home.
May those you love be near you in thoughts and dreams.
Even though we may not get to know you,
we hope that you will be as comfortable and happy
as if you were in your own house.

May the business that brought you our way prosper.
May every call you make
and every message you receive add to your joy.
When you leave, may your journey be safe.

We are all travelers.
From "birth till death"
we travel between eternities.
May these days be pleasant for you,
profitable for society,
helpful for those you meet,
and a joy to those who know and love you best.

Author Unknown

"Heaven on Earth is...

unconditional forgiving across cultures."

Sabine Bredemeyer
Consultant
Germany

"The measure of a nation is what we do with power."

Claude Phipps

Chapter 14

▷ Your Outer World
▶ Co-Creating Heaven on Earth Nation(s)
➤ Uniting a Nation to Resolve an Issue
➤ Uniting a Nation to Co-Create Heaven on Earth for that Nation
➤ Uniting Nations to Resolve an Issue
➤ Uniting All Nations to Co-Create Heaven on Earth

There have been times in history when a nation experienced a renaissance, what could be called a Heaven on Earth period. Scotland in the late 1700s and Germany in the late 1800s had eras of expansive growth in the arts, culture, and sciences. There was an explosion of innovation, and increased well-being. There were contributions to the vibrancy and enrichment of the entire population. These two countries also produced positive impacts well beyond their own borders. Scotland gave the world Adam Smith, David Hume, Thomas Chalmers, and Thomas Carlyle. Germany gave the world Friedrich Nietzche, Max Weber, Baroness Bertha Sophie Felicita von Suttner, Max Planck, Sigmund Freud, and Albert Einstein. Going even further back in time, many other nations experienced similar eras: the Egyptians, Incas, and Polynesians.

Let's say these periods of creative flourishing, these great eruptions of new vitality, were periods of Heaven on Earth. What if today a nation "chose" to enter Heaven on Earth? What if a growing number of people in a country said, "It's time for us to be a Heaven on Earth nation" and what if they proclaim (publicly commit) to do that?

I want to be respectful to those of you who may have a different definition of nation. By *nation*, I mean a specific country (Germany, Brazil, Japan, etc.). I also mean a specific group of people, e.g., aboriginal (Maori of New Zealand, Navaho of the U.S.); geographic (Kurds, Basques); religious (Jews, Hindus); wandering/nomadic (Gypsies/Romani, Tuaregs); or an envisioned larger "nation" (a united North & South Korea). If any of these are your definition of nation, please view the chapter in this way.

A nation — composed of its people, geography, history, culture, and national identity — could choose to co-create Heaven on Earth by proclaiming and establishing it, and then by sustaining and nourishing it.

You could choose Heaven on Earth for your nation. You could choose Heaven on Earth for the nations in your region and for the nations of our world.

To support you in this choice, I asked people all over the world, "What is Heaven on Earth for your nation?" Here are some of their replies…

"Heaven on Earth is...

for **Northern Ireland**,

people crossing the divide and,
in doing so,
realising that at the deepest,
most human level,
the divide never truly existed."

Gillian Caroe
HR Manager
Great Britain

for **Israel**,

in my eyes,
when all wolves and lambs
live together in harmony —
even if they disagree
about many things,
including the question of
who is the wolf
and who is the lamb."

Yehuda Stolov
Director
Interfaith Encounter Association
Israel
www.interfaith-encounter.org

for **South Africa**,

living the Mandela dream of a country
free from prejudice and hatred,
poverty and crime...
a country where people live together
in peace and harmony
and where every human being enjoys
dignity and respect!"

Philip J. Krawitz
Chief Executive Officer
Cape Union Mart Group of Companies
South Africa

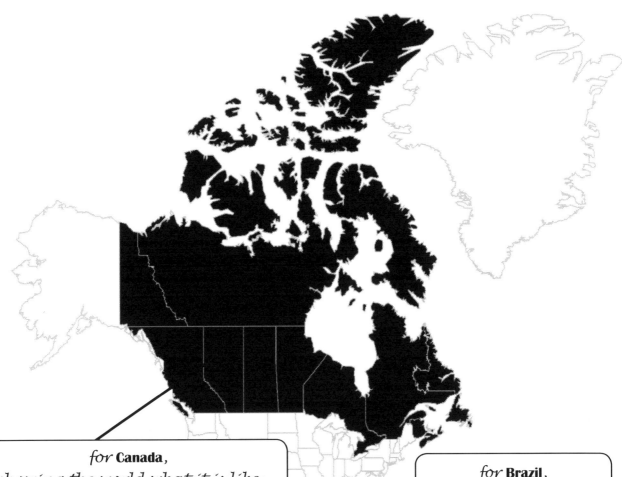

for **Canada**,

*showing the world what it is like
to live in true generosity,
stewardship and love...
by actually living our lives like that."*

Mary Joseph
Lawyer
Canada

for **Brazil**,

*being NATURAL, that
is, being oneself,
authentic, genuine,
enlightened, in love
and loving."*

Robert Wong
Consultant
Brazil

for **Argentina**,

*being an example of Humanity, Love, and
Consciousness, being the mirror for the
world, where peace and joy are reflected.*

*Heaven on Earth is, for Argentina,
being a country where values and
feelings rule our lives.
A place where any citizen can live
up to their dreams and create them
consciously, always thinking about
themselves and others, because we are all
the same, we are all ONE."*

Hernan Pisotti
Consultant
Argentina

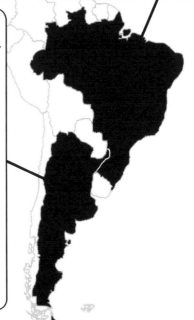

Co-Creating Heaven on Earth Nation(s)

"Heaven on Earth is...

for Germany,

being forgiven by those we've hurt, being proud of our country, and serving healing and peace in the world."

Sabine Bredemeyer
Consultant
Germany

for India,

maintains, not philosophically but experientially, there is a unique purpose of human existence AND to remember our divine home, experience our home, and live life on earth with that vibrant sense of remembrance, thus making heaven on earth possible for all existence."

Nagam H. Atthreya
Consultant/Counsellor/
Sounding Board by profession,
Author by talent,
and pilgrim/seeker by temperament
India
uathreya@bom5.vsnl.net.in

for France,

that there be no beggars in the street starving and that everyone has a roof over his head, that politicians listen to each other in order to lead the country together, that corporations be more open to issues of personal health and the situation of their employees, that people are brought up educated about death, pain and suffering, that people take more time to speak with their neighbors, that money not constitute our greatest priority and reward.

Luc de Belloy
Coach/Actor/Trainer/Director
France

for Japan,

in the year of 2035 people know what is sufficient."

Tachi Kiuchi
Chairman, The Future 500
Japan

for **Mexico**,

the country
and all of its people
being free to celebrate
their passion
for life, family and love —
and having their fear
of violence and hunger
replaced with
full stomachs,
whole hearts
and radiant souls
enjoying all the beauty
the nation offers."

Rob Follows
International Businessperson &
Corporate Philanthropy Expert
Mexico/Canada
www.altruvest.org

for **Venezuela**,

magic water falls,
wonderful people,
beautiful
landscapes,
beaches, jungles,
mountains and
valleys.
Venezuela is
a heaven's piece
on the Earth."

Anahi Peraza Urrutia
Economist
Venezuela

for the **Bolivian people**,

to overcome the Great Heresy of Separateness,
and to live in peace, to work, to prosper,
to educate our children in a loving
environment and to live according to our
utmost human values.

for the **Andean Community**,

to return to our ancestor's strong connection
with the Pachamama (Mother Nature) and
to be able to fly our many-colored Whipala
(flag) and regain our sovereignty."

Nila Tadic de Ossio
Bolivian Unit of Service
Bolivia

"Heaven on Earth is...

for Iceland,

*remaining just the way that it is...
unspoiled and pure."*

Edda Arndal
Body Orientated Psychotherapist
Iceland

for Finland,

*opening up in heart and mind
to goodwill and right human relations
in the realization of
One earth and One humanity."*

Birgitta Svahnstrom
Retired Nurseteacher
Finland

for Uganda,

*a country where there
is respect for human
rights especially for
the children who
are in most cases
innocent of the
conflicts that go on
amongst the adults
but are often caught
at crossroads in these
conflicts."*

Despina Namwembe
Global Council Trustee
United Religions Initiative
representing the
East African sub-region &
Program Manager
for orphans and
vulnerable children
Uganda Orthodox Church
Uganda

for Greece,

*Full Moon on the Acropolis
Sunset on Mt. Athos
A walk in Samaria gorge
A kiss from my love
An evening with mom and dad
Playing with my baby son
Listening in silence
A kid's smile. . .
Listening to Smetana's "Homeland"
No more homeless elderly
Educating Albanian immigrants
Hospitals for all needy
No need for drugs
Zero criminality. . .
Peace with the Turks over Cyprus and Aegean
No more deadly road accidents. . .
Happy marriages for life without divorces. . .
But if I had to summarize all of the above in
one word, I would choose: LOVE.
Get in touch with God within.
Accept everything without!"*

Manolis Trigonis
Manager
Greece

for **Paraguay**,
the end of corruption.
It is the shift of military spending to education and social services for poor people.
It is no children robbed of their childhood
and all children feeling loved by their parents.
Heaven on Earth is a country where everyone has gainful employment.
It does not necessarily mean socialism,
but it has a more equal distribution of wealth.
Heaven on Earth is the end of juvenile prisons without rehabilitation services.
It is education, counseling, and healthcare for youth deprived of their liberty.
It is a place for effective treatment for those who suffer from drug addictions.

Heaven on Earth is restorative justice, where youth learn from their mistakes,
repair the damage they inflicted upon society, and have a second chance at life.
It is more jobs and a more just socioeconomic situation
leading to a great reduction in crime and juvenile delinquency in Paraguay.
It is a place with a police force protecting and aiding
citizens when they are in danger.
There are no more corrupt police who utilize children and youth
to steal and traffic drugs, indoctrinating them for future criminal careers.

Obviously, hunger, disease, and a multitude of other social ills
associated with poverty would also disappear in our Heaven on Earth.
Our first concern is the youth who are excluded from society
and development initiatives.
These forgotten, "throw-away" youth would live normal,
relatively happy lives in the Heaven on Earth we envision.

Heaven on Earth is when you have forgotten about your problems,
because you have focused your energy on helping someone in need.
Heaven on Earth is discovering that you have many talents
that can be applied to make the world a better place,
and then actually putting this information into action.

How can we work together to create Heaven on Earth in Paraguay?
We need a miracle, and a miracle can happen at any time.

Maureen Herman
Executive Director
ProJOVEN (ForYOUTH)
Paraguay

"Heaven on Earth is...

for Sweden,

open minds and open hearts,
open landscapes and open seas,
wisdom open for all and everyone."

Göran Garberg
Consultant in Corporate Missions
Sweden

for Scotland,

not wanting the day to end."

Chris Thomson
Intelligence Consultant
Scotland

for Britain,

— everyone participating to their fullest
capacity for civic responsibility
— genuine neighbourliness
— a government driven by long-term,
compassionate efficiency (especially,
focusing on enlightened parenting and
emotional intelligence in education)
— a foreign policy with consistent and
vaulted morality."

Shoshana Garfield
Perennial Student/Healer/Consultant/
Human whilst embodied
United Kingdom

for Australia,

knowing that we are all spirit in disguise."

Tony Indomenico
Personal Fitness Trainer
& Personal Development Event Promoter
Australia

for **America**,

*being equal partners with the world for
peace, safety, freedom and well being for all.
All the issues that separate us
would be removed
and in its place would be a
universal knowledge that
we are all connected
and all would act accordingly.
To hurt another is to hurt ourselves
and to help another is to help ourselves."*

Maeileen Tuffli Nabb
Business Consultant
USA

for **Chile**,

*human rights for all,
Nature being taken
care of throughout
the country and
restoration of values
for people as once
inherently lived in
everyone's hearts.
Plus the ability
to creatively
experiment with
alternative ways of
right livelihood."*

Carlos Warter, MD
Author/Psychiatrist
Spiritual Activist
Chile/USA

for **Guatemala**,

*the preservation of the environment.
If we don't take care of the environment
there will be no heaven on earth for humans.
'Let's make planet earth our church
and protecting it our religion.'"*

Lorenzo and Emilia Gottschamer
Organic Macademia Nut Farmers
Guatemala

for **New Zealand**,

SANCTUARY FOR THE SOUL."

Pamela Meekings-Stewart
Retreat Facilitator
New Zealand

"Heaven on Earth is...

for Austria,
*reached when all sentient beings living here
have achieved unsurpassed,
perfectly completed enlightenment."*
Dr. Harald Hutterer
Trainer/Coach for
ethics and spirituality
Austria

for Korea,
*elevating and freeing the spirit to the point
where society does not dictate individual identity.
To paraphrase A. N. Whitehead,
then there will be a balance of
individual creative spirit and social order,
supporting change amid order,
preserving order amid change."*
Jinsun Park, PhD
Philosophy of Religion and Theology
South Korea

for Spain,
*everyone
resting happy
with what they
have, and stop
looking at the
neighbor."*
Raquel Torrent
Psychologist
Spain

for Kenya,
*that all Kenyans are able to meet their needs
and voice concerns without fear
in realising their full potential."*
Bikundo Onyari
Youth Planner
Kenya

for **Haiti**,

young and old, living at home or abroad,
following the laws of higher consciousness.
We have no choice than to want the best
for our country, be willing to lend a hand,
project kind and positive energy
and envision the best for ourselves, our country,
and the whole world. There is no going back.

Dr. Carolle Jean-Murat
Gynecologist, Medical Intuitive, Author,
International Speaker
Haiti/USA

for **Cayman Islands**,

a sense of community
where everyone is working together
for the common good of all."

David Luckey
Entrepreneurial Visionary
USA
(My grandmother Doris Ebanks, "Nana,"
is from Grand Cayman)

for the **U.S. Virgin Islands**,

people realizing that
honest communication,
self-responsibility,
true accountability,
and genuine giving
bring them more prosperity
than they could ever imagine."

Brenda Armstrong
Massage Therapist & Bodyworker
U.S. Virgin Islands

Co-Creating Heaven on Earth Nation(s)

"Heaven on Earth is...

for **Kazakhstan**,

people feel secure that they are adequately rewarded for their performance, we have a social system which cares for the retired, the handicapped and the sick, quality public education is provided up to the University level for all who wish to get a degree, and our resources are processed in the country and sold as processed, final product."

Maral Katrenova
Environmental Specialist
Kazakhstan

for **Taiwan**,

people emulating the selflessness of Heaven and Earth, which gives room for all things without partiality; turning human nature toward perfection to help assure peace and well-being for the entire world."

Maria Reis Habito
International Program Director
Museum of World Religions
Taiwan

for the **Arab Muslim World**,

having an open mind, knowing that Islam is a religion of love and peace, remembering Islam's purpose of bringing Peace to the world, building the world, making it a better place. This is our on-going prayer and discipline.

Peace for the region will mean prosperity and the alleviation of poverty. Raising our children with love and acceptance of the world. Our hearts are clean of grudges and pure."

Diana Hamadé
Manager of Communications & Business Development
Dubai, United Arab Emirates

for **Iraq**,
having Peace
and getting rid of all conflict.
People live the normal way
and function right.
Everyone is happy and seeking higher
consciousness and spirit."
Adnan Sarhan
Sufi Teacher
USA & Iraq

for **Bangladesh**,
having all individuals
living a happy life free of
poverty, disaster, hunger,
disease and
human rights violations."
Annisul Huq
Chairman
Mohammadi Group
& President, Bangladesh Garment
Manufacturers and Exporters
Association (BGMEA)
Bangladesh

for **Africa**,
abundant with crops,
green and verdant,
abundant with plenty,
people enjoying peace
and liberty,
and rockin'
as only Africans can."
Elsie Maio
Management Consultant
in brand strategy
USA

for **Philippines**,
united governance of this small country
in the far east, no typhoons coming at
all, and united religions in pursuing
peace initiatives, and rich people sharing
resources with poor, and people in power
going back to the people to feel their
needs and aspirations."
Mario Fungo
Peace Representative
The World Peace Prayer Society, Pathways to Peace
& member United Religions Initiative
Philippines

"Heaven on Earth is...

the experience of your loyalty to the world."

Joichi Ito
Activist/Social Entrepreneur
Japan

"The purpose of national leaders
is to ignite important national conversations."
Michael Valpy

What is Heaven on Earth for your nation?

_____

_____

_____

_____

_____

_____

_____

_____

As people around the world shared their feelings and thoughts about what Heaven on Earth is for their nation, several common themes emerged:

- People want a basic standard of well-being. They want their physical, social, and service requirements met: health, food, water, safety, shelter, education, and work that provides financial self-sufficiency.

- People want freedom and human rights, the rule of law, and honest and transparent institutions that are of service.

- People want to support other nations that are in need — by expressing kindness, generosity, and support.

- People want to be in relationship with other nations and with the community of nations.

Are you willing for your nation to be a Heaven on Earth nation? Are you willing for your nation to become a catalyst for positive growth for the nations in your region? Are you willing for your nation to become a catalyst for the betterment of the entire community of nations?

It is possible to have an entire nation be a Heaven on Earth nation. How? You, a person, or a group of people simply declare that your nation is a Heaven on Earth nation and then get into action by taking the first step(s) to make that real. And then, day by day, keep on keeping on.

The remainder of this chapter explores four other ways to engage in proclaiming, establishing, and sustaining Heaven on Earth Nation(s).

▷ Your Outer World
▶ Co-Creating Heaven on Earth Nation(s)
- ➤ Uniting a Nation to Resolve an Issue
- ➤ Uniting a Nation to Co-Create Heaven on Earth for that Nation
- ➤ Uniting Nations to Resolve an Issue
- ➤ Uniting All Nations to Co-Create Heaven on Earth

The list above shows four Gateways for your involvement in and contribution to proclaim, establish, and sustain Heaven on Earth Nation(s). Let's look at each Gateway in more detail.

➤ Uniting a Nation to Resolve an Issue

Here are multiple commitments to resolving an issue within a nation:

A Nation Free of Nuclear Power by 2022 (Germany)

"Germany's coalition government has announced a...policy that will see all the country's nuclear power plants phased out by 2022."

Environment Minister Norbert Rottgen said, "It's definite. The latest end for the last three nuclear power plants is 2022. There will be no clause for revision."

For more information, visit: tinyurl.com/Germany2022

A Nation Free of Dependence on Fossil Fuels by 2040 (Iceland)

Dr. Bragi Arnason: "...we have been working on the idea of converting Iceland into a country where all the energy consumption comes from domestic energy sources.... We are talking about 2040 or so. And then Iceland will be totally independent of imported fossil fuels and the greenhouse gas emissions will drop to about 45% of the present level.

"We found that we had only 1% of the geothermal energy harnessed. ...we have these large energy sources, but we still imported one-third of the energy for the country."

tinyurl.com/Iceland2040

A Nation Free of Dental Disease in Children by 2020 (USA)

"DentaQuest Foundation 'Oral Health 2020 Goal: Eradicate dental disease in children,' a national movement that will create a new social norm in this country about our oral health....

"Since launching a national systems-change strategy in 2010, the Foundation has, through its investments, facilitated the weaving of a large and powerful network of national, state, and community-based change agents working to improve the oral health of all. Together with over 130 grantee partners in 35 states and at the national level, we have begun to catalyze a network that is poised to transform the national dialogue and re-shape the landscape of action on behalf of oral health. …We are going to eradicate dental disease in children, and improve oral health across the lifespan."

tinyurl.com/DentalDisease2020

A Nation that is Carbon Neutral by 2020 (The Maldives)

"The Maldives…is to become the first country in the world to crowdsource its renewable energy strategy on the Internet.

"In 2009 the Maldives' president, Mohamed Nasheed, announced a plan to make the country carbon-neutral by 2020 — the world's most ambitious national climate change target. Nasheed said he hoped that by adopting the plan, the Maldives would inspire 'other nations to follow suit.'

"…an 80–90% reduction in electricity emissions should be achievable by 2020 without driving up local energy bills."

tinyurl.com/Maldives2020

A Nation Free of Homelessness by 2020 (USA)

"The National Alliance to End Homelessness [seeks to] help reach and maintain the goal of ending family homelessness by 2020.

"The [federal government's] Administration's Homeless Assistance for Families proposal… would give communities exactly what they need to end homelessness for families with children, once and for all."

www.endhomelessness.org/pages/presskit

Nations Committed to Ending Violence Against Women

UN Women, the United Nations Entity for Gender Equality and the Empowerment of Women provides an extensive list of commitments country by country focused on ending violence against women.

tinyurl.com/EndingViolenceAgainstWomen

➤ Uniting a Nation's Vision to Create Heaven on Earth for that Nation

Here are two stories describing a vision for a nation: for Bhutan, the "Maximization of Gross National Happiness," and for New Zealand, Heaven on Earth.

Bhutan

The following is from the 1999 final draft of a report entitled *Bhutan 2020: A Vision for Peace, Prosperity and Happiness*. It was developed by the Planning Commission of the Royal Government of Bhutan.

"The guiding principles for the future development of our nation and for safeguarding our sovereignty and security as a nation state must be complemented by a single unifying concept of development that enables us to identify future directions that are preferred above all others. This unifying concept for the nation's longer-term development is...the distinctively Bhutanese concept of the Maximization of Gross National Happiness, propounded in the late 1980s by His Majesty King Jigme Singye Wangchuck."

"The concept of Gross National Happiness was articulated by His Majesty to indicate that development has many more dimensions than those associated with Gross Domestic Product. ...The concept places the individual at the centre of all development efforts and it recognizes that the individual has material, spiritual and emotional needs."

"The key to the concept of Gross National Happiness...resides in the belief that the key to happiness is to be found, once basic material needs have been met, in the satisfaction of non-material needs and in emotional and spiritual growth."

The report goes on to detail how Gross National Happiness is to be translated into objectives, using these nine domains (and measured by thirty-three indicators):

- Psychological Well-being
- Standard of Living and Happiness
- Good Governance and Gross National Happiness
- Health
- Education
- Ecological Diversity and Resilience
- Community Vitality
- Cultural Diversity and Resilience
- Time Use and Happiness

The report concludes: "There may be those who feel that such a future is beyond our reach. There are those who undervalue our assets and resources and underestimate our determination and commitment to the future of our nation and our children. If we maintain our identity and unity and make full and prudent use of our assets and resources, Bhutan in 2020 could provide an example to the rest of the world. It could demonstrate that with confidence, wisdom, forethought, imagination and above all firm unity and belief in a common purpose, it is possible for even the smallest of countries to rise to challenges of historical proportions and to carve out a distinctive place for itself in the world of the 21st century."

More on Gross National Happiness at: www.grossnationalhappiness.com

The full "Bhutan 2020" report is available in its entirety at:

tinyurl.com/Bhutan2020-1 (Part I)
tinyurl.com/Bhutan2020-2 (Part II)

New Zealand/Aotearoa

Margaret Jefferies is a New Zealander. She wants New Zealand, also called "Aotearoa" in Maori, to take its rightful place in helping co-create Heaven on Earth. As she says, "I have a vision of what New Zealand could be. The more I talk about this the more I see the vision unfolding." Specifically, she says her commitment is: "Aotearoa/New Zealand is a Community, role modeling for the world how to create heaven on earth."

Margaret then details her commitment (note: some words and spellings are New Zealand English): "I see New Zealand as a country where all life is honoured. A community experiencing a 'coming home' feeling — a reconnecting with the natural abundance that surrounds us. A country that has shifted from a perspective of lack and the associated need for greed as we grabbed 'our' portion to a perspective of abundance that also recognises when we have enough.

"I see a community that understands its role in the world — to be fully alive. That is its intent.

"So I see New Zealand living sustainably, understanding the principles of interconnectedness, a country of excellent networkers, celebrating their rich diversity, a people understanding that peace is an active grunty state, not a state of entropy. A people of creative genius, living with advanced innovations that support rather than dominate. A people that recognizes the glue that holds us all together, the 'something other' that has been given many names. A people who relish a diversity of expression of this 'other' and the innate oneness of all."

Saudi Arabia's Vision for 2030

Saudi Arabia has created a bold vision for the country to be realized by 2030, "A vibrant society, a thriving economy, and an ambitious nation."

Mohammad bin Salman bin Abdulaziz Al-Saud, Chairman of the Council of Economic and Development Affairs, says, "It is my pleasure to present Saudi Arabia's Vision for the future. It is an ambitious yet achievable blueprint, which expresses our long-term goals and expectations and reflects our country's strengths and capabilities.

"We are determined to build a thriving country in which all citizens can fulfill their dreams, hopes, and ambitions. Therefore, we will not rest until our nation is a leader in providing opportunities for all through education and training, and high-quality services such as employment initiatives, health, housing, and entertainment.

"We commit ourselves to providing world-class government services which effectively and efficiently meet the needs of our citizens. Together we will continue building a better country, fulfilling our dream of prosperity and unlocking the talent, potential, and dedication of our young men and women.

"We will improve the business environment, so that our economy grows and flourishes, driving healthier employment opportunities for citizens and long-term prosperity for all. This promise is built on cooperation and on mutual responsibility."

http://vision2030.gov.sa/en

➤ Uniting Nations to Resolve an Issue(s)

Here are three examples of nations in a region that have chosen to work together to either resolve an issue by solving a problem (e.g., drugs, crime, environmental pollution) or by developing opportunities (e.g., economic growth, inter-university research).

The fourth example is a group of nations that have chosen to work together to strengthen their economies.

The African Union

The African Union (AU), representing all 54 states in Africa, has aligned on achieving seven aspirations by the year 2063:

> "The aspirations embed a strong desire to see a continent where women and the youth have guarantees of fundamental freedoms to contribute and benefit from a different, better and dynamic Africa by 2063, and where women and youth assume leading roles in growth and transformation of African societies.

> 1. A prosperous Africa based on inclusive growth and sustainable development;

> 2. An integrated continent, politically united, based on the ideals of Pan Africanism and the vision of Africa's Renaissance;

> 3. An Africa of good governance, respect for human rights, justice and the rule of law;

> 4. A peaceful and secure Africa;

> 5. An Africa with a strong cultural identity, common heritage, values and ethics;

> 6. An Africa whose development is people-driven, relying on the potential of African people, especially its women and youth, and caring for children; and

> 7. Africa as a strong, united, resilient and influential global player and partner."

tinyurl.com/AU2063

The Association of Southeast Asian Nations (ASEAN)

ASEAN, consisting of Brunei Darussalam, Cambodia, Indonesia, Laos, Malaysia, Myanmar, Philippines, Singapore, Thailand and Vietnam, represents "the collective will of the nations of Southeast Asia to bind themselves together in friendship and cooperation and, through joint efforts and sacrifices, secure for their peoples and for posterity the blessings of peace, freedom and prosperity."

"The ASEAN Community is comprised of three pillars, namely the ASEAN Political-Security Community, ASEAN Economic Community and ASEAN Socio-Cultural Community. Each pillar has its own Blueprint...."

"The ASEAN Vision 2020...agreed on a shared vision of ASEAN as a concert of Southeast Asian nations, outward looking, living in peace, stability and prosperity, bonded together in partnership in dynamic development and in a community of caring societies."

"The motto of ASEAN is 'One Vision, One Identity, One Community.'"

www.asean.org

The European Union

The European Union (EU) is an economic and political partnership of 28 countries.

Created in the aftermath of World War II, its first goal was to foster economic cooperation based on the underlying principle that countries that trade with one another are economically interdependent and will thus avoid conflict.

Since then, the EU has developed into a single market with the euro as its common currency. It has evolved into an organization covering issues from development to environmental policy to human rights and democracy.

The EU has delivered half a century of peace, stability, and prosperity while raising living standards. It continues strengthening a single European-wide market in which people, goods, services, and capital move freely among member states.

The EU's motto is: "United in diversity."

tinyurl.com/EUMarket

The Group of 20 (G20) – Uniting the major economic nations

(The following is excerpted from tinyurl.com/20United and edited.)

The Group of Twenty (G20), comprising the leading 19 economic nations plus the European Union, is the premier forum for international economic cooperation and decision-making.

The G20 started in 1999 as a meeting of Finance Ministers and Central Bank Governors in the aftermath of the Asian financial crisis. In 2008 the first G20 Leaders' Summit was held, and the group played a key role in responding to the global financial crisis.

G20 leaders meet annually. In addition, Finance Ministers and Central Bank Governors meet regularly during the year to discuss ways to strengthen the global economy, reform international financial institutions, improve financial regulation, and implement the key economic reforms that are needed in each member economy.

Over the past six years, the G20 has framed the world's efforts to restore growth and build the resilience of financial institutions and national economies. It led the world out of an economic crisis and through the initial stages of the recovery. With the world now free from immediate economic crisis, the G20 can increasingly shift its attention to driving practical actions that will lead to sustained global growth while always remaining vigilant to risks and vulnerabilities.

➤ Uniting All Nations to Create Heaven on Earth

On April 3, 2000, the United Nations Secretary-General, Kofi Annan, offered his 21st-century action plan, a detailed report that set the agenda for the United Nations Millennium Summit. The plan called on all Member States to commit themselves to ending poverty and inequality, improving education, increasing security, reducing HIV/AIDS, and protecting the environment.

"We must put people at the centre of everything we do," said Mr. Annan. "No calling is more noble, and no responsibility greater, than that of enabling men, women and children, in cities and villages around the world, to make their lives better."

The report, *We the Peoples: The Role of the United Nations in the 21st Century*, is the most comprehensive presentation of the UN's mission in its history. To view the full report, please visit: tinyurl.com/WeThePeoples

"Heaven on Earth is...

civilization with a heart."

Wayne Teasdale
Monk, Professor, Writer,
Retreat Master, and Spiritual Director
USA

"We will have peace when the love for nation
will extend to a love for the entire humanity and Earth."

Sigmund Freud to Albert Einstein

▷ Your Outer World
▶ Co-Creating Heaven on Earth Nation(s)
> ➤ Uniting a Nation to Resolve an Issue
> ➤ Uniting a Nation to Co-Create Heaven on Earth for that Nation
> ➤ Uniting Nations to Resolve an Issue
> ➤ Uniting All Nations to Co-Create Heaven on Earth

In this chapter we've looked at a number of perspectives and examples of how a nation or nations proclaim, establish, and sustain Heaven on Earth. If this is your Gateway, what simple, easy, concrete step(s) will you take in the next 24 hours to make it happen?

_____

_____

_____

_____

_____

_____

_____

_____

_____

_____

_____

_____

_____

_____

_____

_____

_____

"Heaven on Earth is...

always right here, right now.
Our option is to re-unite and
be the invitation for re-union."

Linda Masterson
Soul Advocate
Hawaii, USA

"There is no other place for Heaven but here
and no other time but now."

Guruka Singh Khalsa

Chapter 15

▷ **Heaven on Earth This-Here-Now**

In the previous chapters we've seen how co-creating Heaven on Earth occurs through the Gateways of the Inner, Relationships, and the Outer.

- **Inner:**
  The more I create and experience Heaven on Earth within myself, the more it will be created and experienced out in the world.

- **Relationships:**
  The bridge between the Inner and Outer — relationships with Yourself, Others, and God/The Divine.

- **Outer:**
  The way to have more Heaven on Earth in the world is by:

  + Ending a Suffering

  + Having Our Institutions Taking Their Rightful Place in Co-Creating Heaven On Earth

  + Co-Creating Heaven on Earth Nation(s)

All these Gateways open the way to making Heaven on Earth real at some time in the future, whether that time is a minute from now, an hour, a day, or longer.

Author and spiritual teacher Andrew Cohen says that we live in two simultaneous "states" in this moment: "Being" and "Becoming." Becoming is about taking action now so the result will be completed in the future. All the Gateways to Heaven on Earth that we've opened have been in the domain of Becoming. We're Becoming *now* in order to have Heaven on Earth be real within ourselves, within others, and for the world in a time after now.

The other simultaneous state we live in is "Being." Unlike Becoming, Being has to do with our consciously being fully present — now — without any future intentions or effort. It's only about existence, essence, essentialness. In short, it's about This-Here-Now. This chapter focuses on *Being* Heaven on Earth, on experiencing Heaven on Earth This-Here-Now.

Neither of the two states is better than the other or more preferred. They co-exist and serve different functions. Both are required, both needed.

At the conclusion of this chapter, we will have opened both the Being and the Becoming Heaven on Earth Gateways. By fully Being (This-Here-Now) and fully Becoming (for subsequent moments of now) we experience the fullness and magnificence that is Heaven on Earth now and in the future.

Let's begin our journey into This-Here-Now by exploring the three realms in which Heaven on Earth occurs:

- In the past, as a memory. (In Chapter 3, the first Heaven on Earth question asked: "Recall a time when you experienced Heaven on Earth. What was happening?") *Heaven on Earth exists in our memories of it.*

- In the future, as a desired outcome, e.g., the end of war, hunger, disease, etc. *Heaven on Earth exists in our vision of it.*

- In the total fullness of this present moment right now. *Heaven on Earth exists in This-Here-Now.*

As we examine our experience of Heaven on Earth in the past, present and future, something fascinating reveals itself. We discover that all three of these realms exist only now. We can remember the past, we can dream about the future, but the only time and the only place they both occur is in the present. And, of course, the present is also happening now. All three — past, present, and future — exist now. So, now is the time to experience Heaven on Earth, the continuing awareness and consciousness that This-Here-Now is Heaven on Earth.

Can it really be that simple? Yes.

Elohim, an Australian magazine, says: "We are spiritual beings having a human experience and we have the power within to manifest heaven on earth in every moment."

Yet still, many people hold onto the belief that Heaven on Earth can only manifest in a future separated from now. Simply put, our belief that Heaven on Earth is not here now, prevents us from experiencing it here, now. If we believe it's not here, it's not here.

Here are some assumptions underlying this belief:

- While we may have experienced some moments of Heaven on Earth in our lives, Heaven on Earth has never been here for us all the time and so it never will be.

- We were kicked out of the Garden of Eden, out of Heaven on Earth, and we can never return.

- Heaven exists only "up there" and/or "after death."

What these assumptions do is leave Heaven on Earth completely out of This-Here-Now. They create a core, underlying belief that no matter what we do, This-Here-Now cannot be Heaven on Earth. The cost of believing this is that, at best, we experience occasional moments of Heaven on Earth. At worst, we experience hell on Earth. This core belief prevents us from unlocking the full potential of Heaven on Earth here and now.

But there *is* another option. What if we simply step out of this limiting core belief? You'll recall from Chapter 4 that the way to step out of a limiting belief is to give your word, to commit to the chosen result you want. In this case the result is to fully experience This-Here-Now, the fullness and vastness of Heaven on Earth.

Committing allows us to step outside our limiting beliefs and begin experiencing Heaven right here, right now. We begin experiencing what we've longed for, and dive continuously more deeply into it.

Are you willing to commit to This-Here-Now being Heaven on Earth?

The experience of Heaven on Earth is available to you and to every one of us...now. Heaven on Earth — This-Here-Now.

In Chapter 3 I wrote about Heaven being experienced, prior to the telescope, as here on Earth. When the telescope was invented and we couldn't "see" Heaven, we concluded that it had to be further than we could grasp or that it only existed after death. As we developed more and more powerful telescopes that could peer further into the deepest reaches of space, we continued looking — and still we couldn't see it.

Could there be another way to interpret both what we've been looking for and what we've been looking at? A new perspective dawned on me when I saw the movie *Gravity*, with Sandra Bullock and George Clooney. It's the story of two astronauts marooned in orbit outside their disabled spaceship far above the Earth. They, and we, spend a lot of time looking down at the Earth.

The majority of human history has been lived from the singular point of view of being on Earth looking up into the sky, into the Heavens. We've believed that since Heaven is up there, it did not include Earth, that we are separate. But in *Gravity*, we look from Heaven's point of view down at the Earth and discover that Earth does not reside in some separate realm outside of Heaven. There is no division between Heaven and Earth. Earth *is* in Heaven — it's *all* Heaven.

Heaven's been right here in front of us, and inside of us, all along. We've been looking for it in the wrong place. We've had blinders on. It's never been anywhere but here, now. Earth is already in Heaven. And if Earth is already in Heaven, then Heaven on Earth exists. Heaven on Earth is This-Here-Now.

We've moved from Heaven on Earth This-Here-*Not* to Heaven on Earth This-Here-*Now*. We've arrived. We *are* back in the Garden.

"Heaven on Earth is...

perceiving the Divine perfection in all that is."

Daniel Kinderlehrer, MD
Physician
USA

"Earth's crammed with heaven...."

Elizabeth Barrett Browning

The thin, translucent veil preventing us from experiencing Heaven on Earth This-Here-Now has been lifted.

It really didn't take effort — just letting go of a mis-belief, a mis-perception, surrendering into what already is.

For example, one morning I was out walking when I suddenly stopped and became aware of everything: the light, the trees, the sound of the wind blowing and the grass rustling, the clouds in the sky, the smells, and the peace of it all. I was fully present, fully in the here and now, fully in Heaven on Earth. What an amazing experience!

That expansive experience is available to all of us in every moment. So let's do that now.

> Stop everything you're doing right now.
>
> Disconnect from your cell phone, computer, TV, and any other distractions.
>
> Notice your body. Any aches, pains? Scan your entire body looking for any tension, then breathe into it and let it go.
>
> Now, notice your thoughts: any concerns, fears, desires, guilt, anxiety, worries, any resentments…just notice whatever thoughts are there… busyness, not enough-ness, too much-ness. Let whatever thoughts that arise be there.
>
> Then, let all your thoughts go. Take four, deep, slow breaths (1…2…3…4)… stop all the mental chatter…stop thinking…let your mind become quiet, at peace.
>
> Once you've achieved that peace, that stillness, observe what's going on around you, what's present: the sounds…the smells…the light…the softness…the sweetness.
>
> Be aware of being aware. Notice that you're observing yourself observing, experiencing yourself experiencing.
>
> Now, allow Heaven on Earth to enter, allow its presence, its fullness to flow in — allow Heaven on Earth This-Here-Now.
>
> Notice what's present…spaciousness, deepening quiet, stillness, peace… This-Here-Now…grace, sweetness…Heaven on Earth This-Here-Now… allowing This-Here-Now…experiencing more Heaven on Earth This-Here-Now…the light of Soul, the emanations of the Divine…Heaven on Earth This-Here-Now…You, This-Here-Now…We, This-Here-Now… Humanity, This-Here-Now…love overflowing, Heaven on Earth This-Here-Now…the laughter of recognition…This-Here-Now…Heaven on Earth This-Here-Now…falling deeper into Heaven on Earth, ever-revealing…This-Here-Now…This-Here-Now…This-Here-Now…

This-Here-Now…

This-Here-Now…

This-Here-Now…

This-Here-Now…

This-Here-Now…

This-Here-Now…

This-Here-Now...

This-Here-Now...

This-Here-Now...

"Heaven on Earth is...

the responsibility of putting form to vision."

Lori Hanau
Corporate Muse
USA

"Having tasted the sweetness of a heaven,
we cannot help but offer it to others."

Rebecca Skeele

Chapter 16

The Heaven Maker Gateways: Your Call to Action

We've looked at Heaven on Earth through the Gateways of Inner, Outer, Relationships, and This-Here-Now. We've explored each one in depth. The creativity each person can express in each Gateway is as endless and varied as the citizens of this planet. The unique contributions you make to help co-create Heaven on Earth are up to you. What you do to make it happen is your choice. It is you responding to your Divine essence's call.

Each of us doing our part, giving our gifts knowing that others around the world are doing the same, gives us all greater power, greater hope, and greater energy to keep going. Collectively, we're growing, expanding, and accelerating the momentum.

The Gateways are yours.

They are vehicles through which you make

your Heaven Making ability real.

On the next two pages, please put a check mark in the boxes for the specific Gateways that resonate with you, the ones you will contribute your energy, talents, and skills to.

The Heaven on Earth Gateways

☐ **Your Inner World (Chapter 9)**
  - ☐ Working on Yourself
  - ☐ Living Your Personal Values
  - ☐ Discovering and Living Your Life's Purpose and Vision
  - ☐ Expressing Your Essence Word
  - ☐ Expressing Your Artistry
  - ☐ Discovering and Giving Your Gift
  - ☐ Enlivening Affirmations
  - ☐ Experiencing The Divine

☐ **Relationships – Co-Creating Heaven on Earth (Chapter 10)**
  - ☐ With Yourself
  - ☐ With Others
  - ☐ With God/The Divine

☐ **Living Your Global Values (Chapter 11)**

☐ **Your Outer World (Chapters 12–14)**
  - ☐ **Ending the World's Major Sufferings (Chapter 12)**
    - ☐ Hunger and Malnutrition
    - ☐ Disease
    - ☐ Lack of Adequate Shelter
    - ☐ War, Genocide, Refugees, & Weapons Proliferation
    - ☐ Illiteracy
    - ☐ Poverty, No Access to Opportunity
    - ☐ Lack of Clean Water and Sanitation
    - ☐ Environmental Pollution and Degradation
    - ☐ Lack of Freedom: Tyranny, Repression
    - ☐ Lack of Meaning and Purpose

☐ **Ending the World's Major Sufferings** *(cont'd)*
  - ☐ Crime, Violence, and Terrorism
  - ☐ Prejudice, Hatred, and Discrimination
  - ☐ Torture, Slavery, Human Rights Abuse, Child Labor, Violence Against Women/Children
  - ☐ Sexual Abuse
  - ☐ Bad Governance, Corruption, and Poor Management
  - ☐ Overpopulation
  - ☐ Animal Abuse and Species Extinction
  - ☐ Spiritual Malnourishment

☐ **Our Institutions Taking Their Rightful Place in Co-Creating Heaven on Earth (Chapter 13)**
  - ☐ Education
  - ☐ Culture: Arts, Media, Sports
  - ☐ Health Care & Medicine
  - ☐ Commerce: Business, Industry, Labor
  - ☐ Resources: Agriculture, Fisheries, Forestry, Mining
  - ☐ Law
  - ☐ Government
  - ☐ Religion
  - ☐ Science & Technology
  - ☐ Civic Organizations
  - ☐ International Intergovernmental Organizations
  - ☐ The Military

☐ **Co-Creating Heaven on Earth Nation(s) (Chapter 14)**
  - ☐ Uniting a Nation to Resolve an Issue
  - ☐ Uniting a Nation to Co-Create Heaven on Earth for that Nation
  - ☐ Uniting Nations to Resolve an Issue
  - ☐ Uniting All Nations to Co-Create Heaven on Earth

☐ **Heaven on Earth This-Here-Now (Chapter 15)**

"Heaven on Earth is...

the grand slam home run we've all been waiting for."

Helice "Sparky" Bridges
The First Lady of Acknowledgment
USA

"The dream drives the action."

Thomas Berry

Now that you've chosen your Gateways, the next step is making your contribution(s) real. Do your part by taking your first step(s) in the next 24 hours. Initiate, add to, and increase the Heaven on Earth results in the world. Get into action — Heaven on Earth needs the unique contribution that is you!

In the rest of this chapter we'll focus on five components essential to integrating your actions into the unfolding new story:

- Your Heaven Maker Leadership Role
- Enhancing the Experience of Heaven on Earth (Being)
- Measuring Our Progress (Becoming)
- It's Here, It's Working, & It's Expanding
- Celebrating Our Accomplishments

Your Heaven Maker Leadership Role

Once you've chosen your Gateways and begun acting on them, you're now a Heaven Maker. Your actions also inspire and support others. You unlock and unleash the Heaven Maker in them. That's how the momentum grows, expands, and accelerates.

As you embark on your Heaven Maker leadership role, you'll notice that:

1. You're clear on what Heaven on Earth is for you and what your Gateways are.

2. You're committed to them. You've given your word that you will fulfill your contributions to Co-creating Heaven on Earth.

3. You're responsible for more and more Heaven on Earth showing up. Responsibility isn't a burden — you're naturally being responsible, it requires no effort, it's joyful.

4. You're a living example of what a Heaven Maker is. You lead from your being, your actions, and your results.

5. You easily enroll others in discovering and expressing what Heaven on Earth is for them. You ask them the 3 Heaven on Earth questions. Then you ask how you can support them in making their contributions real in the world.

6. You look for and find leverage points, those actions or projects where minimum input produces maximum output. You discover what magnifies and amplifies your efforts.

7. You find, and you also attract, others who share a commitment to the same Gateway in order to combine and multiply your results and impact.

8. Your efforts go viral.

You show the world your Heaven Maker leadership. You're no longer waiting for others to do it, or complaining about others not doing it. You've given up finding reasons to explain why it's hell on Earth.

You've stepped up to the plate. You've taken your rightful role in co-creating the new story of what it means to be a Human and what it means to be Humanity. You are a Heaven Maker!

Enhancing the Experience of Heaven on Earth (Being)

When you decide to buy a new car, a blue one, for example, have you ever noticed how you suddenly start seeing blue cars everywhere? Let's use the same effect for Heaven on Earth. Start noticing how Heaven on Earth is showing up, is being expressed. Discover how it impacts your decision making, interactions with others, and your perception of life. Experience how it can be further enhanced by:

- Being aware that Heaven on Earth is occurring This-Here-Now.

- Living Heaven on Earth.

- Observing others creating and experiencing Heaven on Earth.

- Being aware of how Heaven on Earth is globally going viral.

Heaven on Earth exists — it's here now. It's the awareness of your Heaven on Earth state of consciousness in every moment. By you gently affirming, "Heaven on Earth is here now," it shows up in your ongoing intention, awareness, and experiences.

Measuring Our Progress (Becoming)

Our Heaven on Earth results need to be clearly measurable, authoritative, and experientially telling us that "Heaven on Earth *is* showing up." The measurements must have meaning for both our minds and hearts. The format and data need to demonstrate that there is clear progress, that Heaven on Earth is putting down deep roots, is growing, and is flourishing.

We need a continuous stream of evidence showing that Humanity is on the right track, and that a Heaven on Earth wave of momentum is present and accelerating. We palpably see, feel, and hear that things are getting better. We clearly notice where and how Heaven on Earth is showing up and expanding for you, others, and the world.

Here are three concrete examples of the format (*what* by *when*) that measure our progress:

1. In order to measure progress toward the sustainable end of hunger, The Hunger Project uses a specific measurable objective called the Infant Mortality Rate (IMR). The IMR is the number of deaths of children under one year of age per 1,000 live births.

It lets people know where hunger persists, how severe it is, and where it is ending. When a country has an IMR level of 50 or below, it means that hunger as a chronic, persistent, society-wide problem has ended. For example, India between 1946 and 1951 had an IMR of 134[1]. In 2000 it was 66.4[2], and in 2016 it had dropped to 40.50 (est.)[3]. In 1960 Bangladesh's IMR stood at 176.3[4]. In 2000 it had dropped to 64.4[5], and in 2016 it was 32.90 (est.)[6].

2. Free the Slaves (FTS) is an organization whose mission is "Liberating slaves and changing the conditions that allow slavery to persist." *Free the Slaves eUpdate* is their quarterly progress report. It tracks key statistics that indicate how effectively their programs are liberating victims, educating the vulnerable, and bringing perpetrators to justice. In 2015 they recorded these results from their frontline work:

   - 1,106 people freed from slavery

   - 4,051 slaves or survivors receiving support from FTS or our partner organizations

   - 327,135 people reached through awareness raising and rights education about how to protect their families from traffickers

   - 1,709 villages and neighborhoods supported to protect their communities from slavery

   - 1,405 government officials trained on how to more effectively stop slavery

   - 74 traffickers and slaveholders arrested[7]

3. In 2015 the 193-member UN General Assembly adopted the 2030 Agenda for Sustainable Development, along with a set of bold, new Global Goals.

   The framework, "Transforming our world: the 2030 Agenda for Sustainable Development," is composed of 17 goals, 169 targets, and 230 indicators to wipe out poverty, fight inequality, and tackle climate change over the next 15 years.

   UN Secretary-General Ban Ki-moon said, "The 2030 Agenda compels us to look beyond national boundaries and short-term interests and act in solidarity for the long-term. We can no longer afford to think and work in silos. Institutions will have to become fit for a grand new purpose.

   "We must engage all actors.... We must include parliaments and local governments, and work with cities and rural areas. We must rally businesses and entrepreneurs. We must involve civil society in defining and implementing policies — and give it the space to hold us to account. We must listen to scientists and academia. We will need to embrace a data revolution. Most important, we must set to work — now.

---

1   tinyurl.com/India134
2   tinyurl.com/India66-4
3   tinyurl.com/India40-50
4 & 5   tinyurl.com/IMR1960-2000, tinyurl.com/IMR1960-2000
6   tinyurl.com/Bangladesh32-90
7   tinyurl.com/FTS2015

"Seventy years ago, the United Nations rose from the ashes of war. Governments agreed on a visionary Charter dedicated to 'We the Peoples.' The Agenda you are adopting today advances the goals of the Charter. It embodies the aspirations of people everywhere for lives of peace, security, and dignity on a healthy planet," said Mr. Ban.

General Assembly President, Mogens Lykketoft added, "We recognize the need to reduce inequalities and to protect our common home by changing unsustainable patterns of consumption and production. And, we identify the overwhelming need to address the politics of division, corruption, and irresponsibility that fuel conflict and hold back development."

The 2030 Sustainable Global Goals are:

1. No Poverty
2. No Hunger
3. Good Health
4. Quality Education
5. Gender Equality
6. Clean Water and Sanitation
7. Renewable Energy
8. Good Jobs and Economic Growth
9. Innovation and Infrastructure
10. Reduced Inequalities
11. Sustainable Cities and Communities
12. Responsible Consumption
13. Climate Action
14. Life Below Water
15. Life on Land
16. Peace and Justice
17. Partnerships for the Goals

Each of these 17 Goals is broken down into measurable targets. Here are four examples:

Goal 1. End poverty in all its forms everywhere

1.1 By 2030, eradicate extreme poverty for all people everywhere, currently measured as people living on less than $1.25 a day.

Goal 3. Ensure healthy lives and promote well-being for all at all ages

3.1 By 2030, reduce the global maternal mortality ratio to less than 70 per 100,000 live births.

Goal 8. Promote sustained, inclusive and sustainable economic growth, full and productive employment and decent work for all

8.1 Sustain per capita economic growth in accordance with national circumstances and, in particular, at least 7 percent gross domestic product growth per annum in the least developed countries.

Goal 10. Reduce inequality within and among countries

10.1 By 2030, progressively achieve and sustain income growth of the bottom 40 per cent of the population at a rate higher than the national average.

You can get the full report here: tinyurl.com/2030SustainableGlobalGoals. It's inspiring reading, a powerful example of a blueprint, as well as a gauge for Heaven on Earth.

The three measurable examples I've detailed show the format (*what* by *when*) for specifying goals that give us the certainty that progress is being made.

In order to measure your own Heaven Making progress, start by creating your own Heaven on Earth Goal(s) from the boxes you checked on the Gateways page earlier in this chapter. Then break the Goal down into specific measurable objectives with a timeline. This will support you in focusing your energies, discovering and overcoming any obstacles, and observing the progress you're making. It will also help focus your intention and attention on accomplishing your Goal(s) and give others an easy path into supporting you in your goals. It's easier for people to support you when they know what your specific chosen result is.

Keep looking for signs of progress. These signs can be big or they can be small: two warring countries sign a peace accord…three people smiled at you today…a disease is eradicated…a neighbor who has been unfriendly to you for years suddenly speaks to you.

It's important to know that we're succeeding, that Humanity's new story is positively unfolding. By measuring our progress we move from *thinking* we're succeeding to clearly and definitively *knowing* we are succeeding.

"Heaven on Earth is…

Humanity moving into 'The Dream Comes True Stage.'"

Frances Tolton
Consultant
Ireland

"…enlarging people's choices…
To lead a long and healthy life…
To acquire knowledge…
To have access to the resources needed for a decent standard of living…
While preserving it for future generations…
Ensuring human security…
And achieving equality for all women and men."

United Nation's *Human Development Report 2000*

It's Here, It's Working & It's Expanding!

Co-creating Heaven on Earth is Humanity's new story. It has begun and it's building momentum. People are engaging, they're taking it on, they're making it happen, as Heaven Makers and in Heaven Making projects. Some of this is happening by people's direct actions, and some through grace, by occurrences that are unplanned and appear spontaneously.

The examples in this book, and a growing number of others all around the world (e.g., see the interviews on my YouTube video channel: tinyurl.com/HonEInterviews), are evidence of an ever-increasing number of people Co-creating Heaven on Earth. They are creating a growing wave of "workability" — of ideas, innovation and effective, sustainable solutions. And the more people do this, the more Humanity experiences an expansion of the amount of what is working in the world.

And so it grows and builds: more people committed to Co-creating Heaven on Earth, to knowing that it is both their work and the work of Humanity, all helping to build Humanity's new story, the next chapter in our evolution.

Here are two inspiring examples:

The Shift Network

Stephen Dinan is the founder and CEO of The Shift Network, a company that provides transformative virtual and live events. Additionally, they offer programs, media, and virtual courses globally. His was the first major company to incorporate Heaven on Earth into its mission statement:

> "We aim to create a sustainable, peaceful, healthy and prosperous world — what we sometimes call heaven on earth for shorthand.

> "We hold a vision where, not only are everyone's basic needs met while living in peace, but the very best in all of us is expressed and humanity's full creative potential is set free.

> "This is a world in which we know we are one sacred family and are united in our divinity, while celebrating our diversity."

Stephen is deeply committed to Heaven on Earth and has said so repeatedly:

> "Why heaven on earth? Because it's a dream that has been long held in our collective imagination: a time of peace, sustainability, health, and prosperity. It's a natural result of our aspirations for a better life. It's a natural extension of our yearnings to not leave behind a forsaken and denuded planet, but a radiant gem for our children and grandchildren and their grandchildren beyond them. It unites our aspirations to make this world the place of our dreams."

> "I felt awed by the many people who have already been drawn to the vision that we CAN co-create heaven on earth. In our lifetimes. Person by person. Community by community. It's time for the harvest of millions of years of evolution and the creation of a truly beautiful world

in which extreme poverty is vanquished, war becomes a thing of the past, and we remember that we are one human family."

"...we are the people who are now tasked with creating real healing in the world. We are the people who are tasked with turning around the wars and hatred and deprivation. We are the ones who have to figure out how to design and enact heaven on earth (with guidance and empowerment from above, naturally)." (www.TheShiftNetwork.com)

True Purpose Institute

"A home for change agents and messengers called to create heaven on earth."

"Our transformational workshops and powerful training and certification programs equip people to be the change they are meant to create and to spread their personal transformation farther and faster than they ever dreamed possible. Our goal is to help you earn a living as a powerful messenger or change agent: your impact will be much greater if you are making money from living your purpose!

"We are co-creating Heaven on Earth — the creation of a global community which honors the wisdom from our past and the potential of our future, a world in which we live in a state of love, grace and inspiration. Heaven on Earth honors our spiritual connection and through it the realization of our greatest potential — both individually and collectively. We envision a new paradigm world where we live as part of a purposeful, rich and thriving family of humanity.

"We have a deep knowing that the gifts that we individually and collectively bring can and do make a real difference in the world, and that ultimately by truly living our journeys from the heart we will co-create Heaven on Earth." (www.TruePurposeInstitute.com)

Celebrating Our Accomplishments

As Heaven on Earth enters more fully into public conversation globally, and as we begin to see Heaven on Earth accomplishments building in number and impact, remember to...

Celebrate Heaven on Earth becoming a living, expanding rcality!

"Heaven on Earth is...

a choice."

Erick Larson
Property Developer
USA

"The most powerful thing that any individual or organization can do
is to build a visible model of the world they want."

Author Unknown

Chapter 17

Living Our New Story

Huston Smith, the great theologian and academic known for his groundbreaking work on comparative religions, uses a wonderful image for Humanity. He thinks of the physical universe as a horizontal line representing the almost 14 billion light years that is the known universe, and he says, "The horizontal line stands for the physical universe — the material world that science describes. Each of us lives in this material world…." Since light travels at 186,000 miles a second, this is a very long line.

He then sees the vertical line as representing our common Humanity — where we've been, our triumphs, our failures, our awakenings, our continual questing and our evolvement toward wholeness, enlightenment, and the Divine. Huston considers the vertical line longer than the horizontal. The "…vertical line runs directly through the center of each of us, and connects us directly to God — to the divine itself. …Each of us lives in this material world, but at the same time, we're also vertical creatures — spiritual beings. …[the intersection of the two lines is the] meeting place between the spiritual and the material, the worldly and the divine, is actually what each of us actually *is*."

When I heard this for the first time, I was catapulted out of worrying about the minutiae of daily life and into an intense realization of the magnificence of the incredible human journey we're all taking together.

Co-creating Heaven on Earth is the next phase in our human evolution and its time has come. It's the new story of what it means to be a human and what it means to be Humanity — the individual and the collective, the private and the public. It's Humanity's new story, a story designed to inspire and ennoble us. It's the outward expression of our collective heart's deep desire — our mission and, if we choose, our pledge.

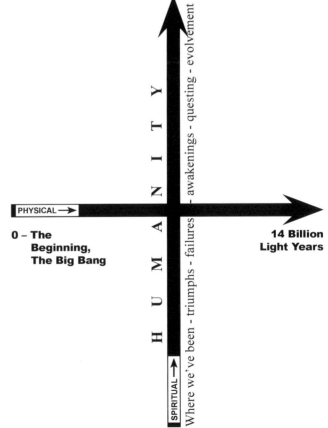

"Heaven on Earth is...

a simple thing."

Melanie Coleman
Manager, Mentoring Services
Canada

"Heaven on Earth is...

both the purpose and the goal of human evolution."

Rev. Joel Grossman
Interfaith Minister
USA

The Heaven on Earth Pledge

We, the People of the Earth,
say with authority, that we are committed
to having the world work.

We, the People of the Earth,
commit to creating sustainable global peace.

We, the People of the Earth,
commit to ensuring our entire family is fed,
is literate, and has access to opportunities for
self-reliance, contribution, and service.

We, the People of the Earth,
commit to supporting and nurturing the
physical, mental, emotional, spiritual, and creative
well-being of all.

We, the People of the Earth,
commit to making our planetary home safe, healthy,
empowering, and enlivening for everyone.

We, the People of the Earth,
commit to being responsible and accountable
to each other and for each other.

We, the People of the Earth,
commit to honoring and valuing our planet's living
biosphere and all life.

We, the People of the Earth,
with the grace of God,
are committed to having Heaven on Earth.

"Heaven on Earth is...

our natural obligation."

Emilia Gottschamer
Organic Macadamia Nut Farmer
Guatemala

"Heaven on Earth is...

*choosing to create it, is choosing to be a partner with the Divine
in the creation of Paradise on Earth."*

Jamie Weinstein
Rabbi & Psychotherapist
USA

What we are clearly and consciously doing is changing our collective story from "This is not Heaven on Earth and we will never have it" to a globally connecting story: "This is Heaven on Earth and we are expanding it."

The work now is to take this new story out into the world. It is talking to people about being part of making Heaven on Earth real. It is producing those tangible results that demonstrate Heaven on Earth is actually happening.

We already have the technological capacity to support us in getting the job done. By adding your unique contribution, we increase the rate at which Heaven on Earth goes viral globally. It's as easy as setting your intention and beginning. You carry the Project Heaven on Earth membership card in your heart, you carry the belonging in your soul, you carry the intention in your actions.

"We are talking of nothing less than reinventing ourselves,
reframing our perceptions, reshaping our beliefs and behavior,
composting our knowledge, restructuring our institutions and recycling our societies.
This is not an impossibly tall order.
Rather, it is routine in the repertoire of human behavior.
Indeed, such systemic social change is the stuff of all human history."
Hazel Henderson

"When you are inspired by some great purpose,
some extraordinary project,
all your thoughts break their bonds;
your mind transcends limitations,
your consciousness expands in every direction,
and you find yourself in a new,
great and wonderful world.
Dormant forces, faculties and talents become alive,
and you discover yourself to be a greater person by far
than you ever dreamed yourself to be."
Patanjali

"Heaven on Earth is...

humankind's natural destiny."

John E. Wade II
Author, Television Producer,
Investor, Philanthropist &
Retired Certified Public Accountant
USA

"Heaven on Earth is...

Humanity's New Enacted Story."

Martin Rutte

The way to begin our new story is to begin.
It's that simple, that easy.

Project Heaven on Earth allows the deep, resonant, heartfelt part of ourselves to come forth and express itself. It emerges as our Soul's expression through our living, working, and being together. It makes real our desire, our longing for our world. As Frances Hodgson Burnett said, "At first people refuse to believe that a strange new thing can be done, and then they begin to hope it can be done, then they see it can be done — then it is done…and all the world wonders why it was not done centuries ago."

Project Heaven on Earth is a global initiative whose time has come.

Can it really be that simple, that easy? Yes.

Michael Madigan is a turquoise miner in Nevada. When I spoke to him about Heaven on Earth, he looked at me and simply said, "The time has come."

We are now free to explore the adventure and the wonder of Heavening on Earth!

"Heaven on Earth is...

*the understanding by every individual
that they can pull a lever large enough to affect the world."*

Catherine Spear
Fundraising Consultant
USA

"The secret of living is to find…
the pivot of a concept on which you can make your stand."

Luigi Pirandello

Now, let's begin!

We'd love to hear from you.
Send us your projects and stories.

Tell us what you're doing to create Heaven on Earth.

Share your Heaven on Earth projects.

It doesn't matter how big or how small, every action, every result adds to the new story of Heaven on Earth.

It adds reality, it gives proof, it shows the evidence.

It gives foundation, structure, example.

Letting us know what you're doing inspires others to jump in, to get into making Heaven on Earth a real, lived, tangible reality.

Your unique contribution to Heaven on Earth does make a difference.

Let us know.

To share your story/project and learn what others all around the world are doing, visit: www.ProjectHeavenOnEarth.com/stories

There are many people from around the world who have chosen
to become Heaven Makers.

You, your family, friends, and colleagues can also join —
and each additional person accelerates the momentum for all of us.

Sign up for my FREE, 7-day e-mail course:

"One Week to Simply Begin Creating Heaven on Earth!"

Sign up at: www.ProjectHeavenOnEarth.com

When you sign up, you'll also receive two bonuses:

1) Access to the "We Heaven Makers" community.

Read about the Heaven on Earth experiences of others,
check out inspiring Heaven on Earth quotes,
and learn about other Heaven on Earth projects.

2) Our weekly blog/video interview.

Each week, you'll receive an inspiring blog that will support you
in expanding the experience and the actions of Heaven on Earth.
Getting the blog deepens your experience and appreciation of
Heaven on Earth as you see how it is showing up,
and as you experience how its momentum is growing, daily, in the world.

Sign up at: www.ProjectHeavenOnEarth.com

Acknowledgments

You have to do it by yourself,
and you can't do it alone.

A book is a solo endeavor and it is not. This book would not have been brought to life without the love and support of many people.

Maida Rogerson, my beloved, my wife, my support, my strength, my comfort, my love, my partner, my playmate, my foundation. I adore you my Maidee.

David Christel, my writing coach and editor. Thank you for supporting my deep Soul's speaking. You made this book happen. Simply put, "No David, No Book, No Kidding!" Thank you, D-Man.
John Dealey, supporter extraordinaire. You embody "being of service."

My Mother, Lily (Fiygeh Rivka Liah). You birthed me. You deeply knew who I am. You are infinite, immense, vast love.
My Father, Harry (Herschel Ben Tzvi). You gave me the freedom to discover myself. You taught me connection, networking, the deep love of religion, and the connection to the Divine.
Fredelle, my sister. An unbreakable, clear bond of love and joy and life.
Adam, my nephew. "Peek," you're the first. Also to my sweet Paola. And welcome to the world, Kiara and Nalu.
Mark, my nephew: Always there with your solid support for my completing this book and for me. Also to my sweet Esha.
Jonah, my nephew: My mirror. Also to my sweet Helen.

Richard Porter, there for me from the very early days, who said, "It's not The Heaven on Earth Project, it's Project Heaven on Earth."
Meg Ellis and Robert Ellis for your generosity of spirit and home. The many, many times you let me stay with you while I worked with David and never once asked for anything in return. You offered me a home away from home and I will never forget that. I love and thank you.
Bob Branscom, my great and wonderful teacher. You saw who I was, you saw my Soul. You brought my essence out into the world. Thank you, Bobbie, I will always love you, and, yes, I do know you will always be in my heart.
Raymond Aaron, my "brother," who, when the book had been on the shelf, unfinished for several years, gave me the swift kick in the rear I needed to complete it.

Tim Clauss, my deep soul brother. Thank you for being there solidly for me all these years.

Barbara Curl, my "Always Twenty Years Ahead of Me" teacher.

Jack Canfield: Thank you for bringing me in to speak at your workshop sight unseen, giving me *Chicken Soup for the Soul at Work*, my TLC soul family, and for being you.

Gordon Allan for being my brother and philosophical wrestler.

Dr. Nicholas Beecroft who, when I was stuck not writing, asked me if I could do just 5 minutes a day…just 5 minutes. I said "Yes," and was back writing again. I would send him an e-mail every night saying how much I'd written that day. Sometimes it was only 5 minutes, sometimes it was more than 2 hours, and sometimes it was nothing. Without judging, he just "got" the communication, and that got me to…go back to writing.

Stephanie Clarke for her "pushiness" in making me set specific goals and keeping my word about them. My ego didn't like it, but my Soul loved it. What a coach you truly are!

Faye Christian (my Fay-zee) for your love, your play, and your being.

Lin Reams (my Lin-ee) for your being and your love.

Mark McKergow of The Centre for Solutions Focus at Work for giving me the 3rd question, "What small, simple, easy, concrete steps will you take in the next 24 hours to make Heaven on Earth real?" Brilliant!

Rabbis: Berel Levertov and Zalman Schachter-Shalomi.

Everyone Who Read, Commented On, and Contributed to the Various Drafts of the Book

Gordon Allan, Raymond Aaron, Pete Bissonette, Karen Bohnhoff, Charles Bower, Geoffrey Caine, Faye Christian, Tim Clauss, Melanie Coleman, Barbara Curl, André Delbecq, Kathy & Harvey Farrar, Tom Feldman, Bob Forman, Bill Gregoricus, David Hawkins, Peggy Holman, Carol Hegedus, Dan Kinderlehrer, Carol Kline, Alan Lurie, Copthorne Macdonald, Susan Millspaugh, Monika Mitchell, Laurie Norris, Don Pachuta, Richard Porter, John Renesch, Max Ritts, Alan Rogerson, Maida Rogerson, Jack Rosenblum, Jasmine Sampson, David Sherman, Mark Silver, Mark Smith, Kate Thompson, John E. Wade II, and John Whalen.

My Wise Teachers & Mentors

Father Tony Firetto, C.R.; Werner Erhard and The est Training.

Bishop Henry Hill: mentor, teacher, wise counselor, jokester, surgical knife wielder. Your Grace. You also taught me the power of "Be complete with your own Religion."

The ManKind Project, Houston.

The Hoffman Quadrinity Process (Bob Hoffman) and my fellow participants who showed me that Heaven here on Earth is possible. Peter & Maureen Kolassa for bringing the Hoffman Process to Canada.

My Transformational Leadership Council (TLC) Soul Family

Especially Shelly & Morty Lefkoe and everyone who showed up at their home for "The New Rutte Map" session: Stewart & Joanie Emery, Stephen & Alice Josephs, Raz & Liz Ingrasci, Matt Weinstein & Geneen Roth, John & Bonnie Gray, Marci Shimoff, Sydney Cresci, Dianne Morrison.

Also to: Deirdre Hade attuned to the vastness of All, counselor Jedda Mali, Ray Blanchard for being the stand for my completing this book, Fred Johnson, Barnet Bain,

Shannon Mel (sh!), Neal Rogin, Lynne Twist, Yakov Smirnoff, Stephen M.R. Covey, Guy Stickney, Tyson Young (who's he?), and the one and only m-J, Justin Criner.

Soulmates

Laurie Norris (Soul whisperer par excellence, AL), James Berry (Jimmy, I miss you), G.P. Walsh (pure consciousness), Elisabeth Ziegler-Duregger (because "It's simple" to make Austria a Heaven on Earth Nation), Sanja Plavljanic-Sirola (Croatia IS a Heaven on Earth Nation…and for "pushing" me to get the book done!), Ava Grace who at age 3 adopted me to be her Grampy, Jeffrey Van Dyk, Peggy Holman (wisdom personified), Julie Claire (surgical clarity in service), Karen Frank (Buddha), Douglas Blair (strength), Josie Gibb, Kerri Lowe (social media maestro), and Tanya Taylor Rubenstein (for bringing out the soul of my story).

The Heaven on Earth Leadership Team

Jennifer Joe, Melanie Coleman, John E. Wade II, Mark Smith, Ross Harvey, Laurie & Jacob Teitelbaum, Tim Kelley for your pioneering leadership, and special mention to Stephen Dinan and the entire staff at The Shift Network.

For Your Direct Help with this Book

Jeff Braucher, copy editor of clarity and precision; Brother Wayne Teasdale for informing me that institutions could also enlighten; Kent Stetson for opening up Heaven on Earth for Nations; Fethi Benhalim for the Sufi interpretation of the ego dying to enter Paradise; Michael Owens for your outstanding research on what the Faith Traditions say, and for your enthusiasm; Rachel Samson for your beauty, and your quotes research; Laurie Timmerman for your research on the world's sufferings; RAI Services Co. for your years of continuing support; Hilary Ramp for your detailed and professional research; Natalie Alexia for your story, "How a Simple Photo Can Change the World"; the Santa Fe, NM, Public Library (Main Branch) for being such a great source of quotation books; www.WorldAtlas.com: Thank you for your gracious kindness and permission to use your map in Chapter 14.

"Heaven on Earth is…" Quotes

Everyone who contributed their definition of Heaven on Earth, whether I've used it or not.

The Solid Friends Team

Diane Fillmore, for teaching me that writing is "Declaration & Discovery"; Robert Lewis; Val & Wally Ford; Avtar Hari Singh Khalsa; Silvana Pagani, gentle, focused ninja destroying the mis-belief of separation from God; Mark Silver; Vikram Budhraja; Michael Stephens; Roberto De Oliveira Braga; Sonia Café, my sister and Minister Responsible for Everything that Doesn't Work; Janice Fiovaranti for her work on the negative beliefs people hold about organizations; Richard James, with me from the beginning and thank you for the Mormon quotes; Joan & Leith Thompson; Marcia & Ken Berry; Christine Barnes; and Patty Aubrey.

The Early Heaven on Earth Supporters

Johanna Lund Montgomery for being the first person to actually jump in her seat when I said, "Heaven on Earth"; Alan Meyer for being the first media person to interview me about Heaven on Earth, for an hour and a half, on radio station CFRB in Toronto; Jennifer Joe for doing the first Project Heaven on Earth website; The Awakened World Conference for hosting my first ever public speech about Heaven on Earth; Mark Victor Hansen for getting it the first time I told him years ago, and for supporting me; Copthorne Macdonald, my writing mentor; and Walter Weinz for your research.

For Giving Me More Heaven on Earth Experiences

Heliconia flowers; Movies: *Amadeus* and *Pina*; Opera: Luciano Pavarotti, Montseratt Caballé, Jussi Björling, Cecilia Bartoli; Comedy: Robin Williams, Abbott & Costello ("Who's on First?"), Bob & Ray ("Slow Talkers of America"), Tim Conway ("The Dentist Sketch").

I also want to deeply thank my country of birth and growth, Canada, and my second home, the United States of America.

I know there are countless other people whom I have not mentioned.
If I have not acknowledged you, please forgive me and know that I am grateful.

Appendix 1

Some Thoughts & Recommendations

a) **Some Things to Consider**

b) **Some Concerns and Things to Watch For**

c) **The Five Most Common Roadblocks and What You Can Do about Them**

d) **Project Heaven on Earth Support Groups**

e) **Project Heaven on Earth Book Contemplation**

a) Some Things to Consider

- The idea of actually co-creating Heaven on Earth is a bold, new idea.

- As Humanity, we are very young at forming a collective vision and making it happen.

- Don't worry if it all doesn't happen today. A former boss of mine, John Thompson, used to ask, "Is it directionally correct?" Are we moving in the right direction? Is it progressing, are we making headway?

- You do have a part to play in creating Heaven on Earth. It is a very important part. Only you can do it.

- Engage with this only if it deeply speaks to you, to your heart, to your Soul, to your intellect. If it doesn't, don't. You don't *have* to do this.

- You may not experience the joy of seeing the fruits of all your labors. Practice patience. Richard Hennessy said, "We must let time penetrate what the present cannot."

- We are focusing our attention on having positive results rather than defending our own particular solution. It's not about being right, it's about getting the job done.

- The impossible does occur, miracles do happen. Terry Molner says, "Evolution has not ended."

- When one person, anywhere in the world, contributes to creating Heaven on Earth, we all get the result.

b) Some Concerns and Things to Watch For

It's important to talk about some potential downsides of Project Heaven on Earth. There are things we need to be concerned about and be careful of:

- **The intentions of the Project could be subverted.**
  I was in an airport where I saw an ad on the wall for a brand of whiskey. The headline said, "Heaven on Earth."

  Watch for those who may take the idea and use it for material greed or perverse reasons. Watch for people using it in a way that debases it.

  These kinds of actions will happen as part of taking this idea into broader public discourse. Simply be aware that it will happen, don't be discouraged, and keep your eye focused on the goal and on your contribution.

- **The Project could become another fad that fades over time.**
  People are very excited when a new idea hits, thinking that it will change the world overnight, or at least by the weekend. Project Heaven on Earth could become a fad. What is more important, though, is: the way the majority of people take ownership of and sustain the Project *over the long run*; that the Project be aligned with the evolution of Humanity; and that the idea of creating Heaven on Earth — organically and naturally — becomes part of the collective expression of Humanity.

- **Gurus might appear to whom we give our power.**
  This Project is not about me. It's about all of us. It's about our home planet. Beware of people who take this on with the mantle of guru. This Project is about, for, and of *all* of us, not one of us. Heaven is God-given and everyone has the right to it. No one person can lay claim to it and use it solely for their own gain.

- **This could turn rigidly dogmatic.**
  Be wary of people who are dogmatic about Project Heaven on Earth being the *only* way to make the world work.

  The concern is that one vision, one person, or one way becomes *the* way Heaven on Earth should be expressed. What we don't want is one vision, person or way to lead, but for the collective to lead — the combination of each of us playing our full, gifted, and noble role *together*. We're looking to have our collective point of view be in the service of what produces increased workability and goodness.

Do you have any concerns?

_____

_____

_____

_____

c) The Five Most Common Roadblocks and What You Can Do about Them

In speaking to people around the world about making Heaven on Earth real, I have heard many of them express thoughts and concerns about roadblocks. What I also hear are their underlying limiting beliefs. In Chapter 4 we looked at several of these. Here are five additional ones that frequently occur, any one of which might be a roadblock for you or people you know. Let's address each one so we can learn how to move beyond it.

1. "It's too idealistic. It's naïve."

Idealistic implies that an idea is too far from hard-nosed, current reality. *Naïve* implies that an idea has been formed from a child's perspective of the world.

Put together, we simply won't be taken seriously as an adult. Our vision is so far outside of the listener's experience that the only rational response is for them to dismiss the idea or us.

When Václav Havel, Nelson Mandela, Mother Teresa and Lech Walesa started out, they were living from their commitment to make their dream, their vision, their heart's knowing real. They were considered idealistic and naïve. But today no one says that about them. Why? *Because idealistic and naïve only exist before a result is produced.* After the result is produced, people immediately stop using those terms. No one believed the Wright brothers until their plane actually flew.

The best way to stop comments about naiveté and idealism is to make our vision for our home planet come true, to manifest Heaven on Earth.

2. "I can't make a difference."

Multiplying this belief by the more than seven billion people on Earth gives you a collective story of powerlessness, futility, and resignation.

To transcend this and other self-limiting beliefs, simply add the phrase "and I do make a difference." For example, "I'm not powerful enough *and* I do make a difference." "I'm not rich enough *and* I do make a difference." "I'm not perfect enough *and* I do make a difference." Begin operating out of this new commitment and watch it become a self-fulfilling prophecy.

When you operate from making a difference, we all get the result and the benefit. We also expand the circle of people experiencing making a difference and helping create Heaven on Earth.

3. "Creating Heaven on Earth is so overwhelming."

When people are confronted with an overwhelming, complex, never-before-accomplished objective, they often let their sense of overwhelm *overwhelm* them. When they think about how hard it will be to accomplish the objective, they stop.

But if we truly want the world to work, we can't let this state of mind incapacitate us.

You can either feel overwhelmed and stop, or feel overwhelmed and get on with helping create Heaven on Earth.

Here's what you can do with overwhelm: just let it be there and begin — take one simple, easy, concrete action and start your journey. Before you know it, you'll find you're accomplishing. My invitation to you: Jump in!

When Pat Giershick, a businessperson I know, feels overwhelmed, she looks at the smallest action she can take and then says to herself, "This will be my gift today." That's how she keeps moving forward.

4. "If the world were perfect, there would be nothing left to do. We'd be bored."

Some people say, "We've never had Heaven on Earth. I'm afraid that if we do achieve it, there wouldn't be anything left to do. We'd be bored."

The problem with this argument is that it results in our not engaging with Co-creating Heaven on Earth now. We wouldn't work to end the major sufferings confronting today's world, e.g., hunger, war, disease, homelessness, etc. because we're worried we'd be bored in the future. But that leaves the sufferings in place. How do we know there'd be nothing left to do? It's so far beyond our current reality. Let's end the major sufferings first and then find out what's next. Laurie Teitelbaum says that we'll go from solving problems to creating more and more of what we love to do — the opposite of boring.

5. "What about evil interpretations of Heaven on Earth?"

Not everyone will have a life-affirming interpretation of Heaven on Earth. There are people whose vision of Heaven on Earth is evil manifesting as terrorism, torture, slavery, sexual exploitation and abuse, child labor, crime, ethnic cleansing, totalitarian regimes, etc.

While evil does exist, it persists among a minority. The vast majority of people in the world want peace, security, goodness, and progress. We need to implement policies and programs that reduce the mechanisms and systems fostering and encouraging evil. As for those manifesting evil, they need to be brought to justice and stopped for good.

The overwhelming majority of people in our world have a vision of Heaven on Earth that is respectful, good, kindhearted, giving, and loving. Let's join with these people in making our dreams come true. Let's build a momentum that is positive, good, and unstoppable.

The context of Heaven on Earth includes doubts, concerns and fears, yet it continues moving forward because it appeals to one of our greatest and deepest desires: a world that works. The energy of individuals committed to this common goal will, in the gentlest of ways, overcome the greatest of obstacles.

d) Project Heaven on Earth Support Groups

A Project Heaven on Earth Support Group is a gathering of people, like you, to:

- Deepen your experience of Heaven on Earth.

- Meet with others who want to expand Heaven on Earth into the world.

- Connect with the energy and commitment of others around the world who are also engaged in this process.

- Engage in direct positive actions so you all feel and see the difference your contributions are making.

Here's a way you can set up your group:

1. Gather together a group of people with an interest in deepening and forwarding Project Heaven on Earth. This can be in your home, place of worship, school, office, or community. It can be in person or on Skype.

2. Take a few minutes to have everyone check in, to say how they're feeling, what they're thinking about, and so on. This supports everyone in being present.

3. Begin a discussion on the purpose of the group and the evening.

4. Have everyone share a time when they experienced Heaven on Earth.

5. Have everyone share what Heaven on Earth is for them.

6. Read a section of this book out loud.

7. Be certain you don't get into debating one way of doing things versus another, but rather keep the focus of the meeting on what action(s) people will take or results they will produce between now and the next meeting to move themselves and Heaven on Earth forward.

8. Discuss what support, both inside and outside of the meeting, you will offer each other to help accomplish actions and results.

9. Discuss progress to date.

10. Discuss what to do about roadblocks. Keep the focus, without criticism or blame, on what can be done about the roadblock so the goal is achieved.

11. Discuss examples of others around the world helping to co-create Heaven on Earth.

12. Enjoy and celebrate your contribution to co-creating Heaven on Earth.

13. Close with a "thank you" and some refreshments.

14. Tell others about the group and its successes.

The next page offers some support reminders for your group.

You have to do it by yourself,
and you can't do it alone.

"Heaven on Earth is
TRUE community."
Andrew Cox &
Martin Rutte

"Heaven on Earth is
agreeing to
make it all work."
Erick Larson

"Heaven on Earth is
bringing out the best
in people."
John Toups

"Heaven on Earth is
the power of one."
Irv Warhaftig

"Heaven on Earth is
people taking care of
our world."
Karina Halseth

"Heaven on Earth is
when people are able to
stand in the creative
and our identity expands
to include all."
Danny Martin

e) Project Heaven on Earth
Book Contemplation

One Christmas, two friends gave me a spiritual-motivational book. They'd studied the book in a highly original manner. They, and the rest of the class, were asked to read the same chapter of the book each day for seven days. On the seventh day, they would all get together and talk about that chapter. The following week they would do the same thing for the next chapter and so on.

They did this for 18 months, going over and over the book, and in the process, delving more deeply into its more profound levels, while gaining greater knowledge, insight, and wisdom.

My invitation to you is that you do the same with this book. You could do this with your Project Heaven on Earth support group, at work with your colleagues, or at home with your family. You'll be surprised and delighted at what you discover. Let me know what happens at: www.ProjectHeavenOnEarth.com/contact

Appendix 2

A Four-Year Undergraduate University Degree in Co-Creating Heaven on Earth

What if education taught students how to create the world they long for by discovering and making real what Heaven on Earth is for them?

Imagine a four-year university program that gives students the skills, knowledge, personal confidence, and practical experiences to help them go out in the world and begin Co-creating Heaven on Earth.

Here is a proposed curriculum for such a four-year degree. Each course is in bold, followed by suggested content.

The Great Literature of Heaven

Appreciating our understanding of "Heaven" through the ages by reading such books as:

Utopian Thought in the Western World, Frank E. Manuel and Fritzie P. Manuel. The Belknap Press of Harvard University Press, 1979.

Heaven: A History, Colleen McDannell and Bernhard Lang. Yale University Press, 1988.

Paradise Lost, John Milton. Buccaneer Books, 1976.

Encyclopedia of Heaven, Miriam Van Scott. Thomas Dunne Books, St. Martin's Griffin, 1998.

(See the Bibliography for additional books.)

Story

- The study of story and myth to appreciate Humanity's story
- The structure and mechanism of belief systems, both personal and collective

Inspiring Heaven Making Leadership

- Empowering others
- Meeting with different kinds of leaders
- Developing your networking skills
- How to leverage ideas, opportunities, new technologies, and the media
- Using social media and the Internet

Ritual & Celebration

- The power of ritual and celebration to bring community together, deepen the experience of connection, expand possibilities and encourage action

Physical Fitness & Optimum Nutrition

- Understanding the necessity and effect of a healthy body through regular endurance, flexibility and strength training, along with a vibrantly healthy diet

Experiencing Making a Difference

- Experiencing your life as meaningful

- Experiencing people and projects that make a difference

- The right use of power

- Designing and implementing your own Heaven on Earth project

Experiencing Humanity

- Encountering, seeing, and feeling our Human family

- Speaking to all of Humanity

- Speaking on behalf of Humanity

Studying the Gateways to Heaven on Earth

- Your Inner World

- Relationships: Co-Creating Heaven on Earth

- Living Your Global Values

- Your Outer World: Ending the World's Major Sufferings

- Your Outer World: Our Institutions Taking Their Rightful Place in Co-Creating Heaven on Earth

- Your Outer World: Co-Creating Heaven on Earth Nation(s)

- Heaven on Earth This-Here-Now

Personal Work/Working on Yourself

- Gaining clarity about your life's vision and your life's purpose

- Mastering how to evoke vision and purpose in others

- Meditation

- Experiencing your own power and using it for good

- Being complete in your relationships

- Being complete with your own religion. Deepening your appreciation of other religions.

- Being complete with the institutions of society: from victim to partnership

- Doing things that are beyond what you believe possible, e.g., the firewalk, hang-gliding, producing greater results in a shorter time

- The experience of giving and getting effective support

- Playing and celebrating
- Appreciating the power of being responsible to, for, and with
- Experiencing the power of commitment
- Keeping your word, the power of integrity

The Experience of Creation & Beauty

- Taking courses in the arts: music, dance, art, poetry, film, digital media, photography, languages, etc.

Enrolling & Marketing

- How to enroll people in your idea
- Enrolling, not as manipulation, but as an act of service
- How to get an idea out into the world as a public conversation
- Marketing your project

Public Speaking & Effective Communications

- Developing powerful presentation skills
- Creative writing
- Having a deep appreciation of and learning how to facilitate healthy and effective group dynamics

Experiencing Awe

- Being exposed to awe: beauty, nature, religious experience, the depth of Humanity

Global History

- Studying history from different perspectives: geographical areas, historical movements, ideas, cultures, culture (literature, theater, visual arts, music), religion, science and technology, philosophy, chronological development

Developmental Humanity

- Studying the development of human beings from the earliest humans to now, to see how Humanity has developed and what our possible future could be

What other subjects would you add?

What subjects or courses would you add to a master's and PhD program?

Bibliography

Ashton, John, and Tom Whyte. *The Quest for Paradise: Visions of Heaven and Eternity in the World's Myths and Religions*. San Francisco: HarperSanFrancisco, 2001.

Bolles, Richard N. *How to Find Your Mission in Life*. Berkeley, CA: Ten Speed Press, 1991.

Cota-Robles, Patricia Diane. *Home: Heaven on Mother Earth*. Tucson, AZ: Bridge Of Love/Angelic Encounter; First Edition, 2003.

Delumeau, Jean. *History of Paradise: The Garden of Eden in Myth and Tradition*. New York: The Continuum Publishing Company, 1995 [for translation].

Jacoby, Mario A. *Longing for Paradise: Psychological Perspectives on an Archetype*. Salem, MA: Sigo Press, 1985.

Kingwell, Mark. *The World We Want: Virtue, Vice, and the Good Citizen*. New York: Viking, First Edition, 2000.

Luskin, Dr. Fred. *Forgive for Good: A Proven Prescription for Health and Happiness*. New York: HarperCollins, 2002.

Manuel, Frank E., and Fritzie P. Manuel. *Utopian Thought in the Western World*. Cambridge, MA: The Belknap Press of Harvard University Press, 1979.

McDannell, Colleen and Lang, Bernhard. *Heaven: A History*. Hew Haven, CT: Yale University Press, 1988.

Muller, Robert. *New Genesis: Shaping a Global Spirituality*. New York: Doubleday, 1982.

Psaki, F. Regina, ed. *The Earthly Paradise: The Garden of Eden from Antiquity to Modernity*. Albany, NY: State University of New York, 2002.

Schneerson, Menachem M. *Bringing Heaven Down to Earth: 365 Meditations from the Wisdom of the Rebbe, Menachem M. Schneerson*. Compiled and condensed by Rabbi Tzvi Freeman. Abm Komers, 1995.

Slaughter, Anne-Marie. *A New World Order*. Princeton, NJ: Princeton University Press, 2004.

Van Gelder, Sarah Ruth. *Saying Yes!: Conversations on a World that Works for All*. Bainbridge Island, WA: Positive Futures Network, 2000.

Van Scott, Miriam. *Encyclopedia of Heaven*. New York: Thomas Dunne Books, St. Martin's Press, 1998.

Wade II, John E., Charlotte Livingston Piotrowski, Daniel Agatino, Michael Nagler, and Martin Rutte, *Glimpses of Heaven on Earth: Inspiring Quotations and Insightful Essays*. Gretna, LA: Pelican Publishing, 2014.

Wade II, John E. *How to Achieve a Heaven on Earth: 101 insightful essays from the world's greatest thinkers, leaders, and writers*. Gretna, LA: Pelican Publishing, 2011.

Zaleski, Carol, and Philip Zaleski. *The Book of Heaven: An Anthology of Writings from Ancient to Modern Times*. New York: Oxford University Press, Inc., 2000.

Websites

(Websites supporting Heaven on Earth)

Alliance for a New Humanity: www.anhglobal.org

    The mission of Alliance for a New Humanity is to connect and inspire people who, through personal and social transformation, are leading a conscious evolution toward a more peaceful and compassionate world and to encourage a new way of thinking about human systems which create conditions for a sustainable global society.

BigPictureSmallWorld: www.bigpicturesmallworld.com

    BigPictureSmallWorld Inc. is dedicated to providing quality educational, training, and consulting programs that inform, inspire and empower. We work with schools, colleges, corporations, and organizations around the world. Our mission is to turn information overload into sensible knowledge that leads to effective action.

Collective Wisdom Initiative: www.collectivewisdominitiative.com

    The Collective Wisdom Initiative began with the publication of *Centered on the Edge: Mapping a Field of Collective Intelligence and Spiritual Wisdom*, an inquiry into group wisdom. This inquiry developed into an exploration of ten arenas of collective wisdom, represented by the following "Doorways:" aesthetics, concepts, cultivation tools, lived experience, maps and mapping, practices, research: group mind, skills and capacities, social application, and vibration.

Foundation for Global Community: www.globalcommunity.org

    The Foundation for Global Community is an educational, public-benefit foundation that provides the funds for grants to a variety of viable projects working to build a sustainable, just, and spiritually fulfilling global community.

Global Art Project for Peace: www.global-art.org

    The mission of the Global Art Project is to joyously create a culture of peace through art. The Project celebrates diversity and multi-culturalism while expressing the idea: We Are All One. Participants create a work of art in any medium, expressing their vision of global peace and goodwill. The art is displayed locally in each participant's community. Global Art Project then organizes an international exchange by matching participants—group-to-group and individual-to-individual.

The Global Simulation Workshop: www.worldgame.org

    The Global Simulation Workshop is a dynamic and innovative learning tool for academic, community, and professional organizations. A direct descendant of Buckminster Fuller's famous World Game™, the Global Simulation Workshop is an interactive game that builds critical skills, social bonds, and global awareness by putting participants into the roles of global leaders who must use creativity and integrated thinking to find individual and communal success in a complex environment.

Humanity's Team: www.humanitysteam.org

    Humanity's Team is a global grassroots movement embodying Oneness with a profound respect for cultural diversity and responsibility for all of life. We are dedicated to raising consciousness through living our individual lives with purpose, each being a loving presence, and serving through authentic leadership.

Kidlink Association: www.kidlink.org/

Kidlink Association promotes a global dialogue among the youth of the world. The Association emphasizes electronic telecommunications, but also supports communications in other forms and media. The Association works to achieve its objectives through several educational, school and classroom projects.

Musicians for World Harmony: http://musiciansforworldharmony.org

The mission of Musicians for World Harmony is to use the healing power of music to reawaken the humanity in the hearts of displaced and distressed peoples affected by war and disease in an effort to promote peace, understanding and harmony.

Omidyar Network: www.omidyar.com

Omidyar Network is a philanthropic investment firm dedicated to creating opportunity for people to improve their lives. We provide grants to non-profits and invest in innovative organizations that are advancing economic and social change.

Paradise Earth: tinyurl.com/ParadiseEarth

This website provides access to Former United Nations Assistant Secretary-General Robert Muller's writings on priorities and objectives for the 21st century and the third millennium. These priorities and objectives are: 1. To make this planet earth a paradise, 2. To stop destroying nature at all cost, 3. To eradicate poverty, miseries and errors engendered by power, greed and egotism, 4. To make out of all humans one united, cooperating family, 5. To create a new social, political world order for Paradise Earth, 6. To attain a life of fulfillment and happiness for all humans, 7. To achieve a human family in harmony with the Earth and the heavens, and 8. To be the ultimate cosmic success of the Universe and God.

Partnership in Statistics for Development in the 21st Century (PARIS21): tinyurl.com/PARIS21st

The Partnership in Statistics for Development in the 21st Century (PARIS21) is a unique initiative that aims to promote the better use and production of statistics throughout the developing world. PARIS21's goal is to develop a culture of Management for Development Results (MfDR). PARIS21 pursues this goal primarily by encouraging and assisting low-income and lower middle income countries to design, implement, and monitor a National Strategy for the Development of Statistics (NSDS).

Radical Middle Newsletter: tinyurl.com/RadMid

Radical Middle Newsletter doesn't just report on innovative political ideas, books, and national meetings. It expresses an emerging political perspective and sensibility that we like to call "radical middle." As a political perspective, it's not a "safe" middle ground between the extremes of left and right. It's off the traditional left-right spectrum...free to gather up ideas from everywhere. It's "radical" because it's seeking solutions that are holistic and sustainable. It's "middle" because it accepts that you can't change people very much.

Robert Muller: www.robertmuller.org

Robert Muller's websites are dedicated to making available the works of Robert Muller for everyone to enjoy, learn from and use to nurture a happier better world for everyone.

The School for Social Entrepreneurs: www.the-sse.org/about-us

The mission of the School for Social Entrepreneurs is to address inequalities and social exclusion by supporting social entrepreneurs from all backgrounds to transform their talent into real social outcomes, in the form of sustainable solutions to poverty and disadvantage in communities. It does this through the use of action-learning based programmes of personal and organisational development.

Search for Common Ground: www.sfcg.org

The mission of Search for Common Ground is to end violent conflict. It's our purpose — our call to action. Instead of tearing down an existing world, we focus on constructing a new one. We do this through a type of peacebuilding called conflict transformation. Meaning: we look to change the everyday interactions between groups of people in conflict, so they can work together to build up their community, choosing joint problem-solving over violence.

Seven Actions to Change the World (PDF): tinyurl.com/SevenActions

These seven actions operate from the empowerment premise that it is we who must create the world we want, stated so well in the phrase, "when the people lead, the leaders will follow." They are created as a menu of choice, with some quite simple and others requiring more commitment. And each invites us to carry on the ancient Hopi tradition of the DreamKeeper — one who stewards the profound belief that humanity can live in harmony with each other and the Earth.

Simpol: The Simultaneous Policy: www.simpol.org

Simpol invites citizens around the world to use their votes in a completely new way to encourage politicians to solve global problems like global warming, financial market regulation, environmental destruction, war, and social injustice.

The Optimist Daily: http://theoptimist.com/

The Optimist Daily is a joint venture between The Optimist magazine and the World Business Academy, pairing an independent international editorial staff with an international nonprofit think tank and business network. This combination brings together solution-oriented journalism and a network of leaders and organizations who are bringing it to the world. With conscious-changing organizations — we partner with aligned non-profit organizations and businesses that share the goal of spreading solutions, catalyzing change, and shifting consciousness.

The TED Prize: www.ted.com/prize

The TED Prize is awarded to an extraordinary individual with a creative and bold vision to spark global change. By leveraging the TED community's resources and investing $1 million dollars into a powerful idea, the TED Prize supports one wish to inspire the world.

United Nations Global Compact: www.unglobalcompact.org

The UN Global Compact is a strategic policy initiative for businesses that are committed to aligning their operations and strategies with ten universally accepted principles in the areas of human rights, labor, environment and anti-corruption. By doing so, business, as a primary driver of globalization, can help ensure that markets, commerce, technology and finance advance in ways that benefit economies and societies everywhere.

We, The World: www.wetheworld.org

We, The World is a non-profit organization that forms international networks of collaboration. We produce and promote events and other programs to increase public awareness and action about critical societal issues such as violence, poverty and ecological damage.

World Future Council: www.worldfuturecouncil.org

The World Future Council is an international forum made up of 50 eminent personalities from around the world. They come from governments, parliaments, academia, civil society, the arts and business. Together they form a voice for the rights of future generations.

Worldwatch Institute: http://worldwatch.org

Through research and outreach that inspire action, the Worldwatch Institute works to accelerate the transition to a sustainable world that meets human needs. The Institute's top mission objectives are universal access to renewable energy and nutritious food, expansion of environmentally sound jobs and development, transformation of cultures from consumerism to sustainability, and an early end to population growth through healthy and intentional childbearing.

Youth Venture: www.youthventure.org/

Youth Venture's mission is to build a movement of young people being powerful now, changemakers now, by: investing in young people to have the transformative experience of launching and leading their own lasting Ventures; creating a critical mass of young people who collectively redefine the youth years as a time of positive contribution; spreading our message that investing in young people to become changemakers is the key factor for success in every part of society; and connecting our Venturers to a global network of changemakers.

Martin Rutte

Martin Rutte is an international speaker, consultant, and author. As president of Livelihood, a management consulting firm in Santa Fe, New Mexico, he explores the deeper meaning of work and its contribution to society. The company's areas of service include: strategic visioning, corporate spirit, stakeholder dialogue, performance management, and creative leadership.

Martin has worked with such organizations as The World Bank, Sony Pictures Entertainment, Southern California Edison, Virgin Records, Esso Petroleum, and London Life Insurance helping them expand their outlook and position themselves for the future.

He addressed the Corporate Leadership & Ethics Forum of Harvard Business School, returning for four consecutive years as a keynote speaker. He also twice addressed joint meetings of the American and Canadian Chambers of Commerce in Hong Kong.

Martin is the winner of the 2014 Excellence in Leadership Award from the Transformational Leadership Council. Established in 2004, the Council was founded so leaders of personal and organizational transformation could support each other in their contributions to the world.

He is a co-author of *The New York Times* business best seller, *Chicken Soup for the Soul at Work*®, with over one million copies sold.

He has contributed chapters on Heaven on Earth in:

- *How to Achieve A Heaven on Earth: 101 insightful essays from the world's greatest thinkers, leaders, and writers* (tinyurl.com/HowToAchieve)

- *Seeking the Sacred: Leading a Spiritual Life in a Secular World* (tinyurl.com/SeekingSacred)

- *Glimpses of Heaven on Earth: Inspiring Quotations and Insightful Essays* (tinyurl.com/ GlimpsesofHeaven)

Articles on his innovative work have appeared in: *Miami Herald*, *The Wall Street Journal*, *South China Morning Post*, *Personnel Journal*, *U.S. News and World Report,* and *The Boston Globe*.

A leader in the management field of spirituality in the workplace, Martin is committed to reconnecting business with its natural source of creativity, innovation, and compassion.

His pioneering work on spirituality in the workplace was featured on the ABC-TV special, "Creativity: Touching the Divine." He has been a speaker in Mexico at all six International Conferences on Spirituality in Business, and has spoken at conferences on this topic in: Canada, USA, Mexico, Brazil, South Africa, and New Zealand.

Martin was a co-founder and the Chair of the Board of the Centre for Spirituality and the Workplace (in operation from 2004–2012), Sobey School of Business, Saint Mary's University, Halifax, Canada.

He has been married to Maida Rogerson, an actor and screenwriter, for over 45 years.

More information on Heaven on Earth is available at:

www.ProjectHeavenOnEarth.com

You can watch Martin interview Heaven Makers on the

Project Heaven on Earth YouTube Channel:

tinyurl.com/PHonEYouTube

We'd love to hear from you.
Send us your projects and stories.

Tell us what you're doing to create Heaven on Earth.

Share your Heaven on Earth projects.

It doesn't matter how big or how small, every action, every result adds to the new story of Heaven on Earth.

It adds reality, it gives proof, it shows the evidence.

It gives foundation, structure, example.

Letting us know what you're doing inspires others to jump in, to get into making Heaven on Earth a real, lived, tangible reality.

Your unique contribution to Heaven on Earth does make a difference.

Let us know.

To share your story/project and learn what others all around the world are doing, visit: www.ProjectHeavenOnEarth.com/stories

There are many people from around the world who have chosen
to become Heaven Makers.

You, your family, friends, and colleagues can also join —
and each additional person accelerates the momentum for all of us.

Sign up for my FREE, 7-day e-mail course:

"One Week to Simply Begin Creating Heaven on Earth!"

Sign up at: www.ProjectHeavenOnEarth.com

When you sign up, you'll also receive two bonuses:

1) Access to the "We Heaven Makers" community.

Read about the Heaven on Earth experiences of others,
check out inspiring Heaven on Earth quotes,
and learn about other Heaven on Earth projects.

2) Our weekly blog/video interview.

Each week, you'll receive an inspiring blog that will support you
in expanding the experience and the actions of Heaven on Earth.
Getting the blog deepens your experience and appreciation of
Heaven on Earth as you see how it is showing up,
and as you experience how its momentum is growing, daily, in the world.

Sign up at: www.ProjectHeavenOnEarth.com

WHY MARTIN IS RIGHT FOR YOUR LIVE EVENT

Martin Rutte has a message of success for creating the life, the work, and the world your audience deeply longs for…he gets people to discover **"What is Heaven on Earth for me and how do I easily get started making that real."** He does this in a fun, entertaining, and in-depth style that will shift your organization/group to its next level, professionally and personally.

If you're looking for a dynamic and inspirational motivational speaker for your upcoming conference, luncheon, retreat or any other live event, then Martin is a great choice.

Martin uses personal experiences, examples, and an engaging style to inspire your audience and get them on the road to Heaven on Earth…simply and easily.

He's presented to such organizations as: Anglia Ruskin University: Lord Ashcroft International Business School; St. Mary's University's Sobey School of Business; The PEI Business Women's Association; The Transformational Leadership Council; The Canadian Society for Spirituality and Social Work; The Shift Network; The Association of Transformational Leaders Europe; Kiwanis Club of Eastern Canada & Caribbean; The Tällberg Foundation.

The **Project Heaven on Earth** program formats can be tailored to fit your needs:

- **The Keynote**: 1–2 hours
- **The Keynote Experience**: 2–4 hours
- **The Workshop**: 4–8 hours
- **The 2-Day Training**: 12–18 hours

For more information, visit: www.ProjectHeavenOnEarth.com/speaking

As an internationally recognized leader in helping people discover and implement Heaven on Earth, Martin delivers **The New Story of What It Means to Be a Human and What It Means To Be Humanity** to enthusiastic audiences globally. People in all kinds of industries have been inspired and empowered by Martin's powerful message. Martin knows how to accelerate the personal, professional, and global achievement of those longing for a better world.

Your audience will be inspired and motivated to achieve beyond what they believe possible, to achieve the dreams of their Soul. Martin will provide the insights and tools necessary to overcome obstacles, adapt to changing circumstances, re-frame perspectives, and solve seemingly impossible problems.

For more information, visit: www.ProjectHeavenOnEarth.com/speaking

(Special discounts apply when 50 or more books are purchased.)

www.ProjectHeavenOnEarth.com